O9-AHU-820

LIFE AND DEATH IN CIVIL WAR PRISONS

THE PARALLEL TORMENTS OF
CORPORAL JOHN WESLEY MINNICH, C.S.A. AND
SERGEANT WARREN LEE GOSS, U.S.A.

J. Michael Martinez

Rutledge Hill Press®
Nashville, Tennessee

A Division of Thomas Nelson, Inc.
www.ThomasNelson.com

This work is dedicated to the late Will Morris (1965–93),
who scribbled in my high school annual all those years ago
that we would be "friends forever." He was right.
Death takes only what must be surrendered.

Published by Rutledge Hill Press, a Division of Thomas Nelson, Inc., P.O. Box 141000, Nashville, Tennessee, 37214.

Library of Congress Cataloging-in-Publication Data

Martinez, J. Michael (James Michael)

Life and death in Civil War prisons : the parallel torments of Corporal John Wesley Minnich, C.S.A. and Sergeant Warren Lee Goss, U.S.A. / by J. Michael Martinez.

p. cm.

Includes bibliographical references (p.) and index.

ISBN 1-4016-0094-8 (hardcover)

1. United States—History—Civil War, 1861–1865—Prisoners and prisons. 2. Minnich, J. W. (John Wesley). 1844–1932. 3. Goss, Warren Lee, 1835–1925. 4. Prisoners of war—United States—History—19th century. 5. Prisononers of war—Confederate States of America. I. Title.

E615.M37 2004
973.7'71—dc22

2003023332

Printed in the United States of America

04 05 06 07 08 — 5 4 3 2 1

Contents

But that I am forbid
To tell the secrets of my prison-house,
I could a tale unfold, whose lightest word
Would harrow up thy soul; freeze thy young blood;
Make thy two eyes, like stars, start from their spheres;
Thy knotted and combined locks to part,
And each particular hair to stand on end,
Like quills upon the fretful porpentine.

—WILLIAM SHAKESPEARE, *Hamlet*, Act I, Scene v

What god can now unfold for me in song
all of the bitterness and butchery
and deaths of chieftains—driven now by Turnus,
now by the Trojan hero, each in turn
throughout that field? O, Jupiter, was it
your will that nations destined to eternal
peace should have clashed in such tremendous turmoil?

—VIRGIL, *The Aeneid*, Book XII, lines 674–81

Foreword

Whether located in the South or the North, a Civil War prison was a tragic scene of suffering and death. As many as 210,000 Northern troops were captured after the Dix-Hill Cartel for prisoner exchanges collapsed in mid-1863, and an estimated 220,000 Southerners became prisoners of war during that same period. Most underwent brutal hardships and grievous suffering. Military prisons were established in converted warehouses in the South, converted fortresses in the North, and hastily constructed prison camps on both sides. There were hellholes aplenty in both the North and the South. Among the deadliest sites for Confederate prisoners were Rock Island Prison in Illinois, Elmira Prison in New York, Point Lookout in Maryland, and Camp Douglas in Chicago. Among the deadliest locations for Northern prisoners were Georgia's Camp Sumter—better known as "Andersonville Prison"—South Carolina's Florence Stockade, and North Carolina's Salisbury Prison. The death rate on both sides was almost equally horrific. Dysentery, starvation, exposure to harsh weather, and brutal mistreatment killed more men than Gettysburg—the war's deadliest battle. An estimated 56,000 prisoners died in captivity—approximately 30,000 Northerners and about 26,000 Southerners.

Such numbers compose brutal statistics, but the gruesome reality of Civil War prison life is found in the personal stories of those who suffered it. Two such victims were Cpl. John Wesley Minnich, a teenager from Louisiana, and Sgt. Warren Lee Goss of Massachusetts. Goss was incarcerated at Libby Prison, Belle Isle Prison, Andersonville Prison, and the Florence Stockade—all Dixie deathtraps. Minnich was imprisoned at an equally hellish hovel—the U.S. government's Rock Island Prison. Although the two men had dramatically different backgrounds and loyalties, their awful ordeals were parallel experiences in horror.

Author and historian J. Michael Martinez chronicles their gripping life-and-death experiences in exceptional detail, transforming two previously unknown soldiers into deeply personal portraits of Civil War soldiers. The two common soldiers become uncommon symbols of the largely untold under-life of the American Civil War. *Life and Death in Civil War Prisons* is a penetrating, unforgettable portrait of the worst of the war—the military prisons of the North and the South. Minnich and Goss come to personalize the American "Everyman" who suffered, struggled, and so often died in a bleak and brutal setting far from home and loved ones.

Life and Death in Civil War Prisons strips the American Civil War of its romance and pageantry. What is left is the hardship and horror of war—and the extraordinary courage of American soldiers from both North and South.

—ROD GRAGG

Preface

I first became interested in the subject of Civil War prisons in 2000, as I searched for a new project after my co-edited book *Confederate Symbols in the Contemporary South* appeared in print. I knew that my hometown, Florence, South Carolina, had been the site of a Confederate stockade, but that was all I knew. As a boy, I had heard stories, but they didn't seem especially interesting to me—just the ruminations of good ol' boys and country raconteurs swapping tales of the "War Between the States." Even if someone had told me more about the Florence Stockade before I was in my thirties, I would not have cared. Like many young people, I could not see beyond myself. I grew up on the north side of Florence and graduated from Wilson High School in 1980. My life in those days revolved around the high school drama club and the Florence Little Theatre as well as the usual teenage ambitions: girls, cars, part-time jobs, and dreams of escaping one day to a bigger, more exciting place. I enjoyed history up to a point, but scampering around a field under a fierce afternoon sun would not have struck me as an ideal use of my time.

Times—and my attitude—changed. The more I read about the prison, the more fascinated I became. I could not believe that the little town where I was born and raised on the Pee Dee River in South Carolina once had been home to such misery and death. Yet the record was clear. Long before I was born, those men squatted in a barren field under cool, breezy South Carolina days and cold, bone-chilling winter nights and died near the edge of a swamp. Their bodies were buried vertically, shoulder to shoulder, in deep trenches—sometimes as many as 140 men per trench—carved out of the black earth of a nearby cemetery.

I tried to imagine the history buried in the prison fields and cemeteries across America. A little less than fourteen decades ago, thousands of wan, starving men clad only in tattered rags endured the volatile times in which they lived and struggled to survive. When I closed my eyes, I could almost see the Civil War prisons in all their horror and depravity. With these scenes in mind, digging through the records of the Florence Stockade became my passion.

When I approached Rutledge Hill Press early in 2002 to ask if a full-length book on the Florence prison might be of interest, the historian and Rutledge Hill Civil War editor Rod Gragg answered my query with a query of his own. Rather than focusing on one prison, how would I feel about comparing the lives of two prisoners—one from the Confederacy, one from the Union? After mulling it over for a few days, I thought the idea had merit. Thus, a concept was born.

Despite the immense pleasure I have derived from delving into times long gone, it is difficult to translate documents and materials so that the past comes alive for contemporary readers. In penning this text, therefore, I have taken the liberty of translating certain terms into modern parlance unless they were used in exact quotations by one of the participants. Accordingly, I speak of the "Civil War," not the "War Between the States." In most cases, I write about "blacks," not "Negroes" (or epithets even more offensive to modern ears). Other examples abound. Although I might be accused of succumbing to political correctness or interfering with the tenor of the times, in my defense I should say that I was trying to make the text more accessible to the average reader. If this were a scholarly text instead of a book written for a general audience, I probably would have made a different decision. Serious scholars of the period can find many other sources that retain the particular terminology of that era.

With each book I write, I realize how many debts I incur along the way. Although my name appears on the spine and I proudly accept all responsibility for the contents of this book, I recognize that many people contributed their time and talents to its production. They may be too numerous to thank by name, but I shall endeavor to pay down my account as best I can.

A comparatively large body of published information exists on the Andersonville Stockade, so I was fortunate to encounter few difficulties in accessing material on that most infamous of Confederate prisons. Sources on the Rock Island Barracks suffered by comparison with Andersonville, but finding information on that Union prison still did not present an insurmountable obstacle. The Florence Stockade, however, was a relatively obscure Civil War prison, and compiling information on the camp that operated for five months in the town of my birth ninety-eight years before I made an appearance proved to be much more difficult than I originally anticipated. Fortunately, I was able to find several Florentines to guide me through rough seas and uncharted waters. First and foremost, I must thank members of the Friends of the Florence Stockade (FFS), a group of local Civil War enthusiasts struggling to preserve the prison site, for providing me with their invaluable advice and assistance. J. R. Fisher, in particular, was generous with his time and expertise. He spent several hours on a Saturday afternoon in March 2000 walking me through the field where the prison once stood, pointing out boundary lines and discussing restoration efforts. He also gave me a tour through the War Between the States Museum on Guerry Street in Florence and spoke with me on the telephone many times, often at his own expense, as questions arose during the writing. The Reverend Albert Ledoux has performed painstaking research and devoted countless hours to identifying Union prisoners who perished in the stockade and were buried in the Florence National Cemetery. He was exceedingly kind and patient in working with me on this project. John Andrews of the FFS also was a faithful and generous correspondent. He steered me in the right direction a time or two when I seemed ready to veer off into unproductive territory.

Two local historians—the late Horace F. Rudisill of the Darlington County Historical Commission and G. Wayne King, a history professor at Francis Marion University in Florence—also went above and beyond the call of duty in providing me with sources of information. I consider it an honor that these two men, who devoted so much of their lives to researching the historical record of the Florence Stockade, assisted me in locating hard-to-find information that I probably never would have discovered through other means. Similarly, George Hobeika of the Florence County Library greatly assisted by providing me with copies of his file on the stockade, including the all-important Walter Woods manuscript placed in the library by the United Daughters of the Confederacy.

Many talented and dedicated researchers and archivists assisted me in delving into primary source material on the lives of John Minnich and Warren Lee Goss as well as the prisons in which they were held. Mary L. Cooper and Cathy Gontar of the Eastbank Regional Library in Metairie, Louisiana, assisted me in locating material on Minnich's retirement years near Grand Isle. Ms. Cooper was particularly helpful. Even as a hurricane bore down on her state, she labored away to find as much data and information as she could locate to complete my portrait. Such commitment continues to astound me. Pamela D. Arceneux, reference librarian with the Historic New Orleans Collection, Williams Research Center, in New Orleans also provided invaluable services in hunting for information on Minnich's life and background. Andrea B. Goldstein, reference archivist with the Harvard University Archives in

Cambridge, Massachusetts, searched the university's records for information on Goss's academic career. Will Elsbury, a reference librarian in the Humanities and Social Sciences Division of the Library of Congress, pointed me toward sources and information on Goss's background, as did Eva Murphy of the State Library of Massachusetts in Boston.

Finding photographs from the nineteenth century often presents unique challenges, but I was fortunate to enlist the help of numerous dedicated archivists and researchers. John W. Kuhl, a private Civil War researcher in Pittstown, New Jersey, graciously granted permission for me to use the photograph of Col. Adolphus Johnson, commandant of the Rock Island Prison Barracks, without remuneration—no small favor considering that I was working on a tight (i.e., nonexistent) budget. Gail Smith, public affairs officer, and Kris Gayman Leinicke, director of the Rock Island Arsenal Museum, Department of the Army, also were kind enough to allow me to use almost a dozen photographs of the Rock Island Prison Barracks. Similarly, Mary Michaels of the Illinois State Historical Library worked with me to find photographs of the Rock Island Prison. Mary Ann Moran of the Lackawanna Historical Society in Scranton, Pennsylvania, and Margaret Kieckhefer of the Library of Congress in Washington, D.C., helped me find and reproduce the James E. Taylor drawings that Ezra H. Ripple commissioned in 1897. Regrettably, I was able to use only a fraction of the photographs I acquired.

Ted Hutchinson of the Massachusetts Historical Society assisted in searching for photographs and information on Warren Lee Goss. Rich Baker and Michael J. Winey of the U.S. Army Military History Institute, Department of the Army, in Carlisle Barracks, Pennsylvania, helped me immeasurably. Mr. Baker provided me with an extensive bibliography, and Mr. Winey searched for missing photographs supposedly taken by the Quartermaster Department at the Florence Stockade in 1866. Although he did not locate the photographs (which apparently were never taken or were lost to history), he was instrumental in orchestrating a thorough search. Kathyrn Hodson, special collections reader services librarian at the University of Iowa Libraries in Iowa City, Iowa, assisted me in reproducing the photograph of Minnich that appears in the opening pages and on the cover of the book. Jo Ann Bromley of King Visual Technology and James W. Martin of the National Archives & Records Administration (NARA) assisted in my efforts to search NARA files, particularly the Still Pictures Branch. Heather Muller, Photographs Librarian in the Special Collections Department at the Alexandria Library in Alexandria, Virginia, was kind enough to assist me in tracking down the photograph of Gen. John H.

Winder that appears in this book. Beverly Brasch of the Kennesaw State University Interlibrary Loan Office in Kennesaw, Georgia, helped me find rare diaries and manuscripts through interlibrary loan.

As the former capital city of the Confederacy, Richmond, Virginia, is home to two invaluable sources of information and repositories of photographs. The excellent staff of the Eleanor S. Brockenbrough Library at the Museum of the Confederacy—especially John M. Coski, Heather W. Milne, and Mark Winecoff—assisted me in locating and reproducing photographs of Confederate military leaders. Dr. Coski helped me in locating research materials as well. As always, his insight into the historical record of the Southern Confederacy saved me from devoting many hours to fruitless avenues of research. The staff at the Virginia Historical Society—Doris Delk, museum shop manager; Eileen Parris, archivist, Division of Manuscripts; Rob Hardee, licensing sales associate; and Patricia Greene, copyright licensing sales associate—assisted me in finding photographs from the Robert Knox Sneden scrapbooks.

Patrick McCawley of the South Carolina State Archives in Columbia was instrumental in locating primary records about events in that state. John O'Shea, a librarian at the Reese Library, Augusta State University, Augusta, Georgia, and Gordon Blaker, curator of the Augusta Richmond County Museum, Augusta, Georgia, found information on the Fifth Georgia Volunteer Infantry Regiment and the Barrett family papers that answered lingering questions about the two guards with the same surname who served at the Florence Stockade. Although we did not discover definitive answers in every case, their assistance certainly helped me to exhaust the possibilities. In the meantime, without assistance from Ken Tilley of the Alabama Department of Archives and History in Montgomery, I would not have discovered so much information on, and so many photographs of, George P. Harrison Jr., the second commandant of the Florence Stockade. Similarly, Martin T. Olliff, assistant archivist, Special Collections & Archives, in the Ralph Brown Draughon Library at Auburn University in Auburn, Alabama, helped me find information on General Harrison's postwar activities. Barbara Townsend of the Darlington County Historical Commission performed the often thankless task of photocopying dusty old files and organizing them for me. Her help was greatly appreciated.

I would be remiss if I did not acknowledge the assistance I received from Dr. Herman Hattaway, an eminent Civil War military historian who teaches at the University of Missouri at Kansas City. I first met Dr. Hattaway when we both spoke at the Fifteenth Annual Deep Delta Civil War Symposium at Southeastern Louisiana University in June 2001. Not only did he read an earlier version of the book, but he also offered words of encouragement that improved the manuscript immensely.

Angela Schneider, a former student of mine at Kennesaw State University, was kind enough to lend me several books that provided background information on the diaries of several Civil War soldiers, especially on the Confederate side. My friend and mentor, Dr. William D. Richardson, a professor and chair of the political science department at the University of South Dakota, encouraged me, as always, in those moments when I lost faith in myself and the manuscript. A friend of almost two decades, Ricky S. Gibson, repeatedly asked to read rough drafts long past the point of politeness; his enthusiasm for the project did much to keep me working. Another long-time friend, Keith W. Smith, also urged me to move forward when I was discouraged at my lack of progress and ready to abandon the project. "Mike, if you could get through law school," he said, "you can get through this." I suppose he was right.

In offering a tale of the parallel lives of John Wesley Minnich and Warren Lee Goss, I hope that I have illuminated an often-neglected part of the historical record and made these two men, long dead, come alive for the reader, if only for a brief, flickering moment.

Acknowledgments

My friends and family have endured all sorts of interruptions and irritations as I have been hidden away in the library on many a weekend. Nonetheless, Paula R. Carter and Laura M. Martinez have been patient and kind in allowing me the latitude to finish the project. Shelby A. Carter, Paula's daughter, good-naturedly assisted me from time to time in making photocopies and performing similar administrative chores.

The noted Civil War historian Rod Gragg has been a tremendous help at every stage of the process. From first recognizing the merits of the book to reading rough drafts and making suggestions for revisions to writing the foreword, he has been a true friend and supporter of the cause. He also graciously granted me access to his treasure trove of photographs, some of which appear within these pages. I will never be able to repay his kindness.

Similarly, I owe a debt of gratitude to Civil War expert and author Paul Fowler of Coastal Carolina University in Conway, South Carolina. As the primary fact checker for the manuscript, he kept me on the straight and narrow, ensuring that I did not embarrass myself too badly in my reading and interpretation of the historical record. The copy editor for the work, Janene MacIvor, assisted in correcting my atrocious spelling, awkward sentence construction, and dangling modifiers. Without their help, the finished product would not be very polished. Nonetheless, I am responsible for all errors and omissions that exist in the final book.

Larry Stone and Geoff Stone, my publisher and editor, respectively, at Rutledge Hill Press have exhibited the kind of patience and encouragement that one reads about but rarely encounters these days. I cannot say enough positive things about their sage advice and assistance. In fact, the entire Rutledge Hill Press staff has been exceptionally helpful in producing this book.

Acknowledgments

INTRODUCTION

The Fires of Sectional Hatred

This book chronicles the parallel lives of two men interned in military prisons during the American Civil War. John Wesley Minnich, a Confederate corporal from Louisiana, spent sixteen months incarcerated in the Rock Island Prison on the Illinois-Iowa border. Warren Lee Goss, a Union sergeant from Massachusetts, was captured twice during his military service. His first stint in captivity found him languishing in the Libby and Belle Isle prisons in Virginia. Later, after he was released and captured a second time, he came to know the stockades at Andersonville, Georgia, and Florence, South Carolina.

In almost every respect, Minnich and Goss were very different men. As far as history records, they never met or faced each other across a battlefield, although both served in and around the same areas of the eastern theater, albeit at different times and under different circumstances. Minnich began his military service as an artilleryman, but he concluded his career in a cavalry regiment. Goss was an engineer during his first enlistment. Later, after he reenlisted following a yearlong convalescence, he served with a Union artillery battery.

A transplanted Southerner, Minnich was born on February 15, 1844, near Spring Mills, a small town of fewer than eight hundred residents, in Center County, Pennsylvania. The state was heavily populated with Minnichs, a variation on the German Menig. His family left Pennsylvania and settled in Louisiana in July 1856, when the boy was twelve years old. He returned to Pennsylvania in June 1865, upon his release from prison, but he moved back to Louisiana in 1870 to live out the balance of his long life.[1]

On January 9, 1861, Minnich first appeared on the scene as a young man living near New Orleans. At mid-century, New Orleans was the South's largest city and arguably its most important seaport. Situated on swampy land at the southern tip of Louisiana, the port was a vital crossroads between the Mississippi

This photograph of John W. Minnich appeared in his memoirs, published in 1908. Reprinted from *Inside of Rock Island Prison* by J. W. Minnich.

River and the Gulf of Mexico. With its decadent Old World charm, the city attracted every kind of person imaginable, from Creoles and Cajuns to whites and persons of color from virtually all social strata in North and South America. It was a romantic, exciting place, especially the French Quarter, filled with men and women of diverse nationalities and ethnicities—rogues and heroes, gamblers, voodoo priestesses, ladies of the evening, merchant marines, riverboat captains, lawyers, politicians, and assorted shady, nefarious characters of uncertain origin.[2]

Many New Orleans residents longed for secession and the glory of battle, and their zeal infected Minnich. Although he had been born and spent part of his childhood north of the Mason-Dixon line, he held no love for Yankees. Instead, he embraced the Confederate cause as earnestly and eagerly as did many Southern men of his generation. On the same day that he offered his services to his adopted state, hundreds of miles away in Charleston, South Carolina, Citadel cadets fired on the *Star of the West*, the civilian ship that President James Buchanan sent to reprovision the defenders at Fort Sumter. Blood had yet to be shed, but the opening salvos of the Civil War had been fired.[3]

Louisiana did not secede until March—and Minnich's enlistment did not become official until March 27—but already men were organizing military units to train for action as state leaders announced their support for Confederate ideals. Minnich did not have to wait long before he found his home in an artillery company. As soon as the Louisiana legislature voted to leave the Union, politicians called for the formation of companies to defend the state.[4]

He was a humble man who could have expected to live his life, pursue his vocation, raise his children, and bury his dead without traveling more than a few dozen miles from his home, had the war not interceded. After the cessation of hostilities, he frequently contributed articles and letters to *Confederate Veteran* magazine, but he did not publicize the entire story of his prison experiences until more than four decades had elapsed.[5]

Warren Lee Goss hailed from Boston, Massachusetts, a city more than fifteen hundred miles from Minnich's home near New Orleans, and even further away in circumstances and sensibilities from the Crescent City. Born on August 19, 1835, in Brewster, a small town in Barnstable County close to Cape Cod—an area sometimes referred to as the "right elbow of Massachusetts"—Goss was one of thirteen children from a prominent New England family. His father, William Whittemore Goss, was a direct descendant of Peter W. Goss, an American soldier and patriot in the Revolutionary War. William, a teacher of local renown, instructed students for more than thirty-six years. He also served briefly as keeper of the Highland lighthouse near Brewster.

In an era when few people attended school beyond the elementary grades, Warren could rightly claim to be one of the privileged elite in nineteenth-century America. Sometime during his childhood, his parents, William and Hannah (Foster) Goss, moved the family to Middleboro, Massachusetts. Afterward, they had the means and wherewithal to send their fourth child to the prestigious Pierce Academy in Middleboro for his preparatory education, no mean feat for such a large family. Later, Warren attended Harvard Law School, the pinnacle of academic achievement. Although he eschewed a career practicing law in favor of writing and teaching—thereby following in his father's footsteps—Warren Lee Goss certainly enjoyed ample opportunities and almost infinite possibilities during his early life.[6]

This drawing shows Warren Lee Goss as he appeared in the late 1860s, a few years after the end of the war. Reprinted from *The Soldier's Story* by Warren Lee Goss.

He was living and teaching near Boston when the war

erupted. Confident that it would be a sixty-day affair, he continued his teaching career as long as he could, leaving the initial fighting to younger men. After the battle of Bull Run demonstrated that the rebellion would not be quelled as easily as everyone originally had thought, Goss felt duty bound to join the Union army. On November 19, 1861, he enlisted as a private in Company B of the U.S. Army Engineer Corps. At twenty-six years of age, he was older than many recruits, and hardly enamored of army life. He recognized immediately that the storybook account of young men marching off to fame and glory on distant battlefields was a far cry from the reality of war.[7]

Judging by his florid prose and extensive vocabulary, he was a garrulous character, perhaps a bit pedantic at times, but also full of hearty, "hail-fellow-well-met" good cheer. In addition to his patrician lineage, he could boast of his legal training at Harvard Law School and his growing list of postwar publications as evidence of his intellect. Unlike Minnich, who claimed that he "did not wish to keep alive the fires of sectional hatred," Goss was satisfied to live out his years regaling old and young alike with historical remembrances and fictional accounts of the war. Although not as bitter as many Union veterans, Goss undoubtedly appreciated the advantages that accrued to an ambitious author who willingly "waved the bloody shirt" for the titillation of paying readers.[8]

For all their differences in lifestyle and temperament, these two men shared similar wartime experiences, and it is those experiences that this book seeks to highlight in tracing their "parallel" lives. First, they answered the call to service in support of their respective causes without waiting for the institution of the draft, no small matter in a war that depended largely on citizen combatants. Both men served at one time in heavy artillery units. Ironically, each soldier suffered terribly during his imprisonment, yet each lived well into the twentieth century. Minnich was eighty-eight years old when he died in November 1932. Goss was even older; he lived to be ninety before he passed away in November 1925.[9]

Aside from the superficial similarities, the paramount connection between these men was that both Minnich and Goss came to know and subsequently write about the horrors of life and death in military prisons of the Civil War. Their works must be read with a bit of skepticism, for they were not neutral observers seeking to plumb the depths of historical archives in search of "objective" truth. Instead, their polemics advance the best and worst of the differing perspectives on Civil War prisons in the postwar period. They each had known fear, starvation, humiliation, and the dark depravities of the human spirit. We can forgive them their histrionic indulgences when we read the more-or-less factual accounts of their experiences, for who could endure what they endured and come away unscathed and unbiased?

The story of life and death in Civil War prisons is a heartbreaking tale of deprivation and suffering—a tale, in Shakespeare's parlance, "whose lightest word would harrow up thy soul." Let us now follow the lightest word to its tragic end by tracing the adventures of two emblematic figures. Through the experiences of Cpl. John Wesley Minnich, C.S.A., and Sgt. Warren Lee Goss, U.S.A., the harrowing tale can be appreciated absent the usual distortion and hyperbole so common in the literature on Civil War prisons.

ONE

Surrendering Just Then Was Not on My Program

He was in a dangerous predicament, and he knew it. His horse was lame, and he had lost his regiment. A cavalryman on foot, separated from his comrades in hostile territory, faced the constant danger of being shot or captured. With his heart thudding in his chest, Cpl. John Wesley Minnich, C.S.A., scurried along the dirt road, casting furtive glances through the heavy pine forest, praying that all would be well.[1]

It was. He might have suffered a terrible fate had he not stumbled upon his company resting by the road. The Sixth Georgia Cavalry had taken terrible casualties as it marched through eastern Tennessee that day. Although Minnich did not know it, his commanding officer, Major Bale, was dead, and their forces had thinned considerably. Only one piece of good news awaited his arrival. His friends had found a stray horse—they dubbed him "Billy Smith"—and the fresh steed was grazing in a field. Grateful for the gift, Minnich saddled up while the Confederates took to the road. The fellows in Company G promised to wait for him over the ridge.[2]

His preparations took longer than he had anticipated. When Minnich finally mounted his new horse and tucked his feet into the stirrups, the unit had disappeared, although it was only a few minutes ahead. With no hesitation, he left the road to follow a shortcut through a heavily wooded thicket.[3]

As he snaked his way through the timbers, he encountered a force of two hundred Union troops trudging through the woods. It was a moment feared by every soldier. He had a split second to act, and his life and fate hung in the balance. If each side drew its guns and exchanged fire, Minnich might take a few Yankees with him, but he was under no illusions: He was a dead man. At the same time, "surrendering just then was not on my program—far from it."

With his decision made, Minnich pulled Billy Smith's reins as hard as he could, swung the animal to the right, and dug in his spurs. Unlike his previous horse, Brownie, who was sluggish even in the best of times, Billy Smith moved with astonishing agility. Minnich charged through the forest as guns blazed behind man and beast; bullets slapped at surrounding trees, sending chunks of pine bark and clumps of dirt skyward.[4]

He remembered the scene vividly. "The bluecoats called upon me in no polite terms, 'Surrender, you Rebel son of a gun,' only they did not say 'gun.'" In his haste to escape, he almost fell from the horse. Billy Smith leapt over a six-foot-high sapling. As the horse landed, Minnich caught his boot on an obstruction. With bullets flying left and right, he held on to Billy Smith for dear life, and somehow managed not to tumble from the saddle.[5]

On horseback, zigzagging through towering pine trees along a gently sloping landscape, he rapidly outdistanced his pursuers. After many minutes of evasive maneuvering, he brought the steed to a halt near a barn. He was surprised to spy his friend and sometime marching partner, Dick Murdock. Like Minnich, Murdock had become separated from the unit and had been thrashing about in the forest, desperate to avoid the enemy. He had come upon the barn just as Minnich emerged from the woods. The accidental companions found they had experienced similar, unexpected encounters with the bluecoats. Recognizing their vulnerability, they agreed to push on toward their comrades' last known position.[6]

A typical Zouave uniform was based on a French design. Reprinted from *Recollections of a Private* by Warren Lee Goss.

Minnich, the clearheaded, courageous, competent nineteen-year-old Confederate soldier of this episode, had come a long way since his enlistment shortly before his seventeenth birthday. In those early days of the conflict, he had been a private in a heavy artillery battery—Company E of the First Louisiana Zouaves—assembled in New Orleans by George A. C. (Alfred) Coppens and commanded by a debonair French entrepreneur, Maj. Paul Francois de Gournay. Zouaves were French army units noted for their unusual uniforms, consisting of a fez, a short blue jacket, and baggy red trousers. They became something of a fad at the beginning of the war, especially in the North, where a zealous law student, Elmer Ellsworth, championed the formation of Zouave units in northern cities in 1860.[7]

Minnich was an enthusiastic recruit in this unusual artillery company. Years later, he recalled the sight of the men in their new uniforms. Although they supposedly were modeled on the celebrated French "Zouaves d'Afrique," the Louisiana Zouaves—nicknamed the "Zoo Zoos" by some of the men—modified their clothing to create a unique appearance for the garments. The fez caps were slightly different than the French version, not tall and straight, but "soft flannel, and close fitting, more like the old-fashioned night cap of our great-granddaddies," in Minnich's words. The deep blue tassel hung down on the side instead of hanging in the back. As for the jackets, the Louisiana unit changed colors, preferring dark blue jackets and vests and red tape trimmings rather than the yellow trimmings on the original Zouave uniforms. Unlike the boots worn by French Zouaves, de Gournay's men "had quite a variety in shape and sizes, black shoes, connecting with the overlapping leggings by white gaiters."[8]

Not long after Coppens organized the First Louisiana Zouaves, the men traveled to Pensacola, Florida, where Gen. Braxton Bragg assumed command. At Pensacola, Bragg's officers reviewed the company roster and decided that Coppens's Zouaves were supposed to be a light infantry unit, which normally would not employ a heavy artillery battery. Thus, they detached Company E from the First Louisiana Zouaves and redesignated the group as the Orleans Independent (Heavy) Artillery Battery.[9]

Minnich was serving as a private in the unit when Coppens and his men were ordered to Virginia. They stayed for a brief period in Richmond—spending their first night there in a warehouse on Cary Street that later would be modified into the Libby Prison—before receiving orders to advance to Yorktown and place themselves under the command of Brig. Gen. John Bankhead Magruder. "Prince John," as Magruder's men nicknamed him, had assumed command of Confederate troops stationed near Yorktown. He fully expected that Gen. George B. McClellan and the Union army would soon arrive at the mouth of the York River on the lower Virginia peninsula and advance toward Richmond. Magruder was charged with erecting defenses to slow Union troops and thereby protect the Confederate capital.[10]

Minnich remained on duty at Yorktown for almost a year. In August 1861, the First Louisiana Zouaves moved to Williamsburg to reinforce the network of defenses built to impede the Union ground advance on Richmond. Not long thereafter, the unit received orders to fall back and protect the outskirts of the

In 1861–62, Confederate Brig. Gen. John B. Magruder erected defenses at Yorktown, Virginia, to stop the Union advance on Richmond. This photograph of Magruder's heavy artillery was taken in June 1862. Courtesy of the Library of Congress.

Confederate capital. In 1862, the Zouaves moved once again, but this time to the western theater of the war as part of the army defending Port Hudson, Louisiana. During all of this movement, Minnich and the men serving in the heavy artillery battalion, now permanently detached from the Zouaves, remained firmly ensconced at Yorktown. As the Zoo Zoos marched toward their new assignment, Minnich and soldiers from the former Company E bid them farewell. "Shortly after my company was detached and sent to mann [*sic*] the heavy guns on the east and southeast fronts of the defenses, our connection with Coppens' Zouaves ceased," Minnich wrote.[11]

It was a depressing time for him. He had been proud of his unit, and now the Zoo Zoos were gone. Time passed slowly as he and his comrades manned the Yorktown defenses waiting for the expected Yankee onslaught. Like many troops on both sides, Minnich originally thought it was to be a brief affair, but the war seemed to drag on with no end in sight. Their wait became interminable as 1861 gave way to 1862, and still an attack did not come. Those months were anything but exhilarating—often rainy, cold, and muddy. Homesickness and disease were constant companions. The men occupied their time reinforcing earthworks that originally had been constructed by the British during the Revolutionary War some eighty years earlier. "I was in the Yorktown works from about June 20, 1861, until 1:30 o'clock Sunday morning, May 4,

1862," Minnich later wrote of that period. "I was a member of the last squad to leave the works."[12]

Union forces advanced up the peninsula from Fort Monroe toward Richmond in the spring of 1862, eventually finding that the Yorktown fortifications were their only major obstacles. But how strong were the Confederate forces there? No one on the Union side knew. A more intrepid general might have attacked immediately, if for no other reason than to test the defenses and assess the size of the enemy army. General McClellan, however, was anything but intrepid; moreover, he became the dupe of an ingenious Confederate plan. Magruder concocted a clever scheme to march his troops in circles and thereby convince his opponent that he had far more than the thirteen thousand or so men he commanded. Amazingly, the ploy worked. Added to McClellan's naturally hesitant disposition, the theatrical display pushed the Union general to conclude that the Confederates had assembled a large group of defenders that would cost him dearly if he ventured an attack. Consequently, the timid Northern commander hesitated for a month, allowing Confederate forces under Gen. Joseph E. Johnston ample opportunity to fall back and shore up the Richmond defenses. When McClellan's forces finally pushed toward Yorktown on May 4, they discovered that the Confederates had abandoned the position.[13]

After leaving Yorktown to the advancing Yankees in the wee hours of the morning, Minnich and a companion, Ed Kelly, hid to avoid capture, and spent the next night in an orchard near Williamsburg. Much of their journey took place in torrential rain through thick, soupy mud. They eventually made a sixty-mile trek to Richmond and rejoined their respective units, which led Minnich to conclude that the Confederates had bested the celebrated General McClellan with their sleight of hand. "I have always been of the opinion that he was overrated. Time has not changed that opinion," he wrote sixty years later. "He could have passed Yorktown before Johnston's army arrived on the scene."[14]

The summer of 1862 marked a period of indecision for Minnich. He seemed to be at a loss about what to do with his military career after he arrived in Richmond. During this time, the Orleans Independent Artillery Battery was reorganized as the Twelfth Battalion Heavy Artillery, while at the same time de Gournay won promotion from major to lieutenant colonel. Curiously, Minnich did not join his revered commander on de Gournay's adventures with the newly reorganized battalion. In fact, Minnich's service record indicates that he deserted the Confederate cause soon after he arrived in Richmond.[15]

Despite official War Department records to the contrary, he did not desert the service, but neither did he join de Gournay's new battalion. It may seem odd

Munnich took part in the Battle of Chickamauga in September 1863. Reprinted from *Prisoners of War and Military Prisons* by Asa B. Isham, Henry M. Davidson, and Henry B. Furness.

that Minnich left the company of a commander he obviously held in high regard. Apart from de Gournay, however, he had little to keep him in the new battalion. The Louisiana Zouaves had moved on to Port Hudson, taking with them his close friends and comrades. He eventually drifted into a cavalry unit, Rowan's Kentucky Rangers, in the summer of 1862. It was during his cavalry service in 1862 and 1863—first with the Kentucky Rangers and later with the Sixth Georgia Cavalry—that Minnich would come under fire and ultimately find himself face-to-face with the enemy. He fought in many skirmishes in Kentucky, Georgia, and Tennessee, distinguishing himself most notably during the first day at the battle of Chickamauga on the shores of a Georgia creek that would become infamous in the annals of military history as the "River of Blood." Finally, in January 1864, he became what many soldiers feared more than anything, even more than death—a prisoner of war.[16]

As Minnich fought his way through the eastern theater, another man served his country in the fight for the Virginia peninsula. "At an early date in the war," Warren Lee Goss recalled years later, "I was a member of the United States engineer corps of the regular army, at that time consisting of one company, and two others partially formed, all under Captain Duane, for some time chief engineer of the army of the Potomac."[17]

Goss's commanding officer, Capt. James Chatham Duane, was a celebrated engineer, a graduate of Union College, and a former instructor at the U.S. Army Military Academy at West Point. Stationed at Fort Pickens when the war began, he had been assigned to the Army of the Potomac early in 1862, where he commanded the engineer battalion during the siege of Yorktown. Duane impressed his superiors as a gifted and creative engineer, especially under fire. He succeeded in building bridges across the Chickahominy River and the White Oak Swamp before taking part in the bloody fighting at Gaines's Mill on June 27, 1862.[18]

Goss joined Captain Duane's battalion at Yorktown, although he found no cause for self-congratulations. He saw little action, finding himself mired down in construction and other dull but necessary activities undertaken by engineers in time of war. "I performed the usual duties as an engineer at Yorktown, at Williamsburg, and on the Chickahominy, until, being in the first stages of a fever, I was sent to Savage's Station, where I was taken prisoner," he wrote in his first book.[19]

A generation of young men enlisted in the Union Army in 1861. Reprinted from *Recollections of a Private* by Warren Lee Goss.

Two weeks before he was captured, Goss had written a letter to friends predicting that he would soon dine in the Confederate capital at Richmond. At the time he wrote the letter, of course, Goss was engaging in a young man's penchant for sarcasm. Like many Union soldiers and officers, he believed that hostilities would be short-lived and the Rebels would soon capitulate. While it was true that they had not been defeated within sixty days, as Goss and his comrades originally had assumed, the matter undoubtedly would be settled quickly once the ragtag Southern army faced a superior fighting force on the battlefield. Little did he realize that his words would be prophetic, although not in the manner in which they were intended. Goss would dine soon enough in Richmond—not as a conquering hero, but as a prisoner of war.[20]

He also learned that his pronouncements on the imminent death of the Southern Confederacy were premature. "On the 27th of June I arrived at Savage's Station," he recalled, "the sound of battle on every side telling how desperate was the nature of the contest." He was confined to the camp hospital, feverish and weak. Outside, twenty thousand troops held the enemy in check along the Williamsburg Road as the Army of the Potomac sought to escape by way of the White Oak Swamp. At five o'clock on the afternoon of June 29, the Confederates advanced on Goss's position. Lying prostrate in the hospital, the private could do nothing but listen to the boom of the big guns as they drew ever closer. "Sometimes the roar of the conflict would almost cease, but only to be renewed with more terrible vigor."[21]

As he lay on his bunk, tossing and turning with fever, he heard a chorus of terrible high-pitched screams. Goss described the noise as the "hyena-like yell of the rebels." It was a ferocious sound, indicating that the enemy was advancing along the Williamsburg Road, and it frightened Goss almost as much as the sounds of artillery fire. The bone-chilling shrieks were his first encounter with the famous Rebel Yell that sent ripples of fear through thousands of Union soldiers on hundreds of battlefields during the war.[22]

The surge of the Confederates late in June 1862 seemed inexplicable to men serving in the Army of the Potomac. Lost in the fog of war, they knew only that General McClellan's Peninsula campaign had not gone as they had expected. Richmond was supposed to fall and the war would end. Yet somehow the Southerners refused to yield. Even as McClellan's forces turned and retreated back toward Washington, D.C., the redoubtable Rebels were far from beaten. They gave chase, an act of such utter audacity that it seemed beyond comprehension.

Goss and his superiors did not yet realize that the war had taken a sudden turn for the worse, at least insofar as the Union cause was concerned, owing to a fortuitous chain of events. Gen. Joseph E. Johnston, commander of the Confederate forces defending Richmond, had been grievously wounded at the battle of Seven Pines on May 31. The next day, Gen. Robert E. Lee—described by one fellow Confederate as "Audacity Personified"—stepped in and assumed command of the newly rechristened Army of Northern Virginia. Although he initially put his men to work fortifying the Richmond defenses, Lee was not satisfied taking a defensive position. Within only a few weeks he had divided his forces—one group defended the capital while another attacked McClellan—and set into motion a series of cunning maneuvers that transformed him into a legend. By war's end, Lee was widely regarded as one of the finest military commanders in American history.[23]

Thus, with the benefit of hindsight, the aggressive Confederate push at the end of June 1862 was not as confusing as it seemed to Union troops at the time. With "Marse Robert" at the helm, Southern forces would take advantage of McClellan's natural hesitancy and draw him away from Richmond. It was only through luck and the valor of Goss's comrades that he survived that interminable day lying in the camp hospital as the enemy repeatedly attacked.

Having momentarily escaped from the clutches of the Confederates, Goss and his hospital mates treated wounded soldiers carried from the field. He was still feverish and weak, but he assisted the surgeons as much as he could to dress wounds and care for the injured. As happened so often during his military service, Goss barely escaped death that day. "At one time, while aiding a young surgeon (whose name I did not learn) who was amputating a limb, as I turned aside to obtain water for his use, the surgeon and patient were killed and terribly mutilated by the explosion of a shell."[24]

The brush with calamity no doubt frightened Goss, but he masked his fear. He would not allow himself to panic when so many young soldiers around him displayed monumental courage under fire. He especially recalled one wounded private from the Fifteenth Massachusetts Regiment, brought into the hospital after he had been slashed across the face with a saber.

"I have been thinking," the young man said when he saw Goss, "how proud I shall be some day of these scars. How proud my mother will be!"

A sudden artillery barrage brought the soldier to his feet. "Where is my rifle?"

Goss was astonished at such exemplary devotion to duty. "Surely you will not go into the fight wounded as you are!"

The private slowly turned and said, in a low, reverential tone as he pointed, "Look yonder! On the hill-side is the flag of my brigade, and I never could forgive myself if I neglected this chance to render service to my country." With that, the young man staggered out to mix with his comrades and defend his position.

Goss stared in wonder at the departing figure. Although he tried to refrain from romanticizing the war, he could not contain his admiration for the young soldier. "He went, and my heart went with him."[25]

Fighting continued to erupt sporadically throughout the afternoon and evening. "When this conflict was over," Goss remembered, "worn and exhausted with sickness and my exertions, yet content in the conviction that victory was ours, I wrapped myself in my blanket and slept soundly." He was confident that the situation would be greatly improved in the morning.[26]

Sometime during the night, Confederate forces moved on the Union position once again. Too weak and too tired to renew the fight, the Army of the Potomac withdrew from the field, leaving behind all persons who could not move without delay. When Goss awoke, he found that the enemy had crept into the hospital and posted a sentry. He had become a prisoner of war.

"During the three or four days we remained here, the treatment experienced in the main was good, although no attention was given us, such as providing rations and medicines," he later reported. Still, Goss fought the fever and felt better despite his dire circumstances. Eventually, Confederate officers appeared to interrogate the captives, but they received little useful information.

The prisoners reacted to their internment in different ways. Most of the sick and injured noticed few differences apart from the lack of attention and the scarcity of rations. As they suffered through pain and weariness, they lost all interest in ideology or causes. One strange fellow even appeared nonchalant, whistling and joking as though he were among friends. Goss wisely kept to himself, refusing to speculate on what the future might hold.

"Our army will be in Washington in a few days," a Southern journalist said casually as he passed through the hospital.

"Undoubtedly," Goss replied, "but they will go there as I shall go to Richmond soon." In uttering this impertinent remark, he was still confident that McClellan would commence a brilliant assault on the Confederate capital within a few days or, at most, a week or two.[27]

While the men waited to be transported to a prison or paroled, a "seedy-looking officer" arrived on the scene. Goss accosted him, asking how the wounded and sick Union soldiers would be taken to Richmond. "In ambulances," the Confederate replied. As the officer rode away, a Rebel guard pointed. "That is Jackson, our general," he said proudly.

Goss was unimpressed with his one and only encounter with the legendary figure. "True enough, as I ascertained afterwards, it was Stonewall Jackson, who proved himself, in the few words of conversation I had with him, to be as big a liar as the rest of the rebels I had met; for he must have known that the rebel army were greatly deficient in the article for the use of their wounded." Needless to say, the prisoners never saw the inside of an ambulance. They rode to Richmond in railroad boxcars.[28]

On July 5 the boxcars set out in sweltering heat. By Goss's calculations, at least twenty men died during the journey. They arrived in Richmond and, despite their pitiful condition, were made to stand at attention. Gazing around, Goss saw that they were a hard-looking crowd of feeble, sick, and wounded men, in most cases barely able to stand. "Many were hopping on rude crutches; others, with amputated arms and shattered shoulders, moved as far as possible from their staggering companions, and were constantly pressed back into the surging mass by the bayonets of the brutal guard." Gone were the gentle Confederates in the field. These rear-guard troops took to their task with relish, pushing the prisoners through the streets of Richmond with little empathy for the plight of the captives.[29]

A mob gathered around the men as they stumbled toward their destination. Goss took note of the crowd's angry mood. Even young children spewed forth a torrent of epithets that would have made him blush under other circumstances. A few women ventured to utter a kind remark and, at the risk of their lives, one or two threw food to the men. A Confederate officer approached on horseback, sneering and asking if this was "Falstaff's army of recruits." Refusing to be cowed, several men answered sarcastically, and the officer rode away in disgust.[30]

Scores of sick and badly wounded men collapsed in the streets from sheer exhaustion, but Goss and the others somehow found the strength to march. By nightfall, they halted in front of their temporary quarters on Cary Street. The guards searched them for weapons and anything of value, which their captors immediately seized as contraband of war. They relieved Goss of his jackknife

Goss was among a group of Union prisoners of war herded into Confederate "prison number two" in Richmond in 1862. Reprinted from *The Soldier's Story* by Warren Lee Goss.

and comb, the only personal items he possessed apart from the ragged, sweat-soaked clothes on his back.[31]

After standing more or less at attention in front of an edifice called "prison number two" for close to two hours, the men stumbled into the interior of the building. Until recently, it had served as a three-story tobacco warehouse. Goss found the place to be filthy and poorly ventilated. As soon as he entered the warehouse, he was forced to fight for each breath of stale air. Other prisoners of war had been housed in the building before Goss and his group arrived, and the lingering odor of feces, vomit, and rotten flesh was almost unbearable. "The room in which I, with about two hundred of my companions, was placed, was too filthy for description," he recalled. "Here, for five days, almost suffocating from want of air, and crowded for room, I remained, having rations issued to me only twice during the five days, and those poor in quality, and insufficient in quantity for a sick man."[32]

With no medication dispensed and little room for sleeping, the men somehow endured the squalid conditions. "Constant interference of some one's feet with another's head or shins caused such continued wrangling as to make night and day more like an abode of fiends than one of human beings." Finally, the guards flung open the doors and marched the captives back into the fresh air. The men savored the pleasant interlude, however brief. Perhaps their fortunes would soon improve.[33]

Any hopes they entertained that they would be transported to a better place or exchanged were dashed when they found themselves standing in front of the Libby warehouse, the most infamous of Richmond prisons. As impossible as it seemed, Goss realized that his current situation was even worse than it had been in the confines of prison number two. Libby Prison "has often been described," he wrote, "and yet from the description given, no adequate idea of the sufferings endured can be formed." In preparing his memoirs in the years following the war, it would be his task to try as best he could to describe the indescribable.[34]

Minnich and Goss were two everyday soldiers caught in the grip of history, hardly unique in tales of the Civil War. Like thousands of their brethren, they fought in the woods and fields of the American landscape, struggled through brutal campaigns in miserable weather, endured almost unimaginable hardships and suffering, and yet survived their experiences to reflect on the meaning of that seminal historical event. Looking back, both men viewed their time in the ranks as the halcyon days of their military careers. Life in captivity, subject to the whim and mercy of the enemy, deprived of adequate food, water, shelter, medical attention, and companionship was another matter. If their days among their comrades at arms were the finest they had known, soon both men would bear witness to a far less glorious side of the war—days of darkness, depravity, and despair.

TWO

The Black and Reeking Pits

On a cold winter morning in mid-January 1864, John Minnich and his marching companion, Dick Murdock, sat on their horses near a field that afforded them a half-mile view of the open road in each direction. The air was so frigid the men could see their breath. Rubbing their hands together, the two sentries shivered, struggling to stay warm.

December and January had been bitterly cold, but the Confederates had shouldered the burden with admirable fortitude. They developed a routine to combat their boredom. Each evening, they crawled from the confines of their tents and thawed out in front of a blazing fire, laughing and joking with each other "with shouts of delight, notwithstanding a cutting north wind, which made our teeth chatter." During those blustery evenings huddled together, seeking warmth from the flames, they traded stories about the rigors of army life, the tenacity of the enemy, and the travails that awaited them in the hard months ahead. Even with such good-natured camaraderie, life was far from pleasant. "Let no one imagine that we were at all comfortable," Minnich remarked of that time. "The ground was wet and cold, and our blankets were only half dry at best."[1]

The men of the Sixth Georgia Cavalry Regiment did not know it when Minnich and Murdock commenced their watch that frozen January morning, but the lull of the East Tennessee winter routine would soon grind to an abrupt halt. "On that particular day I was on vidette [guard] duty with my chum, Dick Murdock, he on the Bay's Mountain road and I on the Morristown-Dandridge road, each at the corner of the field," Minnich recalled. "About 10 A.M. we saw a troop of bluecoats, some 40 to 50, emerge from the woods and ride leisurely toward the main road. Orders were to shoot on sight and fall back to the post at the fork."

In a panic, Murdock called to his friend, "Look out! They're coming."

Minnich did not need a warning. He saw the enemy approach just as Murdock spied the familiar blue uniforms. "As soon as they came into view I started across the field at a gallop, and just as I had reached the crest in the center Dick fired and turned toward camp."[2]

Minnich was not riding Billy Smith. Instead, his mount was a four-year-old sorrel that grew frantic at the sounds of gunfire. No sooner had Minnich discharged his rifle toward the enemy than she was "bucking and rearing like a wild broncho." He fought to hang on, but the horse had grasped the bit firmly in her teeth and refused to relinquish control. At a mad gallop, she dashed into the woods, requiring her rider to duck his head to avoid injury from low-hanging limbs. Just as he thought he would regain control, he lost his rifle. A moment later, he and the horse tumbled to the ground.[3]

The mare got to her feet and scampered off into the woods, leaving Minnich limping and without a weapon. Peering through the trees, he saw the animal encounter a group of Union soldiers, who immediately grabbed her reins. Despite his dire circumstances, Minnich found the scene mildly amusing. "In fact, I considered that she had deliberately deserted, and she Southern born and bred!"[4]

His amusement was short-lived. The bluecoats were not far away, and Minnich knew he was vulnerable. "I thought surely that some of them would detach in my direction, and the fear of capture (I always feared capture more than bullets, and they nearly scared me out of several years' growth) lent wings to my feet. But O such wings!" He threw himself ever deeper into the Tennessee woods, his flight enhanced by the downward slope of the land. Branches and briars slapped at his face and tore at his clothes, but he would not pause. Thinking only of the terrible consequences of capture, he pushed himself long past the normal point of physical exhaustion.

Winded and still limping, Minnich came to a road and stumbled across. His boots were loaded down with mud, which made his mad dash for freedom even more difficult. He found "it was an effort to drag the load to the fence on the opposite side and hoist myself over, where I cuddled up to the bottom of the rails like a rabbit, expecting every moment to see a Yankee trooper looking for me."[5]

To Minnich's amazement, he had escaped. When he caught his breath, he got to his feet, brushed himself off, and headed back toward camp. Except for a bruise on his leg where the horse had fallen on him, Minnich was not injured.

While he limped along the road, a woman came out of her house and stood on the porch, watching him suspiciously. Without a word, he passed by her house and cut into the woods. All the time, he muttered under his breath, "berating myself for being such a 'damn fool' when I might have been with Dick and the rest of the boys and have retained my self respect."[6]

The adventure was not yet concluded. He came upon a small group of Union troops scouring a nearby field. Surmising that they were searching for him, Minnich fell silent and slipped back into the forest while they moved through the high grass close to his position. Not only was he afraid of being captured, but he knew he would be humiliated if they recovered his Enfield rifle—"My 'Old Reliable,'" as he called it.

Holding his breath, he watched them comb through an area he had galloped past only minutes earlier. The men eventually moved on, leaving Minnich alone and greatly relieved. When he was certain they would not return, he ventured past the safety of the woods "and trudged across the field and road, gathering real estate, title free, at every step, and was soon in possession of my hat and trusty Enfield."[7]

He straggled back to camp expecting to be the butt of many jokes, but he was relieved to find that the "boys" had other matters on their minds and "acted decent" about the silly episode. The other matters turned out to be an order to resume marching to forestall the capture of foodstuffs east of Dandridge. Shortly after Minnich returned from his wild adventure, his regiment took to the "Chucky" road toward that little town.[8]

When he awoke the next morning, he was sore and bruised from his misadventures, but otherwise in good health and fine spirits. A low mist hung on the horizon, coating the woods and fields around the Confederate position like a pewter-colored shroud. Sentinels reported that the Yankees had left the field sometime during the night, but Minnich was skeptical. He had experienced the bluecoats' subterfuge on numerous occasions, and he wanted to assess the situation for himself. When he asked his commanding officer, Colonel Hart, if someone should slip into the woods and reconnoiter the area, he received permission to do it himself.[9]

Entering the woods near a small creek, he cautiously stepped through the brush. Had any enemy sharpshooters been in position, he would have made an inviting target. Fortunately, his presence went undetected. This stealth allowed him a rare opportunity to creep up behind a Union soldier. The fellow lay on his stomach facing away from the creek and, at first blush, Minnich supposed him to be dead, left to rot on the cold winter ground. As he drew closer, to his amazement Minnich saw that the man was very much alive.[10]

He must have heard a noise, for the soldier suddenly swung around and reached for his rifle. Before he could raise it and take aim, Minnich pushed a gun barrel into the man's face. The fellow's eyes grew wide.

"Don't do that," Minnich said in a soft voice. "I don't want to hurt you worse than you are."

"I'm not hurt at all," the man assured him.

"Well, then, take your hand off of your gun, and leave it there. I'll take charge of it myself. Get up and step off here, and I'll take you to the rear."

The soldier hesitated as if he did not fully comprehend the circumstances of his capture. Finally, with no option left but to accept the inevitable, he shrugged. "Well, I guess you got me."

"You bet I have." With that terse comment, Minnich waved his rifle at the man, motioning for him to get to his feet.

As they started back toward the Confederate line, the Yankee seemed surprised at his situation. "Where are our fellows?" he asked.

Minnich told him that they had fled during the night. When the soldier refused to believe that he would have been deserted, Minnich adopted a patient, persuasive tone. "How do you think I could get here without getting shot if they were still in that brush over there?"

The logic of Minnich's remark stopped the conversation cold. They trudged through the bushes in silence. A few minutes later, as they emerged from the woods and marched toward the Confederate camp, a general officer wearing a gray uniform approached. Minnich saluted.

"Where did you take your prisoner?" the general asked.

Minnich provided a succinct version of events and offered his opinion that taking the prisoner was not a particularly notable achievement. This self-effacing attitude brought a smile to the officer's face. Turning to the new prisoner, he questioned the man, but got very little useful information from the exchange apart from learning that the youngster was a sergeant in Company I of the 125th Ohio under Colonel Moore's command.

Far from being angry at the soldier's reticence, the general commended him. "You are a good soldier, sergeant, and I cannot blame you for not giving any information about your own troops which might be of some disadvantage to them." Looking at Minnich, he nodded. "Good day."[11]

As the general left the scene, Minnich marched his prisoner to the rear and placed him in the custody of the provost guard. With mixed emotions, he walked away from the fellow and returned to the Sixth Georgia Cavalry. As he departed, he looked back at the sad face of the bluecoat and wondered what

Union troops guard a group of Confederate soldiers that was captured on the battlefield. Courtesy of the National Archives.

fate held in store for the prisoner. Years later, Minnich satisfied his curiosity by examining a copy of Union Colonel Moore's report. "I learned that he was sent to Andersonville, from which 'hell hole' (according to Northern historians) he was released in 1865 and returned home. I was glad to learn that he outlived the war, and though his name was given in the report, my treacherous memory refuses to recall it, much to my regret."[12]

He could not know it at the time, but Minnich had participated in his last extended adventure on the battlefield. He would soon experience a different side of the war, just as the hapless sergeant from the 125th Ohio experienced it—in captivity. On January 27, 1864—less than two weeks after he captured the unfortunate Ohio soldier—Minnich fought in one final engagement at Fair Gardens. As the fighting subsided, he was captured at Hamburg, five miles from Sevierville, Tennessee. His amazing string of good fortune on the field of battle finally, irrevocably, came to an end.[13]

Soon he would be loaded into a boxcar headed for a new prison constructed on the banks of the Mississippi River along the Illinois-Iowa border. Few Americans had heard of Rock Island early in 1864, but the site would enter the public consciousness before war's end. In the sixteen months fol-

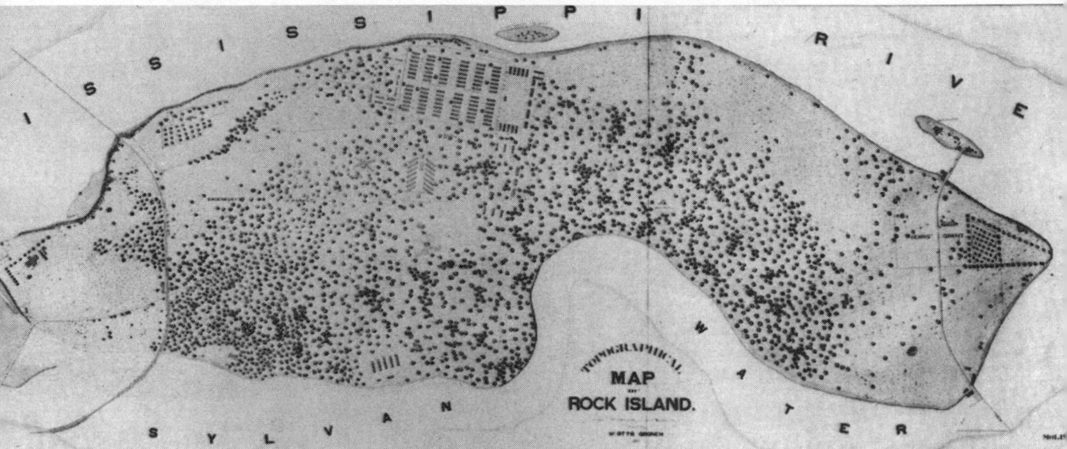

This 1870 topographical map of Rock Island shows the location of the prison barracks on the northern end of the island. Courtesy of the Rock Island Arsenal Museum.

lowing his capture, John Wesley Minnich would have a front-seat view of one of history's most horrific scenes.[14]

While Minnich galloped through the Tennessee countryside with the Confederate cavalry, Warren Lee Goss experienced a far different side of the war. As a prisoner in Richmond, he was feverish and weak, facing bleak prospects for survival. By the time he was ushered into the Libby Prison in 1862, former inmates and an incensed Northern public already had singled it out for notoriety. In the vitriolic words of one Union guest, it was a terrible hellhole, a place known sarcastically as the "Hotel de Libby."[15]

Originally constructed as a brick warehouse on Cary Street by Luther Libby, a businessman from Maine who came to Richmond to try his hand as a ship chandler, the edifice was three stories high in the front and four stories in the rear. It was conveniently located in Richmond's bustling commercial warehouse district and thus accessible by both barge and rail. Set back from the congestion on Main Street, the building was relatively easy to guard and virtually impregnable. As an added benefit, it boasted of running water and three oblong rooms well suited for incarcerating prisoners. Confederate authorities were so anxious to requisition the site for use as a prison that they showed up one day and ordered Luther Libby and his family to vacate the premises within forty-eight hours. The owners left so quickly that they neglected to remove the sign "Libby & Son" displayed in front of the warehouse.[16]

The Libby Prison still displayed the sign "Libby & Son, Ship Chandlers" when Warren Lee Goss arrived in 1862. Reprinted from *Life and Death in Rebel Prisons* by Robert H. Kellogg.

Although Goss and other captives referred to the horrors of the prison as "indescribable," that characterization did not stop them from publishing numerous accounts of the building's physical appearance and the wretched treatment afforded the prisoners. "It is a capacious warehouse, built of brick and roofed with tin," Union Lt. Col. F. F. Cavada recalled. "There are nine rooms, each one hundred and two feet long by forty-five wide. The height of the ceilings from the floor is about seven feet; except in the upper story, which is better ventilated, owing to the pitch of the roof. At each end of these rooms are five windows."[17]

"The sashes from the windows had been removed, and the places supplied by grates made of one-inch rods of iron, passing through three crossbars, two and a half by three fourth inches; the whole firmly imbedded in the walls," prisoner A. O. Abbott wrote. "A flight of stairs led from each room to the one above, but at night those leading to the lower story were taken down, and sentinels were stationed to prevent any attempt to escape that way. A hydrant in each room supplied us with water from the river, and an apology for a bath-tub was placed in each for our use."[18]

A report prepared by the U.S. Sanitary Commission as part of a commission of inquiry in 1864 found conditions in the Libby Prison almost unbelievable. "It seems incredible," the authors remarked. "Ten feet by two were all that could be claimed by each man—hardly enough to measure his length upon; and

Libby Prison was packed beyond capacity with inmates. Reprinted from *The Capture, the Prison Pen, and the Escape* by Willard W. Glazier.

even this was further abridged by the room necessarily taken for cooking, washing and clothes-drying."[19]

"A portion of the lower floor was cut up into small rooms for various purposes," another prisoner remembered. "The lower west room was further subdivided into offices; the middle room was furnished with cook-stoves, and used for a kitchen. The lower east room was the prison hospital." The description does not sound especially harrowing, but the lowest level of the building was infinitely worse. "In the basement were the dungeons in which the recaptured men were confined. These dungeons, or cells, were entirely unfurnished, without fires, with iron gratings for windows, and infested with rats, which the prisoners confined there sometimes caught and procured to be cooked by their Negro attendant."[20]

Physical descriptions, of course, could not capture the true character of the place.

The dungeons especially brought forth the florid prose typical of postwar memoir writers. One commentator wrote, "even a short stay in those dungeons amounted, without a doubt, to an aeon of agony. One person, and one alone, took pleasure in them. With hellish delight—the ecstasy that devils are said to feel about the torment of their victims—Dick Turner [the Confederate inspector] committed helpless people to bread and water in the black and reeking pits." As for the prison in general, a "strong line of sentinels is established around the building with strict orders to fire upon any man who ventures near the windows to get a glimpse of the scenery without, or breathe unvitiated air," Willard W. Glazier recalled. "In these filthy and unfurnished rooms we are huddled together like sheep in a slaughter-pen, awaiting the approach of monsters in human form, who are eager to destroy us by any mode of torture." Cavada observed that "there is something about it indicative of the grave, and, indeed, it *is* a sort of unnatural tomb, whose pale, wan inhabitants gaze vacantly out through the barred windows on the passers-by, as if they were peering from the mysterious precincts of another world."[21]

This drawing, adapted from an 1865 photograph, shows another exterior view of the Libby Prison. Reprinted from *A Prisoner of War in Virginia, 1864–65* by George Haven Putnam.

This was the world that Goss found when he entered the former warehouse. Adding to the descriptions of his comrades, he remembered Libby as a place "where vermin swarmed in every crack and crevice; the floors had not been cleaned for years. To consign men to such quarters was like signing their death warrant." He was filled with dread, wondering if he could survive such torturous conditions in his still-weakened state of health.[22]

As wretched as he felt, Goss recognized that many of his companions were in a far worse condition. On his third day of captivity in Libby, he saw a young soldier, collapsed in a heap on the floor, suffering through the death throes of starvation. "He was covered with vermin," Goss remembered, "the flies had gathered on his wasted hands, on his face, and in the sunken sockets of his eyes." This macabre vignette, as horrible as it was, fascinated him to no end. Still a fairly young man—only in his mid-twenties—Goss had seen few deaths apart from the battlefield carnage he had witnessed along the Williamsburg Road. But this scene in the Libby Prison was up close and personal, a death so immediate and agonizing that it could not be discounted or ignored. "I saw him try to get to his mouth a dirty piece of bread, which he held in his hand: the effort was in vain; the hand fell nerveless by his side; a convulsive shudder, and he was dead."[23]

As ugly as this scene was, it grew worse after the young soldier died. He still clutched the bread in his bony hand as though it were a ticket to salvation or a lifeline to another world. Finally, a Union Zouave with an amputated leg dragged himself over to the corpse and unclasped the fingers, prying the bread from the dead boy's hand. He gobbled up the morsel "like a famished wolf."[24]

Somehow, Goss found the strength of will to exist in these crowded, horrifying conditions for a week. The men who were not unconscious or delirious spoke to each other to relieve their unremitting boredom. Rumor and myth were the currency of prison life. They traded tales of "news" from the front, often speculating on how soon Union forces would whip the Rebels into submission. They

A Russian bloodhound, "Hero," was the subject of many stories, probably apocryphal, told by prisoners in the Libby Prison. Reprinted from *The Soldier's Story* by Warren Lee Goss.

also told stories of sadistic sentries who gleefully brutalized prisoners, each inmate vowing that the cruel beasts would receive their comeuppance at the end of a sword.

One topic of conversation concerned guard dogs employed to chase escaping prisoners. None was more feared than Hero, a massive Russian bloodhound who was said to weigh 198 pounds and stand three feet, two inches from the ground. Hero's exploits were the stuff of legends, and he was thought to prowl the grounds at Libby and at Castle Thunder, another prison in nearby Petersburg.[25]

To wile away the hours, inmates sometimes broke into song. They were hardly melodious or celebratory choruses, but the tunes reminded men of happier times, and so they helped to make prison life slightly more bearable. "It was the custom, after we were all recumbent and there was quiet across the floor, for two or three of the men who had good voices and good memories to raise a song in which the rest of us joined as far as we knew how or when there was an easy chorus," a resident of the Libby and Danville prisons recalled. "The songs selected were, however, mainly of the quieter not to say sadder variety, which did not include choruses. I have the memory that the songs grew sadder as the winter wore on." Although they sometimes chose jubilant songs such as "Marching Through Georgia," the inmates preferred nostalgic standards like "Mother, Will You Miss Me?" "Tenting on the Old Camp Ground," and "Home, Sweet Home."[26]

Surprisingly, the inmates also traded jokes, although they mostly consisted of gallows humor that did not strike the uninitiated as especially funny. One popular chestnut consisted of a one-liner: "We notice a growing disposition among the prisoners to break out, particularly in the pants." "The boys in No. 4, who were so frightened by finding rice in their soup on Thursday, are recovering," one old saying went. "They are assured by the prison keeper that it was a mistake, and he assures them that it shall not occur again." Mocking the guards' constant refrain that the Confederate States Army was vastly superior to Union forces, prisoners particularly enjoyed the joke that said, "The Southern army is always victorious and never fails to fall back when the enemy advances; and it is an utter impossibility for them to lose more than one man."[27]

As the week slipped by with men trading tall tales and watching their comrades slip into oblivion, what once had seemed horrible became commonplace. A sick prisoner's screams of pain and cries for water no longer sent shivers of fear through the ranks. It was just another among a sea of such episodes in Libby life.

Goss might have endured these circumstances until he died or was paroled had an officer not passed through the building asking for volunteers to move to a Confederate prison on Belle Isle. The only requirement was that the inmate had to be able to get up and walk out of Libby Prison so he could be transported to the new pen. "None of us had ever heard of Belle Island as a prison at the time," Goss later reflected, "and we were eager to better our condition." It couldn't be any worse than Libby, could it? "The chance of benefiting myself was irresistible, and so I managed to crawl and stumble down the stairs into the streets."[28]

A well-known resort for affluent residents of Richmond, Belle Isle was a small island of about eighty acres in the James River directly across from Richmond. It was partially visible through the windows on the southwest corner of the Libby Prison. A bridge leading from the mainland to the island could be guarded easily, thus making Belle Isle a suitable site for corralling inmates. Among the prison population, Goss was not alone in assuming that any pen situated on an island would be a distinct improvement over a poorly ventilated, overcrowded warehouse. At least the air would be fresh and the men would have room to move about.[29]

He would soon learn the error of unfounded assumptions.

THREE

He Is Lost, Indeed, Who Loses Hope

Rock Island is a rocky outcropping of land that juts out of the Mississippi River adjacent to three towns: Davenport, Iowa; Rock Island, Illinois; and Moline, Illinois. Measuring three miles long by half a mile wide, the small island sports limestone cliffs that loom twenty feet above the water. River rapids roar past the area for almost fourteen miles, making entry to and exit from the island by boat exceedingly difficult. During the nineteenth century, lush vegetation decorated the rocks, suggesting a romantic, tropical locale. Many visitors of a bygone era found it aesthetically pleasing. One early observer even concluded that Rock Island was "the handsomest and most delightful spot of the same size, on the whole globe."[1]

The U.S. government assumed ownership of the island in 1804, but it remained vacant until the War of 1812. In 1816, the U.S. Army constructed a fort on the western edge of the island named in honor of President Madison's secretary of war, John Armstrong. Troops were garrisoned at the fort until 1836. At the time, it was a frontier post, far removed from anything resembling civilization, and duty there consisted of wiling away the hours engulfed in boredom. From time to time, soldiers at Fort Armstrong took part in campaigns to fight local Indian tribes, most notably during the Black Hawk War of 1831, but such activities were the exception rather than the rule. For a five-year period beginning in 1840, the army stored ordnance on the island, but otherwise it remained deserted. In 1862, the Union decided to build an arsenal there and Rock Island became a permanent locus for military activities.[2]

A year later, during the summer of 1863, Lt. Col. William H. Hoffman, commissary general of Union prisons, was desperate to alleviate overcrowding in the camps under his command, most of which existed in the east. He faced

Early in its history, Rock Island served as the location of a military installation, Fort Armstrong. Courtesy of the Rock Island Arsenal Museum.

several daunting obstacles. The agreement for exchanging prisoners had unraveled in May, shortly before Union victories in July at Gettysburg and Vicksburg. Along with these victories, the Union gained record numbers of Confederate prisoners. Looking around at available facilities, Hoffman found that Rock Island was an attractive site for a new prison. It was relatively isolated from the general population—which meant that security would not be a major problem—and Union soldiers already occupied the island as they worked to establish and maintain the arsenal. The only practical methods of entering or leaving Rock Island were by crossing a 1,550-foot, government-owned bridge to the Iowa side or using two smaller bridges on the Illinois side—one leading to Moline and the other to the town of Rock Island.[3]

Hoffman informed Gen. Montgomery C. Meigs, quartermaster general of the army, that the site was suitable to meet Union needs, and he wasted no time in acting on Hoffman's recommendation. In July 1863, Meigs ordered Capt. Charles A. Reynolds of the Quartermaster Department to survey the land and begin constructing barracks to house ten thousand prisoners of war. This was a tall order, for it required Reynolds to oversee construction of eighty-four buildings and a wooden fence around the site in a relatively short time.[4]

Reynolds had enjoyed an up-and-down career in the U.S. Army by the time he received Meigs's order. He had served as a private during the Mexican War before his discharge from military service in 1848. Although he had not attended the U.S. Military Academy at West Point—the traditional venue for career soldiers—Reynolds had been enthralled by the allure of life in uniform.

Late in 1863, Capt. Charles A. Reynolds of the U.S. Quartermaster Department came to Rock Island to build the prison barracks. Courtesy of the Gil Barrett Collection, U.S. Army Military History Institute.

In March 1855, he returned to the service as a second lieutenant in the Ninth Infantry. Advancing up the ranks, he briefly served as a captain before the outbreak of war. Finally, he accepted the temporary rank of lieutenant colonel while serving as General Grant's quartermaster in 1862–63. Reynolds and Grant eventually had a falling-out; as a result, Reynolds was relieved of duty in April 1863. He again served as a captain when Meigs sent him to Rock Island.[5]

Although he did not know it when he received his assignment, the politically naïve captain would soon find himself in an untenable position. Control of the island was anything but clear as three separate government authorities exercised command over different administrative departments. A government agent on duty, T. J. Pickett, operated a small farm and allowed local citizens to board horses on the island, but his duties did not extend beyond these minimal activities. At the same time, Maj. Charles Kingsbury assumed command over the island as well as the arsenal, and his imperial attitude did little to endear him to anyone. In the words of commentator Benton McAdams, "During the war many West Pointers looked down on their volunteer counterparts. Kingsbury was not so narrow: he looked down on everybody." Later, Col. Richard H. Rush of the U.S. Invalid Corps briefly served as the prison commandant, although he was replaced after only a few months by Col. Adolphus J. Johnson of the Eighth New Jersey Regiment, who remained in command until the prison closed in July 1865.[6]

From Reynolds's perspective, the rivalry that sprang up between the towns on the Illinois and Iowa sides of the river was a greater problem than the confusion over the military chain of command. When Reynolds placed an advertisement for lumber in the Rock Island *Argus*, the Democratic paper on the Illinois side, Meigs and other Republicans loyal to the Lincoln administration called the hapless colonel to task. To placate his superiors, Reynolds began working with Republican citizens in Davenport, on the Iowa side of the river, to purchase necessary supplies and matériel.

This action prompted J. B. Danforth, the Copperhead, or pro-Southern, editor of the *Argus*, to take pen in hand and attack Reynolds savagely. In a typically scathing editorial questioning even the smallest decisions that Reynolds made in constructing the barracks, the *Argus* hinted at the officer's suspect motives. "Can anybody tell what influences were brought to bear to induce Capt. Reynolds to locate the military prisons on the north side of the island, exposed to the bleak northwest winds, and in a position where they will be partially cut off from this end of the island?" The only logical answer, according to the newspaper, was patently obvious: Reynolds displayed unconscionable favoritism. "Was the proposed location, on the north side, selected to please Davenport['s] political shoddy contractors?"[7]

In this tense atmosphere of backbiting and political intrigue, Reynolds's superiors constantly interfered, micromanaging every stage of the project. Reflecting Colonel Hoffman's legendary thrift, Meigs reminded Reynolds that "the barracks for prisoners at Rock Island should be put up in the roughest and cheapest manner. Mere shanties, with no fine work about them." Later, when he received word that construction on the barracks was being handled with too much care and attention to detail, Meigs admonished his subordinate that "very rough work only is needed; light frames and sheds."[8]

Despite these taxing conditions, Reynolds managed to complete his assignment. By October 1863, only two months after he arrived, he could report that the camp stood ready to receive the first shipment of prisoners in the near future. At that time, he had completed most of the exterior work on the buildings, although some delays on the interior work had occurred because of a lack of materials and squabbling among local residents as they competed for Union labor and materials contracts.[9]

When construction was finally completed early in 1864, each of the eighty-four barracks was one hundred feet long, twenty-two feet wide, and twelve feet high. They were arranged in six rows, north to south, of fourteen buildings each. Following a uniform plan of construction, Reynolds ensured that every building contained twelve windows, two doors, two roof ventilators, and a kitchen. Each edifice was designed to house 120 inmates, with eighty-two feet of sleeping space. The site also included two hospitals—one for jailers and one for prisoners—and pesthouses to treat communicable diseases, although the pesthouses were built after the completion of the barracks.[10]

A stockade encircled the prison barracks, extending fifty feet from the sides of the outermost buildings. Constructed of wooden boards, measuring twelve feet high and placed on their ends, the stockade walls included a parapet four feet from the top that allowed Union guards to patrol the camp. Prisoners were permitted relative freedom of movement along a main avenue ninety feet wide that ran east to west throughout the prison. As long as inmates stayed on the designated road or in the barracks, they generally went unmolested. One notable exception to their freedom involved a trench, deemed the "deadline," that ran parallel to the walls at a distance of twenty-five feet. It was designed so that any inmate who ventured too close to the wall could be detected and shot by a guard before the prisoner could escape.[11]

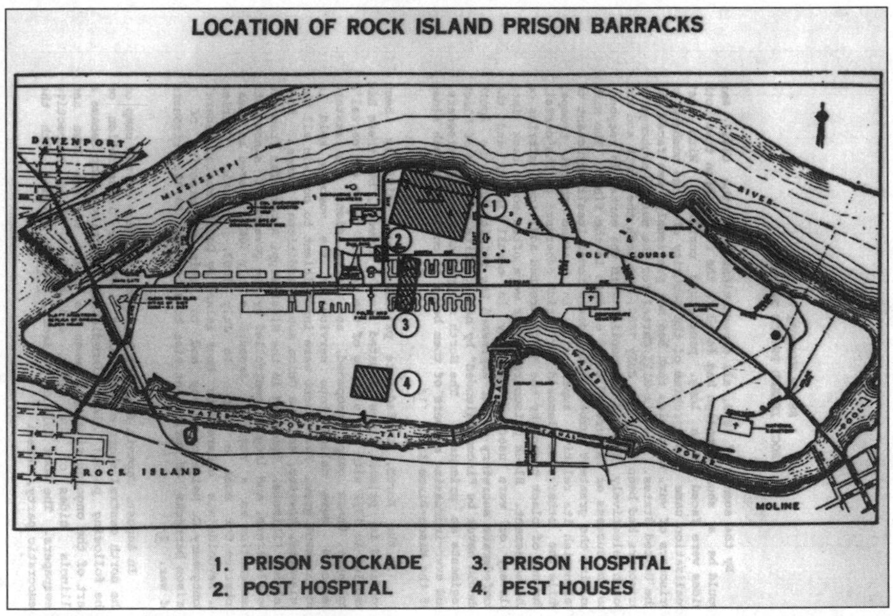

The Rock Island Prison consisted of a stockade, a series of barracks, a hospital, and pesthouses. Courtesy of the Rock Island Arsenal Museum.

November proved to be a busy time at Rock Island. On the second day of the month the first soldiers arrived for guard duty, although it was another seventeen days before their commander, Lieutenant Colonel Shaffner, the provost marshal of prisoners, made his way to the camp. In the meantime, Colonel Hoffman arrived on November 17 to inspect the empty prison and determine whether it was ready to accept prisoners. He was on a tour of the West and had little time to visit the new camp. During his whirlwind inspection, Hoffman found Reynolds's work sufficient to meet the needs of a new prison, although he ordered the construction of two more barracks for the guards. Of course, the prisoners could be used to provide the labor for construction once they arrived, thereby saving on expenses. Building costs for other parts of the camp totaled $125,000, and Hoffman did not wish to invest more funds in the enterprise.[12]

After the visit, Hoffman wrote to the secretary of war that the Rock Island Prison was open for business. Had he spent more time inspecting the camp, he might have hesitated to reach this conclusion, for much work remained to be completed. In fact, even as the first inmates arrived, construction crews labored to finish their tasks. Nonetheless, Hoffman felt enormous pressure to relieve overcrowding at existing prisons. Moreover, a fire that swept through the Camp Douglas Union prison near Chicago a few days before Hoffman's visit to Rock Island left 1,000 inmates without shelter. Hoffman intended to send those men to Rock Island as soon as possible. Thus, the first trickle of prisoners appeared in mid-November, followed by larger shipments: 466 men on December 3; 830 on December 5; 1,300 on December 9; and 1,000 on December 11. By the end of December, 5,592 inmates resided in the new camp. General Grant's forces at Lookout Mountain and Missionary Ridge captured a large percentage of the first Rebels interned at Rock Island.[13]

The arrival of the prisoners was an auspicious occasion, exciting a crowd of local residents who, despite bad weather, turned out to inspect the load of enemy soldiers humbled by their sordid circumstances. "It was a dark, raw, gloomy day, December 3, 1863, when the first Confederate prisoners came," recalled Kate E. Perry, a Southern sympathizer who witnessed the affair. "I promise you, it was a day fraught with intense excitement, never to be forgotten. Real, live Rebels were coming and, ridiculous as it may seem, it is a fact that many citizens were actually afraid of a disarmed foe. Still, they had curiosity to see how he looked, blankly disappointed, no doubt, to find him minus the horns and cloven hoofs."[14]

Most prisoners arrived by train. Stuffed into railroad cars without adequate food and water, the men huddled together while the weather grew increasingly cold as they traveled north away from the mild Tennessee climate. Rock Island was the most distant Union prison yet constructed, and the trip was especially long and arduous. Some men remembered that, at the request of the inmates, guards opened the doors as the train sped past Lake Michigan, affording the Confederates an impressive view. This seemingly kind gesture degenerated into a cruel, sadistic maneuver when the guards refused to close the doors after a few minutes. As the cold wind whipped off the lake, the captives piled onto each other in the hopes of conserving the heat from their bodies to stay warm. To make matters worse, they arrived at a partially completed camp that did not yet have provisions to handle the load.[15]

Col. Richard H. Rush served as the prison commandant when the first prisoners arrived. Recognizing the poor conditions of the barracks, he complained to Hoffman that a lack of sufficient construction materials and guards placed the prison in a precarious position. He also requested guidance on the appropriate chain of command, explaining that he and Major Kingsbury already had disagreed on their overlapping responsibilities. Hoffman was not interested in such minor administrative problems. In a series of dispatches, the commissary general essentially told the commandant to improvise and somehow find a way to operate the camp with the limited resources on hand.[16]

In a flurry of activity, Colonel Rush issued orders and scrambled to accommodate the influx of prisoners, churning out detailed regulations on inmate inspections and the makeup of guard regiments. Although some of his activities smacked of melodrama, Rush appeared to be a competent, reasonably diligent administrator. One commentator has speculated that "had he remained, perhaps much of the coming horror would have been avoided; unfortunately, Rush did not remain." By early December 1863, Rush had been shipped off to Chicago for a new assignment. His replacement, Col. Adolphus J. Johnson, assumed command of Rock Island on December 5.[17]

December can be a hard, bitterly cold month in the Midwest, and it certainly proved to be true in 1863. Virtually every prisoner who arrived at Rock Island during the first four months of the prison's existence commented on the harsh weather. For Confederate soldiers who arrived that month, it was not the handsome, lush tropical paradise that early tourists had enjoyed. "The winter of 1863–64 was intensely cold," inmate Charles Wright of Tennessee recalled years later. "During this time some poor fellows were without blankets, and some even without shoes. They would huddle around the stoves at night and try to sleep." With few blankets or other garments provided to them, the Rock Island captives had to make do with whatever provisions they brought with them into the prison. Those prisoners who came with only the shirts on their backs faced the grim prospect of trying to survive in subzero temperatures. "The feet of those who had no shoes, or were poorly protected, became sore and swollen," Wright

Rock Island was a desolate, uninviting place when the first Confederate prisoners arrived in 1863. Courtesy of the Illinois State Historical Library.

explained. "In one case I saw, mortification no doubt ensued, for the man was taken from my barrack to the hospital and died in a few days."[18]

On December 18, the river began freezing, and by December 21, the ice was thick enough to walk from the mainland to the island without using the nearby bridges. On December 29, a raging winter storm charged through the area, depositing rain, sleet, and snow well past New Year's Day. Newspapers reported that temperatures plummeted to twenty degrees below zero. During this time, the inmates of the Rock Island Prison tried to sleep by "spooning," a process that involved huddling together to take advantage of each other's body heat. When the prisoners were awake, they huddled inside the barracks around stoves that gave off limited heat, but not enough to stave off misery and illness. Frostbite was a common complaint, and any man who ventured outside was almost certain to lose part of an ear or nose as well as exposed fingers or toes.[19]

Although he was not among the first prisoners to arrive, John Minnich echoed the sentiments expressed by Charles Wright and other Rock Island inmates. "As for myself," he wrote, "I was captured in East Tennessee on the 27th of January in shirt sleeves, a light cotton undershirt, with a captured knit woolen overshirt, and many were no better off and some even less warmly fitted." The prisoners prayed that the weather would improve and they might enjoy a much-needed respite from brutal winter conditions, but little did they know that they would soon face a far worse problem than the terrible vicissitudes of a midwestern winter. Epidemics of disease, especially smallpox, swept through the barracks, leaving the weakened, malnourished men fighting for their lives.[20]

—~—

Rock Island bore an uncanny resemblance to the Belle Isle Confederate prison poised on the banks of the James River across from Richmond, Virginia. Both outcroppings jutted incongruously from the surrounding waters, offering idyllic vacation spots in times of peace and horrific prisons in times of war. Their names became infamous in Civil War history.

Belle Isle's physical features were a study in contrasts. The upper portion of the land rose to a high bluff littered with trees, but most of the island was a sandy, barren beach close to the river. The Confederates constructed earthworks three feet high to hold inmates on ten acres of the sandy beach. A narrow lane lined with rows of boards twelve feet high led from a bridge to a heavy gate connected to the earthworks. To improve interior security, the jailers also cut a ditch around the prison site, thus preventing prisoners from tunneling under the earthworks without considerable difficulty. As in other prisons, a line drawn three feet from the ditch became known as the "deadline"; captives were not allowed to move close to the line or the guards would shoot them down.[21]

The Belle Isle Prison could be viewed, at least partially, from the nearby Petersburg Railroad in Manchester, Virginia. Courtesy of the D. Scott Hartzell Collection, U.S. Army Military History Institute.

Prison administrators never constructed permanent housing. They initially provided tents to the men, but they quickly exhausted the available supply. As a result, prisoners who arrived after the first two weeks were forced to brave the elements without shelter of any kind. The more ingenious fellows fashioned homemade "shebangs"—makeshift hovels—from cloth, rags, and remnants of old uniforms, but not everyone could find suitable materials. To add insult to injury, the Confederates planned to reconfigure the camp and pack additional inmates into the space. What began as an improvement on conditions in the Libby Prison rapidly degenerated into a different kind of hell.[22]

As much as they hated Libby, inmates who served time in both prisons reserved their most vivid descriptions and vituperative prose for Belle Isle. "No verdant spot here greets the eye, or softens the glare of the fervid sunlight; on every hand is the glistening, barren sand," one prisoner remarked. As bad as it was in the heat, the winter conditions were even worse. "Those who were outside the tents were in much worse condition. The river was covered with a thin crust of ice, and the camp with snow during part of the time. Need it be said, that many of these half-naked wretches froze to death, or that large numbers lost fingers, ears, and feet from frost?"[23]

Calling the place "one of the Rebel's hells," Sam Boggs remembered that as late arrivals he and his fellow inmates were given "not a tent or shelter of any kind, and without fire; having fasted all day, we were hungry, cold and miserable in the extreme; some had neither pants, coats nor blankets, and we huddled in bunches like shivering swine." They were not allowed to cross the deadline, so men perished from thirst. "Although the James River was within a few yards of us, it would be certain death to try to get to it." The rations were pitifully small. The day after Boggs and his comrades arrived, they received food consisting of "a piece of unsalted corn-bread, about the size of a half-brick given to each man; we were then allowed to get water from the river."[24]

Inmate John McElroy remembered being confined to a former tobacco warehouse known as the "Pemberton Building" in Richmond as his friends shuffled off to the new prison. He wrote in his memoirs, "our men were suffering terribly on that island. It was low, damp, and swept by the bleak, piercing winds that howled up and down the surface of the James. The rations had been much worse than ours."[25]

Arriving in the summer of 1862, Goss shared the general assessment of Belle Isle. He suffered through a notably horrible experience before he even arrived on the island. Stumbling through the streets toward the new pen, he felt lightheaded and fell to his knees. Someone led him into a nearby shop and there a kindly Irishwoman fed him raspberry wine and baker's bread until he came to his senses.

When the old lady asked him if the Union army would soon invade

Richmond, he surmised that they would liberate the city within a week or two. "I hope they will," she told Goss, "for this is a devilish place, and I wish I was in New York."

A guard appeared with a bayonet and ordered Goss to fall back into line. He struggled to his feet and walked outside, falling onto the pavement once again. This time the old woman was not allowed to come to his aid.

"I guess you'd better not go down there, old hoss," the Rebel guard said as he stood over the fallen prisoner. "Belle Isle's a right smart hard place, and I reckon you won't any more'n live to get down thar, anyway."[26]

With further prodding from the bayonet, Goss somehow got to his feet and rejoined the procession of weary Union inmates trudging through the streets of Richmond. As they approached the bridge leading to the island, a torrential rain commenced, drenching the men. This final obstacle was almost too much to endure. Goss thought he would fall again but, much to his amazement, the Rebel guard held him up until they crossed over to the island.[27]

No sooner had Goss stepped off the bridge than he again felt dizzy and confused. The guard was no longer there to prop him up, and so he collapsed into the mud. For the ensuing four or five days, he was engulfed by a feverish delirium. His companions called him "old crazy" because he raved and muttered to himself. When he finally recovered enough to realize what had happened, the scene was like someone's bad idea of hell. According to Goss, "I found myself lying on the damp ground, with no shelter from the driving rain, and hundreds of others around me in the same situation." He endured prison life without shelter—without even "a poor imitation of a tent"—for three weeks.[28]

During those weeks, Goss regained his strength, despite the lack of sufficient food or adequate shelter. "Our rations at this time consisted of one half loaf [of bread] to each man per day, and beans, cooked in water in which bacon had been boiled for the guard—usually containing about twenty percent of maggots—owing to scarcity of salt; thirty percent of beans, and the remainder in water." This meager fare was not enough sustenance to keep a healthy man alive for long, much less inmates in a weakened condition. Against this backdrop, Goss marveled at the enormous lengths to which men resorted to survive.

Bartering occurred among prisoners and guards as the captives sought to gain extra food. Although the rules were explicit that captives and captors were not to fraternize, almost no one adhered to the strict regimen. For prisoners who had nothing to trade, the thin line between life and death became indistinguishable; starvation was a common feature of life on Belle Isle. It is little wonder that many of the drawings and photographs of "human skeletons" that so enraged the

Northern public late in the war featured men who had served their time at the island prison.[29]

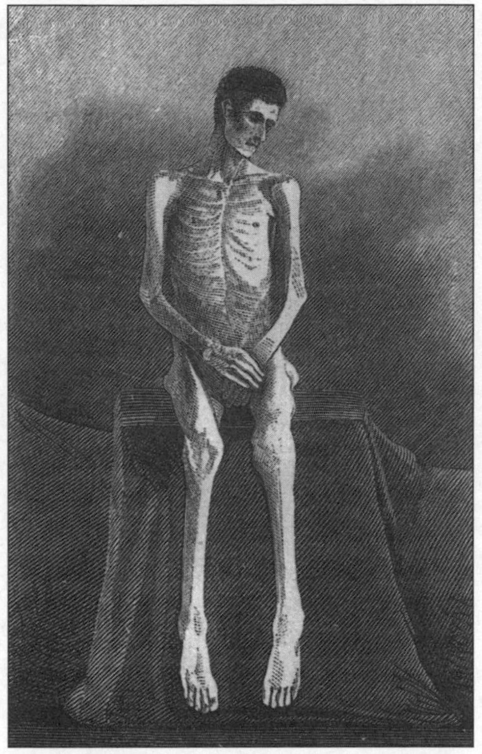

The Northern public was horrified when photographs and drawings circulated showing "human skeletons" who almost starved to death while they were incarcerated on Belle Isle. Reprinted from the U.S. Sanitary Commission's *Narrative of Privations and Sufferings of United States Officers and Soldiers While Prisoners of War*.

Goss recalled one incident that typified the struggles of hungry men. He stumbled upon an "Irish acquaintance" one day and noticed that the fellow was nursing a bacon bone with a bit of meat on it, but it looked almost alive because it was crawling with maggots.

"What are you doing, Jim?"

The man looked at Goss with a comic leer. "Quarrelling with maggots to see who will have the bone," he said as he brushed them away and "went in for a meal."[30]

As repulsive as this scene appeared, Goss understood that desperate men undertake desperate measures. He was one of those desperate men, but he was determined to make his way without "quarrelling with maggots." "As soon as I obtained sufficient strength to walk around, I entered into competition with others, and after trading away my shoes and coat for food, set up as a kind of commission merchant, for dealing in boots and any other article of clothing of trading value." The Rebel guards and officers eagerly greeted Goss's new business, as did prisoners who had something to trade but were too weak to transport their goods to the market near the deadline. For a small fee—an extra johnnycake, potato, or onion—Goss took temporary custody of a sick man's clothing, negotiated the best deal possible with a guard, completed the transaction, and brought food back to the original owner.[31]

Goss's trustworthiness served him well. Owing to his business acumen and his honest dealings, the consignment venture sustained him through the summer of 1862 when weaker men died. His health improved despite the impoverished conditions, and he allowed himself to hope for a better future for the first time since he had been taken captive. He was not naive, however; he recognized that he was suffering from a severe case of "exchange on the brain." Although he hoped that he would be home soon, he knew that he might succumb to the cruel fortunes of prison life at any time. Such was the precarious nature of existence on Belle Isle.

In a thoughtful, if somewhat melodramatic, passage in his postwar memoirs, Goss summarized his philosophy of suffering and hope for the future. "The contemplation of misery teaches the necessity of hope; cut off from comforts and tender sympathies, from the daily intercourse of friends, from the habitual avocations of life—shut out from social pleasures, doomed to mental and physical sufferings, to the lethargy of the heart—he is lost, indeed, who loses hope." Yet a man must face reality. "While preserving hope, we should not build expectations on frail foundations and in disappointments lose it." It was this mixture of hope and prudence that kept Warren Lee Goss alive.[32]

"During the last of July our sufferings were intense," he later recalled. "All other thoughts and feelings had become concentrated in that of hunger." It was the overriding preoccupation of inmates dying in the Belle Isle Prison. The men spoke of little else but johnnycakes, sweet potatoes, beans, ham, and anything even marginally edible.[33]

Lying under the sweltering summer sun, his stomach growling in agony, his lips parched from thirst, Goss had little to do but consider the predicament of the captives. "There were three stages of hunger in my experience," he wrote. "First, the common hungry craving one experiences after missing his dinner and supper; second, this passed away, and was succeeded by headache and a gnawing at the stomach; then came weakness, trembling of the limbs, which, if not relieved by food, was followed by death." It was a common refrain. Littered all about him were the frail corpses of men who had succumbed to their dire straits.[34]

When faced with such extreme conditions, human beings sometimes shed the last vestiges of decency. No behavior is beneath a man if he thinks it will relieve his misery or ease his suffering. Goss observed the brutish behavior of his fellow man firsthand one afternoon when he discovered a young German soldier dying near the deadline on the west side of the camp. "No one was there to care for him and soothe his dying moments; the parched, filthy ground was his deathbed; over his wasted hands and sunken face the flies were gathering, while the disgusting sores of his flesh swarmed with maggots and other vermin."[35]

Moved by the pitiful spectacle, Goss knelt and wet the young man's lips with water from a canteen he had found. Witnessing the scene, another inmate suggested that Goss remove the dying man's boots to make the poor wretch more comfortable. No sooner had Goss done this than the inmate grabbed the boots and scampered off into the swarming crowd, probably to sell the items and profit from the soldier's impending death. Later, when Goss chanced to encounter the opportunist, he castigated this behavior. The shameless fellow merely shrugged and explained that a dying man had no need of boots. "There was some show of reason in this," Goss admitted, "and so much effrontery that I made no reply."[36]

This drawing depicts a scene from the Belle Isle Prison. Reprinted from *Prisoners of War and Military Prisons* by Asa B. Isham, Henry M. Davidson, and Henry B. Furness.

The Darwinian world of a Civil War prison where only the strong—and cunning—survived sometimes brought out human ingenuity in addition to bestial behavior. One afternoon, Goss and his fellows noticed that parts of Belle Isle were a sanctuary for wild geese. The Confederate sentinels claimed nominal ownership of the animals, but did little to enforce their edict. In the meantime, the tempting fowls landed and rested in the tall grass just beyond the deadline. Hungry men looked on the birds with naked greed, but the geese seemed to sense their precarious position. The flock always remained just beyond the reach of the prisoners until one enterprising man concocted a simple, yet stunningly effective plan.

After procuring a handful of corn—no doubt acquired at usurious rates—the entrepreneur sprinkled his investment as close to the deadline as he dared move. He then withdrew a safe distance to observe the scene. Several unsuspecting geese moved to the corn and began eating. With a swiftness and agility surprising in men so weakened by hunger, numerous inmates dashed for the birds, grabbing a goose and a gander as the more fortunate animals took flight. Another group of prisoners made noise away from the scene so that the Rebel guards would be distracted from the cackling. In a few short seconds the birds were strangled and their bodies were set to boil. The innovative fellow received a handsome return on his investment that afternoon, as did his partners in the enterprise.[37]

Each day the men struggled through this routine of talking about food, scheming to acquire more food and, not surprisingly, plotting an escape. It was not beyond the realm of possibility that a man might dash across the deadline and hurl himself into the James River before a careless sentry could raise his rifle and get off a shot, but the reality of surviving the torrents of the mighty James dissuaded many a fellow from risking such a bold maneuver. Only one viable avenue of escape remained: exchange.[38]

Unlike later stages of the war, when the exchange cartel between North and South was suspended, prisoners in 1862 could look forward to being paroled or exchanged after they had served only brief periods of incarceration. In fact, some of the more seriously ill men already had been released from Belle Isle. Goss and his comrades were infected with hope each time the prison gate swung open and the Confederates swarmed in to look for men eligible for exchange. The irony, of course, was that the healthier men usually were left in the prison while their more desperate brethren were removed. No man wanted to be at death's door, but it was an effective strategy for leaving Belle Isle. Thus, the men became master thespians, submitting performances that would have earned them critical acclaim in any theater. In time, distinguishing between real and feigned illnesses became an almost impossible feat.[39]

While the men waited anxiously to be exchanged, they noticed that conditions within the prison were deteriorating at an alarming rate. The guards who originally ushered them through the gates gradually disappeared as the war dragged on and the need for increasing numbers of Confederate troops on the battlefield required their reassignment. They were replaced by citizens of Richmond, many of whom were adolescent boys with little or no training. These new sentries were far more unpredictable and dangerous than their predecessors, for they were not restrained by a soldier's sense of duty and propriety. Acts of wanton cruelty became commonplace.

"One of these citizen soldiers one day ran a bayonet through a New York boy, from the effects of which he died in a few hours," Goss remembered. Outraged by this random act of gratuitous violence, the prisoners retaliated at once. "A soldier of the Hawkins Zouaves sprang at the guard, and, reaching over the railing, seized him by the throat, lifted him from the ground, shook him until the 'rebel brave' was black in the face, then hurled him like a dog." Another guard, coming to the young Confederate's defense, was knocked to the ground by the force of a brick hurled from the crowd. Needless to say, no one in the prisoners' ranks could be found to testify as to the events of that day.[40]

When it seemed that matters could not get worse, the battle of Fair Oaks brought even more prisoners into the already overcrowded spaces of Belle Isle. Originally designed for three thousand men, by mid-July eight thousand inmates were stuffed into the holding pen. With poorly equipped, untrained young guards and a growing number of desperate, starving inmates, the prison seemed like a powder keg ready to ignite. It would not have taken much for the Belle Isle captives to rush the guards and attempt an escape. They might have done this if they had found enough strength to fight, but most prisoners could not take such bold action in their weakened states of health. Goss found hope dwindling as he gazed at the hollow cheeks, sunken eyes, and gaunt faces of his comrades. He realized that he looked the same to them.[41]

Goss never quite gave up hope and, as fate would have it, his salvation was at hand. One day someone passed a Richmond newspaper through the camp and Goss learned that the men would soon be exchanged. It was almost too good to be true. Nonetheless, the story was confirmed a few days later when Goss was instructed to write out parole forms for himself and his fellow inmates. His task dragged on through the night, but he persevered without complaint. In the morning, the prisoners lined up and once again marched through the streets of the Confederate capital. Goss recalled that "as we passed through its streets, skeletons in form, from which almost all semblance of humanity had fled under the torture of imprisonment, we excited pity among even the virulent women of the capital."[42]

They were pushed along the roadway for hours until it seemed impossible to take another step. As Goss felt himself slipping into a fatal lethargy, he caught sight of a Union transport ship in the harbor. Other men spotted it as well, and a feeble cheer rang through the ranks. "The feeling was too deep to be expressed in words or cheers," he wrote years later. "Tears of joy started to eyes unused to weep at misery; the voice that attempted expression was lost in choking sobs." As they waited to board the ships, the men collapsed in a heap. Goss could not control his sobbing, nor did he try.

"What are you blubbering about, old fellow?" a comrade asked.

Goss was unashamed. He told the fellow "that I was crying because folks were such fools to live under a flag with three stripes, when they might have one with thirteen over them."[43]

The men were loaded onto a ship and transported to Camp Parole, a Union facility in Annapolis, Maryland, used to nurse former prisoners of war back to health. Goss stayed there for three months until he was granted a disability discharge from the service at Camp Banks, Virginia, on November 15, 1862—four days shy of a year after he first enlisted.[44]

This last episode ought to have been the end of Warren Lee Goss's Civil War experiences. The remainder of his life should have been devoted to other endeavors—reclaiming his health, marrying, raising a family, pursuing an occupation, and so forth. During most of the year 1863, as John Minnich galloped through the Southern landscape with the Confederate cavalry, Goss seemed to follow the expected course—and yet, incredibly, he returned to military service as the year drew to a close.

In the second phase of his service to the Union cause, he was captured again. Thereafter, he came to know two more prisons, perhaps the worst ever built by the Southern Confederacy—the stockades at Andersonville Station, Georgia, and Florence, South Carolina.[45]

FOUR

The Exigencies of the Moment

In 1864, when John Wesley Minnich and Warren Lee Goss entered their respective prisons, the administrative systems on both sides were in disarray, and rapidly deteriorating. The noted Civil War historian William Best Hesseltine once concluded that Civil War prisons "came into existence, without definite plans, to meet the exigencies of the moment." This disturbing development occurred because few contemporary observers expected the fighting to last more than a few months. Even when it was clear that the conflict would drag on into the indefinite future, most military planning and resources were devoted to prosecuting the war. Consequently, the prison systems on both sides initially developed a chaotic series of plans haphazardly designed to handle a fluid situation on a mostly *ad hoc* basis.[1]

Civil War prisons are among the least studied aspects of the war. Not surprisingly, political and military events are the preferred subjects of most Civil War histories. The dramatic effect of the events of the 1860s is undeniable. Nonetheless, more than 674,000 men—almost 16 percent of the total number of soldiers who served in uniform—passed through prison camps during the war. In the early years, most captives were exchanged shortly after they were incarcerated, as was the case when Goss left the Belle Isle Prison. In the twenty-three months leading to Appomattox, general exchanges were suspended, although special exchanges of sick and wounded prisoners continued. This breakdown of the exchange cartel between North and South in mid-1863 left between 410,000 and 430,000 men interned in approximately 150 prisons of various designs, sizes, and conditions.[2]

One commentator, Lonnie R. Speer, has classified Civil War prisons into seven categories. Existing jails and prisons comprised the first category. Whenever possible, administrators on both sides sought to hold prisoners in existing structures. Thus, early in the conflict the city jails in Selma, Alabama; Savannah, Georgia; and Columbus, Ohio, among others, were used to hold prisoners.

The second category of prisons consisted of existing coastal fortifications such as Fort McHenry in Baltimore, Maryland, where Francis Scott Key penned the immortal words of the "Star Spangled Banner" during the War of 1812, and Castle Pinckney in Charleston Harbor, adjacent to Fort Sumter. The advantages of using these structures were readily apparent: They already existed and had been built to be impregnable. Moreover, because they were located near coastal shipping lanes, transporting prisoners to the prison sites was relatively convenient.

If existing jails and prisons or coastal fortifications were unavailable, the next best option was to retrofit other buildings. This was more burdensome than using existing fortified structures, but it was preferable to constructing new prisons from the ground up. Thus, some Union prisoners were held in a converted tobacco warehouse in Danville, Virginia. Libby Prison in Richmond and Castle Thunder in Petersburg, Virginia, were typical of this third category, as were Gratiot Street Prison and Myrtle Street Prison in St. Louis.

A fourth prison category was used for camps well into the twentieth century. Prison authorities constructed a series of barracks surrounded by fences, although sometimes the site was an old military training ground converted into a prison. The North used these types far more than did the South. Their names became infamous: Camp Douglas in Chicago; Camp Chase in Columbus, Ohio; Elmira Prison in New York; and the Rock Island Prison on the Illinois-Iowa border, among others.

If scarce resources prevented authorities from constructing barracks, they sometimes housed prisoners in tents pitched behind high fences. Obviously, this fifth option was considerably less expensive than providing barracks, and it held the advantage of allowing administrators to change the camp structure and organization as increases and decreases in the size of the prison population required. Belle Isle in Virginia and Point Lookout in Maryland were prime examples of prisons that used tents to house inmates.

If the above options were unavailable, prisoners could be placed in an open field and guarded by armed soldiers with orders to shoot and kill anyone who tried to escape. The South used this arrangement late in the war. The North occasionally herded captured enemy soldiers into a field, but it was only a temporary method of holding prisoners after a major battle. It was the least expensive and most versatile option, but it was unworkable over any length of time.

This led to the seventh—and arguably the worst—category of Civil War prison: The open-air stockade. Used exclusively by the Confederacy, an open-air stockade was a variation on the option of housing prisoners in a field. However, placing prisoners in a field was a temporary measure; the construction of an open-air stockade was designed to be more or less permanent. Generally, the Confederates selected a site close to a transportation hub, preferably a railroad line, but far enough away from a major population center to discourage escapees from blending into the local landscape. Because the men were exposed to the elements and were not provided with any shelter except what they could create for themselves, incarceration inside a stockade resulted in far higher mortality rates than those found in other prisons. It was no accident that the inmates held in stockades in Salisbury, North Carolina; Andersonville, Georgia; and Florence, South Carolina, suffered higher mortality rates than men held in other prisons. This unfortunate statistic also partially explains why so many Union prisoners' accounts after the war argued that Confederate authorities deliberately sought to kill them.[3]

Whichever type was used, Civil War prisons were horrific places, as postbellum writers made abundantly clear. A large body of literature appeared in the years after the war ended—at least five hundred ex-prisoners recalled life and death in captivity in numerous speeches, diaries, memoirs, pamphlets, articles, romans à clef, and sermons—although most sources were anything but factually accurate or objective. Some commentators attempted to describe their experiences dispassionately, but many former prisoners were intent on venerating their government's actions and vilifying the other side's conduct. As a result, much of the overblown, stilted prose, which relies on religious allegory, mixed metaphors, and demonstrably false hearsay, makes these works almost unreadable today. Moreover, the sources are so melodramatic and dripping with vituperation that they strain credibility, even in those instances when the events described can be corroborated through other documents. It is no wonder Civil War prisons have been so seldom studied; the sources are so shamelessly unreliable that distinguishing fact from myth is almost impossible.[4]

Despite the suspect accuracy of these sources, historians generally agree that Northern memoir writers garnered more favorable publicity than their Southern counterparts. Northerners enjoyed greater access to publishers, and their lives in the postwar period were not disrupted by the economic, social, and political decimation that plagued the South during Reconstruction. If victors write history, then Union veterans like Goss told their stories with a vengeance that could not be matched by ex-Confederates like Minnich, although certainly Southerners tried to tell their stories.[5]

The propaganda of the period argued that Confederate prisons were infinitely worse than Union prisons, but modern historians believe this assessment to be oversimplified. Statistics from the Civil War era are notoriously suspect, for records in the nineteenth century were not kept with the same sense of precision that has become today's standard. Based on the best available data, however, it appears that the Union army captured between 210,000 and 220,000 Southern soldiers during the period after general exchanges were suspended, while 200,000 to 210,000 Northern prisoners passed into Confederate hands. Using the most conservative estimates, Union prisons claimed the lives of 25,796 Confederates, or approximately 12 percent of the men incarcerated there, while Southern prisons claimed 30,218 lives, or slightly more than 15 percent of the inmates. As a point of comparison, the number of men—56,014—known to have perished in Civil War prisons was almost equal to the total number of American servicemen who died in the Vietnam War over a century later.[6]

Regardless of the postwar battle for public opinion, the truth is that neither side was equipped to handle prisoners when the conflict erupted in 1861. Existing prison facilities quickly filled to capacity and beyond. In those early days, military prisoners sometimes found themselves sitting side by side in the same cell with convicted murderers and other civilian criminals. The Union held an advantage in housing military prisoners because many Northern states could use prisons, military forts, and other preexisting edifices. In the South, the Davis administration was forced to confiscate warehouses and tobacco barns to be used as makeshift prisons, but the supply was severely limited.[7]

As the war continued, disparities between North and South became more visible. The Union struggled with administrative questions, especially concerning the development of a centralized prison command system, but eventually those questions were answered relatively effectively, at least compared with the Confederacy. The task of preparing U.S. military prison facilities initially fell to Gen. Montgomery C. Meigs, quartermaster general of the U.S. Army. In July 1861, General Meigs contacted Secretary of War Simon Cameron and recommended that the Lincoln administration appoint a commissary general of prisoners. The administration initially ignored the general's recommendations, but in October the situation changed as the prison population exploded. Recognizing that a unified command held distinct administrative advantages, the War Department promoted Lt. Col. William H.

Hoffman of the Eighth U.S. Infantry to colonel and ordered him to take control of military prisons.[8]

William Hoffman served as the Commissary General of Union prisons. Courtesy of the Roger Hunt Collection, U.S. Army Military History Institute.

Colonel Hoffman was a relatively obscure player in the drama of the Civil War, and yet for those who have studied his career, his reputation can only be characterized as strange. During his time in the service, he was reputed to be the most frugal man in the U.S. Army. In his defense, he managed the Union prison system with a ruthless administrative efficiency that avoided logistical problems that plagued his counterparts in the Southern Confederacy. Had this natural-born bureaucrat been employed to mass-produce war matériel during one of the world wars of the twentieth century, he might have left a legacy that rivaled the achievements of great public entrepreneurs in American political history—David Lilienthal, Hyman Rickover, and Austin Tobin, for example. Like those men of a later time, Hoffman understood how to use the mechanisms of government to accomplish his objectives, and he would not be dissuaded from performing his tasks with alacrity.[9]

But he was not in charge of mass-producing war matériel. Instead, he oversaw the conditions and treatment of Confederate prisoners with an almost fanatical parsimony that bordered on obsession. In a typically terse communication with General Meigs, Hoffman outlined his administrative goals in no uncertain terms: "In all that is done the strictest economy consistent with security and proper welfare of the prisoners must be observed." Similarly, he told a prison commandant from Indiana, "So long as a prisoner has clothing upon him, however much torn, you must issue nothing to him." Here was a man who would not waste words or dollars. He worked relentlessly to ensure that economic considerations were afforded great weight, but some question exists whether the welfare of prisoners received similar attention. Today he is remembered as a man who so zealously championed frugality that he cut costs when he easily might have eased the suffering of Confederate prisoners.[10]

When hostilities commenced in 1861, Hoffman was held briefly as a prisoner of war in Texas, finally leaving after the state passed a secession ordinance that, among other things, forced U.S. troops to flee the jurisdiction. A careful, meticulous administrator, he immediately brought order to a chaotic system as soon as he accepted his new assignment. Hoffman began by centralizing control of the prison structure under his command and instituting an elaborate system of procedures designed to standardize the method of handling inmates. His efforts greatly impressed his superiors, and he remained secure in his position for the duration of the war. According to one commentator, "Hoffman's reputation is that of an inhuman fiend who intentionally denied care the Union was perfectly capable of providing. But Hoffman was not evil: he was narrow. He was unimaginative, humorless, hidebound, and very wise in the way of army politics. He had extremely strict ideas of duty, obligation, and his own career, and he followed those tenets blindly."[11]

Although organizing the prison system was taxing for the North, the South faced a far more difficult challenge. Armed with fewer resources and possessing almost no preexisting facilities, the Confederacy simply could not house, clothe, and feed the influx of Union prisoners. Richmond became the locus of prisons in the early years because the capital city was home to warehouses that could be converted into holding pens comparatively quickly. Warren Lee Goss experienced those prisons firsthand when he suffered through incarceration in Prison Number Two, the Libby Prison, and Belle Isle in 1862. The overflow of inmates in those early years was sent to Castle Pinckney in Charleston Harbor or to a hastily constructed stockade in Salisbury, North Carolina.[12]

As sordid a reputation as William Hoffman acquired, he was no match for his counterpart, Gen. John H. Winder. Originally a career army officer from Maryland, Winder accepted a commission as a brigadier general in the Confederate States Army after he resigned his commission in the U.S. Army at the outset of the war. Not long thereafter, Confederate President Jefferson Davis appointed his old friend, a fellow West Point graduate, to serve as provost marshal of Richmond. As a result of his appointment, the sixty-one-year-old general was in command of the Richmond prisons. A strict, gruff, white-haired curmudgeon who never suffered fools gladly, Winder administered the Richmond facilities with a heavy hand that infuriated the public on both sides but won praise from his superiors as effective and efficient.[13]

When Winder assumed his duties in Richmond, he realized that overlapping responsibilities and confusing jurisdictions had muddled the Confederate chain of command. Different commanders exercised responsibility for different parts of the prison system, but no one was in charge of overall planning and coordination. As a result, prison expansion proceeded in disorganized, uncoordinated fits and starts that wasted what few resources were available. To rectify this situation, Winder dispatched his relatives to scout for remote locations so prisoners could be housed outside of Richmond in places like Belle Isle. He also sent a few prisoners to Danville, Virginia, thereby providing temporary relief. Despite his early efforts, Winder realized that the prison system remained wasteful and inefficient and contributed directly to the inmates' suffering. Unfortunately, he did not know how to resolve the enormous logistical problems he faced. He had neither the authority nor the ingenuity to take the decisive action necessary to reorganize and thereby improve the unworkable prison structure.[14]

Beginning in November 1864, John H. Winder served as Commissary General of all Confederate prisons east of the Mississippi River. Courtesy of the White-Wellford-Taliaferro-Marshall Papers, #P-1300, Southern Historical Collection, the University of North Carolina at Chapel Hill.

In the face of an ever-growing crisis, Winder's authority expanded by default, and he served as the *de facto* head of prison facilities for the South throughout much of the war. This confusing command structure created many needless and silly disputes about who was in charge of the prisoners in certain parts of the Confederacy. Recognizing the need for a centralized prison authority, the Confederate high command finally appointed Winder commissary general for all prisons east of the Mississippi River in November 1864. The general's defenders have argued that this centralization of command came far too late; the abominable prison conditions already existed when Winder took charge. He did what he could to cope with an untenable set of circumstances, but he faced an impossible task. With few resources as the Southern Confederacy fought for its life during the last five months of its existence, Winder was doomed to fail. Jefferson Davis probably was Winder's most loyal supporter, concluding that the old general was "a man too brave to be cruel to anything within his power, too well bred and well born to be influenced by low and sordid motives."[15]

His detractors have taken issue with this kind assessment of the man's character and actions. In their view, Winder either deliberately mistreated prisoners or, at best, turned a blind eye to their suffering. For many supporters of the Union cause, he became the embodiment of all that was vicious and evil in the Confederate prison system. The diaries and memoirs of former Union soldiers held in Confederate prisons speak of Winder as a monster in human form. One of the most embittered alumni of Southern prisons, John McElroy, wrote that "His cold blooded cruelty was such as to disgust even the Rebel officers." Sam Boggs, a former prisoner who cited McElroy's work at length, agreed with this characterization, noting that Winder exercised "full power to torment and murder as he pleased." Boggs implored his readers, "If you have one spark of humanity in your soul, you will never express your admiration for that perjured murderer and his traitorous advisers." Writing shortly after the end of the war, Augustus C. Hamlin lamented that "Winder has already been summoned to his God, without affording to the tribunals of men the opportunity to judge of his justification or his shame." Even a supposedly dispassionate congressional investigation of Civil War prison systems adopted this same high-handed moral condemnation of Winder. "We shall not dwell upon the career of this wretch," the congressional report concluded. "He deserves execration, not history."[16]

Physically, Winder was an ideal symbol for the contempt that many postwar observers felt for the Southern cause, for he looked the part of the aged, bloodless villain. Critics of the Confederacy stare at old photographs of the wrinkled face and menacing countenance—as though somehow physical attributes and outward appearance can provide a window into a man's character—and detect great cruelty. His shock of white hair, thinning and in disarray, and his considerable girth at a time when Union prisoners were emaciated and ravaged by starvation and disease complete the portrait of a sinister, deliberately brutal old man who cared nothing for the suffering of Yankees. Winder probably would have been tried for war crimes had he not suffered a massive heart attack and fallen dead at the Florence Stockade in February 1865.[17]

Even as Hoffman and Winder struggled with the question of how to handle their prisoners, administrators on both sides recognized the benefits of mutual cooperation. Thus, Union and Confederate representatives met early in the conflict to eke out an exchange agreement. On July 22, 1862, they formally signed the Dix-Hill Cartel to exchange prisoners on a regular, ongoing basis. The news triggered almost universal joy and enthusiasm. Yet, despite the wide acclaim for prisoner exchanges, the cartel was plagued with problems from its inception. First, the Lincoln administration refused to recognize the Confederacy as a separate government. In his speeches and public proclamations, President Lincoln was careful to refer to the hostile forces as "rebels" or "insurrectionists." Captured Confederate sailors were treated as pirates, and captured Confederate soldiers were deemed to be traitors who had taken up arms against their country. Throughout much of American history, those offenses had been punishable by hanging.[18]

A formal exchange cartel signed by both sides placed Lincoln in an awkward position because it implied that the Southern Confederacy was a sovereign entity that could enter into legitimate formal agreements. An unofficial agreement between field commanders to exchange prisoners on a case-by-case basis was one thing, but a general exchange was an altogether different matter. Despite the logical inconsistency of refusing to treat the Confederate States of America as a separate nation and yet simultaneously entering into a formal agreement with Southern leaders, Lincoln recognized that public opinion strongly favored the ratification of an exchange cartel, and so he acquiesced on the matter.[19]

Before the formal agreement could be signed, agents for both the Union and the Confederacy faced a perplexing legal question: Which documents or precedents should serve as the basis for prisoner exchanges? Eventually, a fifty-year-old agreement between the United States and Great Britain during the War of 1812 provided a suitable precedent. Under the terms of that arrangement, inmates were exchanged on the basis of rank. Consequently, a prisoner who held the rank of a commanding general could be exchanged for 60 privates. A lieutenant general was worth 40 privates; a major general, 30 privates; a brigadier general, 20 privates; a colonel, 15 privates; a lieutenant colonel, 10 privates; a major, 8 privates; a captain, 6 privates; a first lieutenant, 4 privates; a second lieutenant, 3 privates; and a non-commissioned officer was worth 2 privates. The formula was not without its critics, but it was as logical a system as anything else that could be found.[20]

To ensure a smooth exchange of men, each side appointed exchange agents to handle the administrative details. Robert Ould, a former district attorney from Washington, D.C., became the Confederacy's exchange agent in the East. The new U.S. secretary of war, Edwin Stanton, delayed appointing a Union exchange agent; in the meantime, the Union ordered Gen. John A. Dix to travel up the James River at Aiken's Landing and prepare for the exchange. Shortly thereafter, Stanton ordered U.S. Adj. Gen. Lorenzo Thomas to assume the duties of the exchange agent in addition to his other duties. Together with General Dix, Thomas reached an arrangement with Ould to swap 3,000 captured Confederates for 3,021 Union prisoners. In the West, Confederate Maj. N. G. Watts, acting under orders from Ould, arranged for exchanges at Vicksburg, Mississippi, with Union Capt. Henry M. Lazelle, who served as a *de facto* exchange agent.[21]

The Dix-Hill Cartel never lived up to expectations because each side believed that the other was not acting in good faith. The Confederates were especially incensed by the actions of several Union leaders. Stanton issued orders to military field commanders that they should confiscate the property of any "disloyal citizens" who fell under their commands; as a practical matter, enforcement of this order left many pro-Confederate civilians destitute. In addition, Maj. Gen. John Pope, the commander of Union forces in northern Virginia, followed up Stanton's order by commanding his commissioned officers to arrest all disloyal male citizens. Disputes also arose concerning the appropriate calculations used to determine which officers and which ranks should be exchanged. These difficulties threatened to destroy the cartel before it was implemented.[22]

Even when the cartel worked, it created enormous administrative burdens for both sides. Exchanges were supposed to occur within ten days of capture, but often a month or more went by before they occurred. The paperwork and logistics were overwhelming as officers struggled to retain information on prisoners' names, rank, places of internment, and provisions. Both sides incessantly bickered over the treatment of prisoners and the terms of parole. Because record keeping was difficult to verify, each side accused the other of violating their carefully constructed agreement and dealing in bad faith.[23]

Despite the many problems involved in exchanging prisoners, the issue of black Union soldiers probably more than anything else drove a wedge between the two sides and finally led to the collapse of the cartel. Although blacks had served in the armed forces in many American wars, their appearance in the Civil War was especially controversial. Southerners had long feared that slaves might be induced to rise up and slay their masters. This fear seemed real in the antebellum period when slaves revolted many times, most notably in 1739, 1800, 1822, and 1831. The thought of free blacks marching into battle against the South horrified the Confederates, for it was the realization of their worst ancestral fears of racial unrest and violence.[24]

The Union could hardly claim the moral high ground on the question of black participation in military service. The North initially rejected the use of black troops, but this position changed as the nature of the conflict evolved. In 1862, Congress passed two statutes that altered the war almost as much as President Lincoln's subsequent, and more famous, Emancipation Proclamation. The first statute was a militia act that allowed the president to enroll "persons of African descent" for any purpose or "any war service for which they may be found competent." The second statute, the Confiscation Act, authorized punishment for "traitors" by confiscating their property, including slaves who "shall be deemed captives of war and shall be forever free."[25]

If the Union was not quite ready for black soldiers in the summer of 1862, the stage was set for their future participation. After President Lincoln announced his preliminary Emancipation Proclamation in September, the first black soldiers, the First Louisiana Native Guard, were recruited into the service of the Union cause. Shortly thereafter, the Second and Third Louisiana Native Guard regiments were formed. These troops later were designated the First, Second, and Third Corps d'Afrique under Gen. Nathaniel P. Banks and, later still, they were known as the Seventy-third, Seventy-fourth, and Seventy-fifth U.S. Colored Infantry.[26]

After the final Emancipation Proclamation went into effect on January 1, 1863, blacks increasingly enlisted in the Union army. By war's end, 178,892 blacks had worn the blue uniform of a Union soldier, and 32,369—more than 18 percent—died in the service of their country. The most celebrated black regiment of the war was the Fifty-fourth Massachusetts Volunteer Infantry, which led an assault on Fort Wagner near Charleston in 1863 under the command of Col. Robert Gould Shaw. Although Shaw was killed in their unsuccessful bid to capture the fort, the regiment's heroic actions demonstrated the valor of black troops in combat.[27]

The Confederacy's treatment of black soldiers captured in battle was, and remains, a source of controversy. Certainly the Southern rhetoric was vehemently opposed to this new type of soldier. Jefferson Davis called it "the most execrable measure in the history of guilty man" and proposed to treat captured black soldiers as escaped slaves to be returned to servitude. A white Union officer captured while leading a regiment of black soldiers would be tried for inciting a slave insurrection. Under the laws of the Southern Confederacy, if he were found guilty he could be sentenced to death. Confederate Gen. P. G. T. Beauregard was even more direct; he called for black soldiers captured in battle to be executed "with the garrote."[28]

Although Confederate actions generally fell short of the fiery rhetoric, it is true that the mortality rate for black prisoners was higher than the rate for white prisoners. Of the nearly 800 blacks taken prisoner during the war, 35 percent—284 men—died while incarcerated. Many more failed to make it to prison because they perished from disease or at the hands of their captors. Perhaps the most notorious incident occurred following the Confederate attack on Fort Pillow, Tennessee, on April 12, 1864. After assaulting the earthworks, the Confederates captured 226 Union prisoners from several units, including the Thirteenth Regiment, West Tennessee Volunteers, and the U.S. Light Artillery (Colored Troops). Of the 226 prisoners, 58 were black. The blacks were slaughtered. The question of whether they were killed in battle or summarily executed after they threw down their arms to surrender has never been fully answered, although execution was a plausible scenario. Similar atrocities occurred in other places, including Poison Spring, Arkansas, and Saltville, Virginia.[29]

Blacks who were not killed on the battlefield faced a far more terrible experience in prison than did their white counterparts. Any white man who claimed that a black prisoner was his slave could turn up at the prison and take possession of his property. If black inmates were not claimed, they could be sold on the auction block as slaves, even in instances when their captors knew them to be freedmen. Those who were not claimed or sold died in alarming numbers in Southern prison camps for many reasons, including the refusal of Confederate doctors to treat them. Moreover, blacks were forced to perform the most menial and demeaning tasks imaginable, such as burying dead bodies. They generally died much more rapidly than did their white comrades because the black prisoners came into such close contact with diseases and endured exhausting, abysmal working conditions.[30]

The brutal treatment of black prisoners as subhuman beasts of burden continued throughout the conflict. In fact, the Confederacy did not recognize black prisoners as soldiers until February 1865, two months before the war ended. According to the Confederate government, blacks were not subject to the terms of the exchange cartel because they were escaped slaves, not soldiers. The Union government disagreed, and demanded that blacks be treated equally.[31]

As much as anything, the Confederates' policy toward black soldiers became a point of contention that could not be compromised. On May 25, 1863, Union Gen. Henry Halleck ordered that exchanges be halted. Although this was hard on prisoners, the Union's decision to dissolve the cartel also held a strategic advantage for the North. Because Confederate soldiers who were released from Northern prisons generally returned to the ranks in higher numbers than their Union counterparts, the cartel may have lengthened the war as the same Confederate soldiers fought in battles, were captured, exchanged, and fought again. Union commanders, especially General Grant, believed that the severe shortage of Southern men to serve as combat soldiers would be exacerbated if Confederate prisoners were not exchanged.[32]

Although this reasoning may or may not have been specious, the failure of the exchange cartel in 1863 greatly increased the burden on the already overburdened prison system on both sides. The prison population exploded during the next year. By August 1864, the Confederacy held 50,000 Northern prisoners and the Union held 67,500 Southerners. As men who previously would have been exchanged were forced to wait for special exchanges or, worse yet, the end of the war, prison conditions rapidly deteriorated in direct proportion to the swelling of the ranks.[33]

This was the post-cartel prison system that John Wesley Minnich and Warren Lee Goss entered in 1864—Minnich in January and Goss in April. Neither man could realistically hope for exchange or parole in the immediate future. Like most prisoners captured during that time, they would have to tough it out and hope that the war would end soon. In many ways, their nightmarish time in captivity would be among the most formative and traumatic experiences of their lives, and each man would reflect on his time in prison often in the long years that followed.

FIVE

We Were Ushered into What Seemed to Us Hades Itself

The unenviable task of overseeing the operation of the Rock Island Prison fell to Col. Adolphus J. Johnson, a Union officer who originally hailed from Newark, New Jersey. He seemed an unlikely choice to serve as a prison commandant. Born in 1816, Johnson had fashioned a career as a merchant—mostly a hatter and a barber—during the antebellum years. After the Rebels fired on Fort Sumter in April 1861, he appeared in Trenton, New Jersey, and enlisted in the First Regiment, New Jersey Militia, where he was commissioned a colonel and regimental commander. Although he might have avoided military service owing to his age—he was in his middle forties at the time—Johnson seemed intent on performing his duty. When his initial enlistment ended after three months, he remained in active service. Beginning in September 1861, he held the rank of colonel in the Eighth New Jersey Regiment.[1]

He was a large man for the time. Standing five feet, eleven inches tall, he was an imposing physical presence to all who saw him. With a balding head, an angular face, and whiskers that crept down his cheeks like a vine encircling a pole, this stolid, humorless man carried himself with an air that could be characterized either as the haughty authority befitting a commissioned officer in the U.S. Army or a rigid, aloof bureaucrat zealously devoted to following convoluted military rules. As many officers on both sides discovered during the postwar years, Johnson found that his stint as a prison commandant besmirched an otherwise sterling reputation.[2]

His military career began with great promise. He proved his courage under fire during General McClellan's ill-fated Peninsula campaign in the winter of 1861–62. The Eighth New Jersey fought valiantly during the siege of Yorktown in April and May 1862 before Johnson fell victim to a bullet wound at the battle of Williamsburg. A Confederate Minié ball entered his hip through the left side of his back and exited out the other side. After five months in recovery, he still sported an unhealed, open wound, but Johnson nonetheless seemed anxious to resume his duties. Amazingly, he rejoined his unit and took part in the battle of Fredericksburg in December 1862.[3]

By March 1863, when it was clear that he would never be fit enough to endure another arduous campaign, Johnson reluctantly resigned from the service. His superiors regarded his resignation as a severe loss for the Union army. By all rights he should have spent the rest of the war watching from the sidelines, but Johnson was not content to assume such a passive role. In September, when he felt that he had sufficiently recovered, he reenlisted and received a commission as a major in the Veteran Reserve (Invalid) Corps. He suffered pain in his legs for the rest of his life, but he was able to perform his duties. For two months, he spent time at Camp Chase, Ohio, learning the procedures for operating a prison. In November 1863, he was ordered to serve a brief apprenticeship under Col. Richard H. Rush at Rock Island before he assumed command on December 5.[4]

Colonel Adolphus J. Johnson served as the commandant of the Rock Island Prison Barracks. Courtesy of John W. Kuhl and the U.S. Army Military History Institute.

Johnson has been criticized for his numerous managerial flaws, but he brought a measure of professionalism and stability to the administration of the camp. Unlike many prisons, especially Confederate stockades constructed toward the end of the war, the Rock Island Prison did not feature a parade of commandants rushing through the post on their way to bigger and better assignments. After he succeeded Rush in December, Johnson was in command during the entire existence of the prison. Moreover, he was a man of sober judgment who took his duty seriously.

Johnson was not a power-hungry megalomaniac anxious to assert his authority over a captive population, but a man who had a job to do, distasteful though it may be, and he undertook his duties, for the most part, diligently and thoughtfully.[5]

Never a fan of the Rock Island commandant, even John Minnich begrudgingly admitted that Johnson was not always an ogre. After overhearing a fellow prisoner talking with Colonel Johnson about receiving wages for inmate work performed outside the stockade walls, Minnich remembered the reaction. "Colonel Johnson's back was turned to me, and I could not see his face. But others told me he turned red in the face, and finally agreed to adopt the Confederate's plan and call for volunteers. This was done and wages paid." Johnson might have refused the request and retaliated against the inmates, but he did not. Despite his reluctance, he responded to the entreaties of the prisoners by meeting their demands.[6]

Johnson's reputation suffered because he served as the head of a camp that, rightly or wrongly, came to symbolize the worst characteristics of Civil War prisons, at least on the Union side. Castigated by pro-Confederate newspapers and former prisoners late in his tenure and most especially during the Reconstruction years, Johnson represented in the minds of many observers the Northern equivalent to Andersonville commandant Henry Wirz. In addition, his road to infamy no doubt was shortened by a war of words with the editor of a local pro-Confederate newspaper, the *Argus*. J. B. Danforth, a relentless gadfly who liked nothing better than to wield his pen as a sword while slinging his vitriolic prose toward the prison administration, condemned Colonel Johnson in several editorials in the *Argus* in 1864.

A typical criticism appeared in a November 21 diatribe. Reflecting on Johnson's deliberate mistreatment of prisoners, Danforth mused, "It is a shame that, in this enlightened age of the world, white men, our own countrymen, should be confined in a pen, fed on such scanty and improper food, and reduced down almost to starvation point, until disease and death ensue." To ensure that the point was not lost, the editorial concluded with a blatantly incendiary charge: "There is no excuse for this deliberate torture of human beings, and the hand that does it or the heart that prompts it is hardened against the common instincts of humanity." He assigned blame predominantly to the Lincoln administration because it possessed the means with which to ease the prisoners' sufferings, yet declined to alleviate their misery. Still, Danforth reserved no small measure of contempt for the prison authorities. "We do not know where the censure should fall for this inhumanity, nor do we care. Whoever is guilty of it is guilty of a great crime. . . . Whoever is guilty of this deliberate torture and death ought to be execrated by all mankind."[7]

Johnson generally chose to ignore Danforth's barbs, but he had endured all he could stand by the time this scathing indictment appeared. With barely suppressed fury, he took pen in hand and responded to the charges. "Up to the present time I have passed unnoticed the numerous erroneous articles that have appeared in the papers," he wrote, "but in this case I will deviate from an established rule, and give your article of the 21st inst. the notice it seems to merit." Foreshadowing the debate between survivors of Union and Confederate prisons that would occur in the postbellum years, Johnson chastised the *Argus* for focusing exclusively on the plight of Southern prisoners when stories of atrocities inflicted on Union soldiers in Confederate camps had begun to circulate. Highlighting what he saw to be Danforth's pro-Southern sympathies, Johnson remarked, "Did it occur to you that while you can spend the necessary time to pen an article like that . . . that your files may be searched in vain for the smallest editorial paragraph in condemnation of the rebel authorities for the brutal treatment of our men in their hands?"[8]

Johnson was well aware that rumors had arisen claiming that the Rock Island Prison was the "Andersonville of the North" and that he, as commandant, deserved to be excoriated no less than his Rebel counterparts who commanded Confederate prisons. Incensed at what in his judgment was such an unfair comparison, he directly challenged the characterization of his administration as deliberately cruel and heartless. He then explained that whatever shortages the prisoners might have suffered were through no fault of his own. Stung by Danforth's criticism, the commandant then wrote a stream of ill-considered words in a letter he would have occasion to regret sending to the *Argus*.[9]

In a curious twist of logic, he remarked that the prisoners could not have been deliberately mistreated because had he chosen to do so—and had it been left to his discretion—the deprivations would have been infinitely worse. "In the first place, instead of placing them in fine comfortable barracks, with three large stoves in each, and as much coal as they can burn, both day and night, I would place them in a pen with no shelter but the heavens, as our poor men were at Andersonville; instead of giving them the same quality and nearly the same quantity of provisions that the troops on duty receive, I would give them as near as possible the same quantity and quality of provisions that the fiendish rebels give our men; and instead of a constant issue of clothing to them I would let them wear their rags, as our poor men in the hands of the rebel authorities are obliged to do." In short, Johnson vowed, "had I the power, strict retaliation

This photograph shows a bird's-eye view of the Rock Island Prison as it appeared during the Civil War. Reprinted from *Rock Island: In Peace and in War* by B. F. Tillinghast.

would be practiced by me."[10]

Danforth was delighted to receive this missive, especially owing to the impolitic ending. Johnson admonished him to "oblige me by publishing this communication entire," but he need not have asked for such consideration. As anyone engaged in a battle of verbal repartee can attest, often it is the more aggressive combatant who comes off sounding mean-spirited and vindictive. If Colonel Johnson had hoped to rehabilitate his image in the eyes of the surrounding community or his progeny, he was sorely mistaken in his poor choice of words and the attention afforded them in a hostile venue. He was his own worst enemy, and Danforth knew it.[11]

Striking exactly the right balance between sorrow for the imprisoned men and perplexed empathy for the confused, tormented soul who administered their pen, Danforth waxed eloquent in his published response. He noted that at times in the past—very few times, to be sure—the *Argus* had praised "the humanity of Col. Johnson, in the treatment of prisoners" and was impressed when the commandant had "shown a feeling of humanity creditable alike to him as a soldier and as a fellow-countryman," but the vicious letter forced a new assessment of the man's character. "We do now 'blush' to say that his letter shows that he has sadly changed in that respect."[12]

If Danforth and the *Argus* responded to Johnson's foolish prose with bewildered sadness, the prisoners themselves seized upon the letter as evidence of an evil Union conspiracy to brutalize and perhaps extirpate them. Comparing Johnson to the Andersonville commandant, Minnich found little to distinguish the two men. "If Wirz was truly guilty, having himself shot a prisoner with or without cause," he wrote, "was he any more guilty than was Col. A. J. Johnson, who never punished a single one of his men for having wantonly and without the least cause shot prisoners to death in broad daylight or in the night?" Like crimes of commission, crimes of omission were still offenses perpetrated against humanity.[13]

Citing Johnson's reply to the *Argus*, Minnich argued that the commandant had confessed that he wanted to see the prisoners at Rock Island murdered. "It will not do to endeavor to exonerate Colonel Johnson on the ground that he was ignorant of the actions of the troops under his command," Minnich observed. "That would put upon him the brand of utter incompetency and his utter unfitness for the command of even a very limited number of men in any capacity whatever." Judging from Johnson's strong military record before he came to his post at Rock Island, he was anything but incompetent. "To what, then, are we to ascribe his utter indifference to the acts of his men as herein stated? There is but one answer; and the key to that answer, revealing the whole character of the man, is to be found in his letter of November 23, 1864."[14]

Minnich found Johnson's confession of cruel intentions to be positive proof that Union prisons were every bit as horrible as their Confederate equivalents—and Union leaders were a good deal worse, in his view. At least Southern prison commandants could offer up a defense that they had few resources and provisions at their disposal. Men like Colonel Johnson could only point to bulging Union warehouses and supply depots as well as their own recorded remarks when asked why they allowed suffering to continue under their watch. If Johnson had been given a free hand, Minnich concluded, "Verily, I would not be here to-day inscribing these bitter, cruel truths which for forty-four years I have kept locked away that none but the most intimate friends might see, and no one has ever yet seen the whole."[15]

As Minnich's comments made clear, Adolphus Johnson's reputation was forever tarnished by his reign as the commandant of the Rock Island Prison. The question remains whether he was as dastardly as he was portrayed. Like his boss, Commissary General Hoffman, he certainly carried frugality past the point of good sense. At the conclusion of his prison duty, Colonel Johnson returned more than $181,000 to the prison fund established for the operation and maintenance of the camps. This amount is all the more astonishing when one realizes that it represented almost 10 percent of the entire operating budget for the Rock Island Barracks. The statistic is especially damning evidence for those men, like Minnich, who argued that Johnson could have done more to ease the suffering of the inmates under his command if common decency and a concern for humanity had prevailed.[16]

Johnson bore no small measure of responsibility for the events that occurred in the Rock Island Prison during his tenure. Even if he did not actively countenance the atrocities that Minnich and his brethren recorded, he turned a blind eye to sordid episodes that he might have prevented—or at least mitigated—had he been so inclined. While he might have treated the men worse, he also might have treated them better. If he did not exactly rise to the level of a Satan, in the eyes of Confederate prisoners he was unquestionably on the order of a Pontius Pilate.[17]

While John Minnich and his fellow inmates struggled with the camp administrators at Rock Island in the early months of 1864, Warren Lee Goss rejoined the Union army after recuperating from his experiences in the Richmond prisons. "Possessed naturally of a strong constitution, I recovered with almost marvelous quickness from disabilities which an able board of medical men had pronounced incurable. With returning health came the desire to be again with my companions in the field. The clash of arms, the excitement of battle, the hurried military parades and displays, awoke all the pleasurable recollections, and there are many in the soldier's life. Hardships suffered were remembered only to revive my hatred of the enemy who had caused them."[18]

As inexplicable as Goss's actions may appear to later generations, his decision to reenlist was not entirely unreasonable. Like many young men of that time and place, he was not satisfied to sit by idly as the most profound event of nineteenth-century American history occurred. If Northern men marched into battle, Warren Lee Goss was determined to march with them; therefore, on November 30, 1863, he presented himself a second time for Union military service. He was mustered into the ranks on December 7 as a sergeant in Company H of the Second Massachusetts Heavy Artillery Regiment.[19]

No sooner had he joined his regiment than they moved southward to assume garrison duty at Fort Williams, a small post in North Carolina along a coastal front that had changed hands several times early in the war. The area had been under Union command for a year and a half, but the Confederates had decided to wrest control from the enemy not long before Goss and his unit arrived on the scene. Southern resistance in eastern North Carolina was unexpectedly heavy in 1863–64; consequently, the Second Massachusetts experienced numerous delays during the journey. After weeks of frustration and slow progress, the men arrived late in the winter of 1864. Not long thereafter, the Confederates launched a combined amphibious and ground assault on the Union position.[20]

The Confederate commander, Gen. Robert E. Lee, had long recognized the danger of allowing Union troops to occupy the coastal areas of North Carolina, but he had not been able to offer effective resistance. The bluecoats repeatedly disrupted the vital railroad link that brought supplies to the Army of Northern Virginia and continued to serve as a nuisance to Lee's troop movements. During a winter lull on the Virginia battlefields in 1863–64, Lee finally dispatched several units to rectify this lingering problem.

Commanded by Gen. George E. Pickett of Gettysburg fame, a Confederate fighting force of some forty-five hundred men descended on New Bern, North Carolina, and fought Union troops in the winter and early spring of 1864. Although the Confederates met with some successes, ultimately the campaign was a failure. The Union army remained firmly ensconced behind coastal fortifications.[21]

This initial setback prompted Confederate Gen. Braxton Bragg to replace Pickett with a twenty-six-year-old aggressive commander, Robert Hoke, who had performed well during the New Bern attack. Hoke immediately switched his operations from New Bern to Plymouth, a small town situated at the point where the Roanoke River flowed into Albemarle Sound near the state's outer banks. Plymouth was an inviting target for the Confederates; it was strategically situated and it could be taken with Hoke's available forces, which outnumbered the Union garrison nearly three to one. Moreover, Hoke could count on naval support from a Confederate ironclad, the *Albemarle*.[22]

By April 1864, Goss and his regiment had settled into Fort Williams not far from Plymouth. On April 18, while Hoke's batteries fired on the town, Goss's unit was instructed to pass through the area en route to the river. As the regiment marched along the assigned route, they found Plymouth in a tattered condition, scarred by the ravages of war. It reminded Goss of the Rip Van Winkle story—a hamlet suspended in time. Most of the quaint log cabins and houses had been destroyed, but a few wooden shacks still stood, despite an ongoing and ferocious artillery barrage.[23]

Plymouth residents already had abandoned the area, leaving mostly escaped slaves and Rebel deserters in their wake. The remaining denizens professed their love of the Union and scrambled forward seeking rations and supplies from the current occupants. Goss had few items to spare, but he contributed what he could. As he left their town, he looked at the people behind him. The lean, hungry, frightened outcasts hunkered down in shacks and bungalows, preparing to weather the rising storm as best they could.[24]

After passing through Plymouth, Goss boarded a Union ship, the *Dolly*, and set sail for nearby Fort Gray. Later that same day, he returned from the fort carrying Union corpses for burial. Goss and another soldier buried their comrades until 2:00 A.M., when the two men stumbled off to bed. The next day's work promised to be grueling. Rebel soldiers were known to be lurking nearby, and Union forces had a long day ahead of them.[25]

He was jolted awake an hour after he retired. The sounds of Confederate cannons firing on Fort Gray were unmistakable. Still groggy and tired from the previous day's labor, he roamed the camp until he found a group of men reviewing the grim situation. Rumors of an impending Rebel invasion abounded, but the small Union force could not hold the line against a unit of any size or strength. Soon enough, the rumors proved to hold a measure of truth.[26]

During the night, the Southerners had constructed a pontoon bridge and crossed the river. With their arrival, the loss of Plymouth was inevitable. The question facing Goss's unit was whether the men should fight the incoming forces or surrender in the face of insurmountable odds. At that hour, Confederate artillery surrounded Fort Williams. Union troops outside the fort surrendered without delay, leaving only the men inside to hold the tide against the invaders. Although the Rebels summoned the men to lay down their arms or suffer "no quarters" if they failed to comply, stubborn Union defenders refused to give up the fort.

They fought valiantly through a long, hot afternoon, and Goss was impressed with the efforts of his comrades in arms. "It is a pleasure to know that most of the men and officers of the second behaved with gallantry, as did other regiments in the field," he later wrote. He reserved special praise for Margaret Leonard, the wife of a private in Company H, who prepared hot coffee and food for the men all through that interminable day, even under intense fire and at considerable personal risk.[27]

As the afternoon waned, however, surrender became their only realistic option. The men ran low on ammunition, food, and supplies. Faced with few alternatives, they would not sacrifice their lives needlessly. When the Confederates again summoned the Union commanding officer to surrender, he agreed to their terms. For the second time in his career as a soldier, Warren Lee Goss became a prisoner of war.[28]

As soon as they laid down their arms, the men of the Second Massachusetts and their comrades were forced to march through two lines of Rebel infantry. The triumphant Confederate soldiers, intoxicated by victory, were boisterous and rowdy, grabbing hats from their prisoners' heads and offering their own in return. Goss did not want to part with his hat, but he had no choice under the circumstances.[29]

As the captives shuffled past an assembled throng, he was greatly disturbed by the behavior of the men and women of Plymouth. Their professed loyalty to the Union—so vocal and emphatic in recent days—had dissolved, like mist, in the morning light. They had transformed themselves into ardent secessionists, assuring their new commanders of their singular devotion to the Confederate cause. As they had demonstrated to Goss the day before, these sunshine patriots eagerly accepted rations and supplies, this time from a new army of occupation.[30]

Not every Plymouth resident embraced the Southerners and their cause, and the defiant ones paid dearly for their devotion to principle. Along with the soldiers taken as prisoners, Union loyalists were marched into an open field at the point of a bayonet. Small children, old women, and persons of all colors and creeds huddled together, fearing that the Rebels might prove as fiendish as rumors suggested. Fortunately, the Confederates as a general rule did not extract vengeance on the soldiers or the local population. Anyone who attempted to escape was punished harshly, but the captives were not mistreated if they obeyed.[31]

Black Union soldiers were not afforded such generous treatment. They were drawn up in a line and marched away, single file, beyond the reach of eyewitnesses. The Rebels assured their white prisoners that the blacks would be shot without mercy for donning a soldier's uniform. Like his comrades, Goss was horrified by the prospect of summary executions. "There were about twenty Negro soldiers at Plymouth, who fled to the swamps when the capture of the place became certain," he recalled. "These soldiers were hunted down and killed, while those who surrendered in good faith were drawn up in line, and shot down also like dogs." Although such events may have occurred, Goss and the other prisoners did not witness them firsthand. The Confederates wisely decided to take whatever action they deemed necessary away from the surviving captives.[32]

The prisoners spent the night in the field where they had been assembled, lying under the stars, contemplating an uncertain future. The next afternoon, they were given hardtack and pork, formed into a line, and marched about fifteen grueling miles, where they again rested in a field. On April 22, without receiving further rations, the men and women were taken to the little town of Hamilton, North Carolina. The citizens of the village, mostly women, poured into the streets to catch a glimpse of the captured Yankees. They milled about, examining the prisoners and plying them with questions.

"Has you'uns Yanks got any snuff?" someone in the crowd inquired. Other voices joined in the cry for tobacco, food, clothing, or whatever held value. The captives carried few items, apart from Union dollars, so the crowd gradually dissipated, disappointed at the meager offerings.[33]

They camped at Hamilton for several days. It was an uneventful time. Early in the morning of April 24, after four days in Confederate custody, the prisoners were marched to another town, Tarboro, and given rations of meal, beans, and bacon. Another prisoner, Sgt. Maj. Robert H. Kellogg of the Sixteenth Regiment, Connecticut Volunteers, recalled the Plymouth Pilgrims' early experiences in captivity. "The indolence and monotony which characterized these days was unpleasant in the extreme," he wrote. "Sometimes we found little variety in spicy debates with rebel officers, upon the war and slavery. They seemed to be very fond of arguing with us, although our boys almost invariably got the better of them."[34]

Goss made the most of the idle hours. Recalling his previous experiences in the Richmond prisons, he knew that he would need utensils if he hoped to survive. He traded his overcoat for a two-quart pail, which he believed would be a priceless commodity. It proved to be a wise transaction. That night, his comrades pooled their rations to use the pail for cooking mush. The concoction tasted bland and unappealing without salt, but they knew they were lucky to have any warm food. As the owner of the pail, Goss ensured that his portion of the food was generous. Once again, his business acumen proved to be a blessing.[35]

The next morning, the captives were on the move again, this time marching through the streets of Tarboro. Southerners streamed out from their houses to observe the prisoners and comment on their predicament. Ladies in torn and frayed crinoline and homespun hoop skirts traded with the captives, exchanging shoes, buttons, and cooking utensils for Union greenbacks. They had many kind words for the men and women suffering from the ill fortunes of war. Curiously, the townspeople seemed as impoverished and needy as the prisoners. Perhaps women on the Southern home front were ailing almost as much as soldiers on the front lines. The ladies of Tarboro, lifting their skirts lest they become muddy and entangled in the brush, followed the prisoners to the outskirts of the village, waving good-bye.[36]

Not long after they left the little town, the captives found themselves standing at a train depot. They were crowded into boxcars, sixty and seventy persons to a car. Robert Kellogg recalled that the men "longed for a little sleep; to lose ourselves in grateful unconsciousness for a little while, but we found there was not room for us all even to sit down, much less to place our bodies in such a position as to experience anything like rest." When the prisoners had been loaded, the engine sounded, a whistle blew, and the train lurched forward, headed farther south into enemy territory.[37]

They squinted through the slats in the boxcars and observed the surrounding countryside. Tarboro dropped behind them as though it were a dream, a landscape that existed only in the realm of imagination. The cars swayed back and forth on the track with hypnotic predictability like a pendulum keeping time; in this way, the hours crept by with glacial speed. Gradually, they collapsed into a heap of jumbled arms and legs, each man panting for air amidst the heat and smells of so many bodies crowded together without sufficient ventilation.[38]

To pass the time faster, they speculated on their destination. Many captives held out hope that they would be taken to another depot and placed on a Union train for prisoner exchange. This optimistic assessment seemed borne out by a conversation that the prisoners overheard between two Confederate guards. Goss had some experience in these matters; he believed an exchange of prisoners was unlikely. In his opinion, the conversation was staged for the benefit of the prisoners so they would remain docile in hopes of procuring an early release.[39]

As he took measure of his surroundings, Goss noticed a hole in the side of the boxcar large enough for a man to crawl through. He contemplated an escape under cover of night. He and his fellow inmates could wriggle through the opening and wait for the train to pass a patch of woods that would conceal their flight. At exactly the right moment, they could hurl themselves into the darkness. It was a risky plan. Eagle-eyed Rebel guards who would love nothing better than to drive a Minié ball through a Yankee prisoner might spot them. They might hit the ground at a wrong angle, breaking their legs and lying in the middle of nowhere, helpless, victims of their own ingenuity.

Even if they managed to land safely and travel under the cover of darkness, it was unfamiliar terrain in a land populated by the enemy. The chances of engineering a successful escape seemed remote, at best. Still, it was something to consider.

Several prisoners objected to the plan for another reason. "We shall be shot by the guards if you escape," one man said. Others murmured their assent. The general agreement seemed to be that the group should keep quiet, make no trouble, and if by chance they arrived in a prison camp, they would receive better treatment for having been model prisoners.[40]

Goss thought these hopes were naive and foolish. He tried to dissuade the group from following such a passive course of action, but he did not succeed. Several prisoners even threatened to disclose the escape plan to the Confederates if Goss persisted. The captives were so anxious to believe that they would not endure harsh treatment they accepted any story, no matter how implausible, that would confirm their brightest hopes. Later, when a Rebel guard assured them they were being shipped to a new prison—a beautifully laid out camp, with luxuriant shade trees filled with birds, and a running stream stocked with fish—the prisoners accepted the statement at face value. As one of the few men who had survived the brutal conditions in a Confederate prison, Goss told his comrades that the guards' comments were a not-so-subtle form of chicanery. In his view, no Rebel guard could be trusted. Despite his impassioned plea to listen to reason, he could not convince the desperate men that their conditions probably had worsened. "Although I informed them of the manner in which prisoners were treated, they could not be brought to believe it was so bad after all."[41]

The prison system had changed markedly since Goss first had been captured almost two years earlier. During the intervening months, prisoner exchanges had become the exception rather than the rule. As a result, military prisons on both sides of the conflict were strained almost beyond capacity. To accommodate the burgeoning inmate population, Northern and Southern administrators scrambled to build new facilities. The captives were headed through the Carolinas and deep into the heart of Georgia. There, in the southwest corner of the state, they would be confined to a new Confederate prison, Camp Sumter, a stockade located near a small railroad junction with a name that soon would become infamous in the annals of Civil War history—Andersonville.[42]

Goss and his comrades were not the only Union prisoners who heard the stories about idyllic conditions at Andersonville. Many arriving inmates were

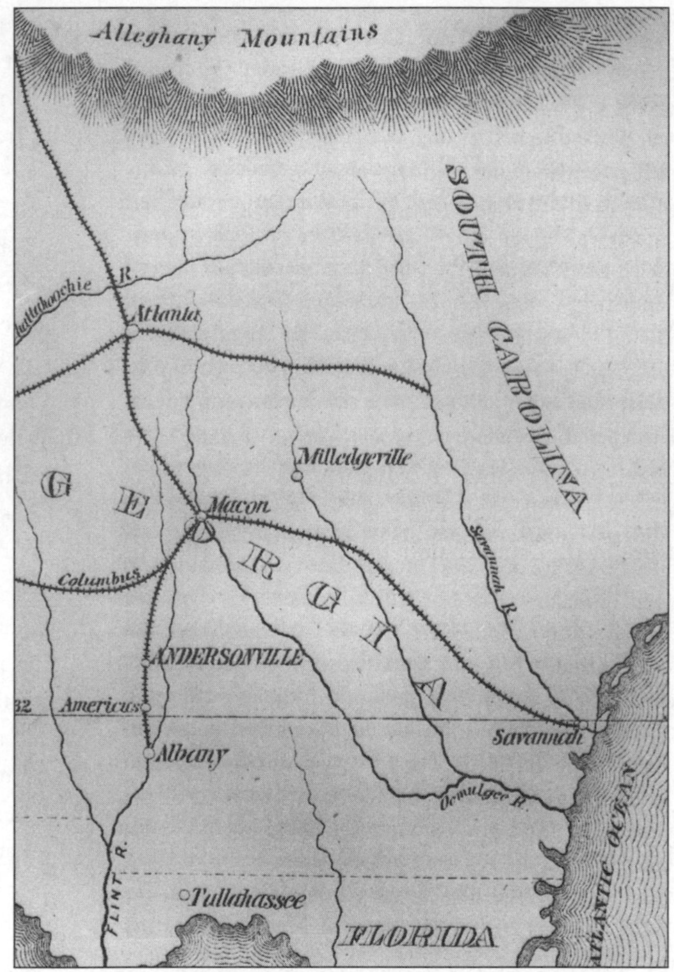

When he was recaptured in 1864, Warren Lee Goss was sent to a new Confederate prison, Camp Sumter, constructed at Andersonville Station in southwest Georgia. Reprinted from *The Soldier's Story* by Warren Lee Goss.

told en route that the new prison was a marked improvement over Belle Isle, where most of the first occupants had been held before their transfer. "On our way from Atlanta down, some of the guards described it to us as a large open field with plenty of good shade, plenty of rations, plenty of good water and green grass to wallow in," Charles A. Smith of the Eleventh Iowa Volunteers recalled. "I was foolish enough to look forward to it as a 'sweet field arrayed in evergreens,' for that was the native timber there." Smith and the prisoners found a far different situation than what they had been led to believe. "There too was the plenty of green grass and plenty of nice shade, but for some reason they were both separated from the prisoners by a heavy stockade built of hewn timbers standing on end in the ground, deep enough to stand firm, and reaching 15 to 18 feet above the surface. Add to this the smoke rising from their little fires all over the camp and then fancy to yourself my sinking heart." Sgt. Daniel Kelley of the Twenty-fourth New York Cavalry remembered that "we longed to get there, for the guards told us that the stockade was well shaded by pines; that there was a beautiful creek running through it with plenty of fish; and that we would have good tents, and receive rations in abundance." [43]

As anxious as the exhausted captives were to arrive at their new luxury accommodations, they had to survive the long train ride, no mean feat for sick and starving men. Goss reported that the train briefly stopped in Wilmington. To their relief, the prisoners received more rations of bacon and hardtack. When they were off-loaded near a large stack of cotton bales, Goss and his friends set fire to the bundles undetected. Even in their time of dire need and desperation, they were determined to create as much mischief as possible. Passing through on a later train, Sergeant Kellogg witnessed the damage firsthand. "A short time before our arrival the place had suffered from an immense fire," he recalled. "Remains of buildings and docks were still smoking and burning. One of the prisoners who went through in advance of us placed a lighted pipe in a bale of cotton, and before it was discovered the fire had made too much progress to be easily arrested. The loss was estimated to have been about six millions of dollars, one million of which belonged to the Confederate government." After the prisoners arrived in Charleston, Goss and his fellow inmates were gratified to learn from the Rebels in a harshly worded missive that "a large amount of cotton had been destroyed, supposed to have been fired by malicious Yankee prisoners, who passed through the place en route for Andersonville."[44]

They saw Florence, South Carolina—where some men would be imprisoned later in 1864—for the first time during the trek to Andersonville, but probably thought little of it at the time. After crossing the river on a ferry at Wilmington, the prisoners halted at Florence and received additional rations, this time consisting of Indian meal. Goss did not record his initial impressions. By nightfall, they had left Florence and arrived in Charleston, where they were kept in a workhouse yard.[45]

Goss believed that he and his comrades were treated kindly by the Charlestonians, who seemed to take pity on their plight. The picturesque city had been destroyed by Union artillery, and the captives felt genuine regret for the damage inflicted on so lovely a place. As they were loaded into boxcars for the continuation of their journey to Andersonville, they hated to leave a city where the people had showed them so much Southern hospitality, a rarity under the circumstances of confinement.[46]

The next day found the weary travelers in Macon, Georgia, a town that reminded Goss of New England—perhaps Augusta, Maine. The weather was drizzly, and the sky was gray. Watching the scene from between the slats of the boxcars, the captives realized that soon they would be behind the walls of another Confederate prison. The group fell victim to a pervading sense of melancholy that mirrored the color of the sky. As the train drew closer to the site of the prison, the Confederates increased their guard. Whatever window of opportunity the prisoners might have had to escape was closed.[47]

They reached the Andersonville Stockade around four o'clock in the afternoon on May 1, 1864. A torrential downpour heralded their arrival. As they stepped from the boxcars, the prisoners caught sight of a ferocious, round-shouldered little man riding a bay mare. Surrounded by guards, he rode upon the scene swearing and raving in an almost comical manner. He seemed to be the caricature of a prison commandant; his movements were jerky and uneven, like the spasms of an out-of-control puppet. Several prisoners burst into laughter before they could help themselves.

Henry Wirz served as the commandant of Camp Sumter, Andersonville Station, Georgia. Courtesy of the Museum of the Confederacy.

"By Got! You tam Yankees," the man screamed, wiping his face, which was saturated with rain. He held one arm to his side as though it were a useless appendage. "You won't laugh ven you gets into the bull pen."

The laughter died at once. Something in the man's savage tone of voice overrode the farcical German accent. The prisoners realized their predicament was dire, and the little fellow's words contained a grim prophecy.[48]

They had just caught their first glimpse of Capt. Henry Wirz, the commandant of Camp Sumter, Andersonville Station, Georgia. In many ways, he was the comical figure he appeared to be, bearing no small resemblance to Charlie Chaplin's character, the Little Tramp, which would become popular fifty years later. Wirz sported a dark beard—much darker than the rest of his hair—and almost always donned a gray army cap, probably to conceal his premature baldness and his unusually thin head. On many days, he waddled around the camp wearing a tattered Confederate uniform, the cap pulled just above his eyebrows, carrying a revolver in a holster strapped to his waist. His beady eyes and constant twitching could be unnerving to those who chose not to laugh, and his thick accent, which made him all but incomprehensible when he was enraged, which was often, transformed him into an enigmatic presence among the soldiers and prisoners under his command. On first encountering this peculiar man, a prisoner did not know whether he should laugh or cry. Wirz's mercurial temperament meant that he could appear tender and thoughtful one moment, and ferocious and vindictive the next. With his foreign lineage, his thick German accent, his strangely proportioned body, his right arm held at his side or stuffed into his shirt à la Napoleon, and his volatile, unpredictable temper, he was anything but a typical Confederate officer.[49]

This curious little man, forty years old when the camp opened, was born in Zurich, Switzerland, on November 25, 1823. He emigrated from Europe to the United States in 1849, arrived in Massachusetts, and took to roaming the countryside. He eventually turned up in New Orleans, where he worked as a bartender. Wirz was interested in pursuing a career in medicine, so he began an apprenticeship with several physicians in Kentucky before returning to Louisiana around 1856. Practicing as a homeopathic doctor in Madison Parish, Wirz managed to eke out a living during the antebellum years, although he was far from affluent. When the war erupted, he enlisted as a private in the Fourth Louisiana Infantry—nicknamed the Madison Infantry—on June 16, 1861.[50]

His military career was as strange as his accent and odd appearance. He rose through the ranks to become a sergeant, but much of his later career was shrouded in mystery. Commentator Ovid Futch concluded that Wirz suffered a grievous injury at the battle of Seven Pines, May 31–June 1, 1862, which rendered his right arm incapacitated and required his absence from further frontline duty. A later commentator, William Marvel, found that Wirz did not arrive in Virginia until many days after the battle ended; therefore, he could not have been wounded at Seven Pines. As is the case in so much of Wirz's life and career, it is difficult to know where the facts end and the myths begin.[51]

However he was injured, by June 1862, Wirz had been promoted to the rank of captain and was serving as adjutant general to Gen. John H. Winder, provost marshal of the Richmond prisons. During that time, he learned much from the elderly general regarding prison operations and discipline. After a brief interlude, during which he searched for missing records in Alabama and served as commander of the Confederate prison in Tuscaloosa, Wirz traveled overseas as Jefferson Davis's special plenipotentiary to Paris and Berlin. Once again, it is difficult to know the true purpose of Wirz's European excursion. His daughter later contended that he was on official business on behalf of the Confederate government, but how much of his mission was at Davis's behest and how much was for other reasons is impossible to know with any accuracy or precision. It strains credibility to view the temperamentally unstable Wirz as a Confederate diplomat, and he was so striking and unusual in his appearance and mannerisms that it seems unlikely that he served as an effective espionage agent, assuming that European espionage could have gained any advantages for the Confederacy. Whatever his duties, they required his absence for the entire calendar year of 1863.[52]

Not long after he returned to the Confederacy early in 1864, Wirz met with General Winder and learned that he had received a new assignment. To relieve the overcrowding in prisons that resulted from the suspension of the Dix-Hill Cartel, the Confederate government had constructed a stockade in southwest Georgia. Winder ordered his loyal subordinate to report to the new post and assume command of the prison interior.

At the time, Lt. Col. Alexander W. Parsons of the Fifty-fifth Georgia Regiment was in charge of the prison guard and the exterior grounds. To assist in the transition, Winder sent Wirz on his way with a letter to Parsons explaining that Wirz was experienced in prison administration, and a good man to have on hand. Despite the letter of introduction, Parsons and Wirz quarreled frequently because Parsons believed that Wirz's arrival was a sign that Winder and the Confederate government lacked faith in Parsons's abilities. In June, the lieutenant colonel departed from Andersonville, leaving Wirz to replace him.[53]

When Wirz arrived at Andersonville in March, he went right to work. During his tenure at what became the most infamous of all Civil War prisons, he established a reputation among the Northern public as a dastardly, inhuman fiend, one of the worst villains in American history. The diaries and memoirs of former Andersonville inmates excoriated Wirz even more than they did

Winder, finding no saving grace among his many faults. "I must say that he was the most inhuman and abusive man I ever met," the Rev. M. V. B. Phillips recalled. "The compunctions of humanity passed over his seared and unfeeling conscience, with no more effect than when the waves surge over the huge rocks which form the bed of the deepest ocean," Augustus Hamlin wrote in the typically overwrought style of the day. Josiah Brownell concluded that "a more brutal coward I never saw. Kicking and cursing the sick who from inability to walk lay down on the ground outside the gate of the prison, revolver in his hand, he ran from one place to another, as we were being driven, like a flock of sheep, within the gate, threatening, striking and cursing with the ferocity of a bulldog." John McElroy, one of the most embittered Andersonville alumni, was typically effusive in his virulent portrayal of the commandant. "He was simply contemptible, from whatever point of view he was studied. Gnat-brained, cowardly, and feeble natured, he had not a quality that commanded respect from any one who knew him. His cruelty did not seem designed so much as the ebullitions of a peevish, snarling little temper, united to a mind incapable of conceiving the results of his acts, or understanding the pain he was inflicting."[54]

Predictably, the Southern view of Wirz and Andersonville was far more charitable. Always the foremost apologist for the Confederate cause, Jefferson Davis lamented in his memoirs that "this unfortunate man" improved conditions at Andersonville, but fell victim to the quest for vengeance exhibited by emancipated prisoners after the war. In Davis's view, history would vindicate Wirz when it became clear that "under the severe temptation to which he was exposed before his execution, exhibited honor and fidelity strongly in contrast with his tempters and prosecutors." If this description of Wirz's treatment at the hands of Union army officers sounds vaguely reminiscent of the situation at Calvary, the oblique allegorical reference was no accident. Dr. R. Randolph Stevenson, chief surgeon of the Confederate States Military Hospitals at the Andersonville Stockade, was another postwar writer who took it upon himself to rehabilitate Wirz's reputation and the conditions in Southern prisons. Writing in 1876, he concluded that "when the web of falsehood, concealment and perjury called 'the Wirz trial' shall be rent, and the truth known, it will be seen that the real responsibility lies with the [Union leaders] who sacrificed these poor wretches to their own ambition."[55]

Although Wirz's name is forever linked with Andersonville in the pages of history, the stockade already existed when he reported for duty in March 1864. It had been constructed at the behest of General Winder, who dispatched his son, Capt. W. Sidney Winder, in November 1863 to find a site deep in the heart of the Confederacy far away from the reach of Union liberators. Captain Winder reported to his father that Station Number 8 near what was then called "Anderson Station" in southwest Georgia was a suitable location. Benjamin Dykes, a mill owner in the area, even offered to lease the Confederacy a wooded site approximately a mile and a half from the railroad line that could be cleared of trees and used for the prison. Captain Winder believed that the tract was well suited as a stockade site; it gently sloped down to a small stream, a branch of the much larger Sweet Water Creek, itself a tributary of the Flint River.[56]

The Confederates called the new facility "Camp Sumter," naming it after the powder keg that ignited the war, Fort Sumter in Charleston Harbor. Preparations for constructing the new camp remain controversial to this day. Confederate officers have argued that Winder and his men always intended to construct barracks for the prisoners, but time and money were in short supply. With the disruption of major railroad lines throughout the Confederacy and the shortage of supplies such as lumber and construction materials, it was impracticable to build anything other than the most rudimentary prison. Thus, beginning in January 1864, the Confederates felled trees and hammered them vertically in the ground to serve as the walls of a simple stockade.[57]

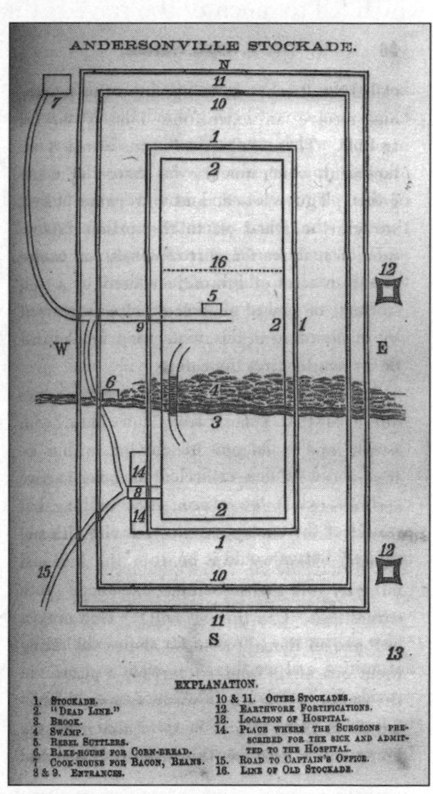

The Southern Confederacy began operating the Andersonville Stockade early in 1864. Reprinted from *Life and Death in Rebel Prisons* by Robert H. Kellogg.

The stockade was a large open field, bounded by logs and a "deadline" eighteen feet inside the enclosure to prevent prisoners from venturing too close to the walls. When construction was completed, it en-compassed sixteen and a half acres of land with no buildings for the inmates and only two trees left standing in the prison interior. The pine logs were jammed into the ground so close together that no one could see through the spaces beyond the stockade grounds. At the top of the stockade walls, roofed sentry boxes were placed at regular intervals with ladders so that guards could oversee activities in the prison interior. The stockade was a hollow rectangle inside a second, larger hollow rectangle, which meant that the prison walls were enclosed by a second set of prison walls, both of which were entered through a pair of massive wooden gates on the west side of the camp.[58]

The only visible feature of note inside the prison was a small five-foot-wide stream that cut through the gently sloping prison grounds. Prison administrators intended for the stream to serve as both the source of drinking water at the upper end and the prisoners' latrine at the lowest point of the prison. As the inmates poured into the stockade in ever-increasing numbers, the Confederates' instructions on appropriate uses of the stream went unheeded, which led to much of the tragedy that followed. When the twin functions of the stream overlapped, scores of men fell victim to disease and died.[59]

A low, marshy area surrounded the stream. John McElroy called it "a quaking bog of slimy ooze one hundred and fifty feet wide, and so yielding that one attempting to walk upon it would sink to the waist." In his diary, Sgt. Eugene Forbes of the Fourth New Jersey Volunteers, a young man who died in the Florence Stockade in February 1865, observed that "a considerable marsh occupies the very centre of the pen, which, if not drained, will be apt to create disease among us." "At times this swamp would be so alive with wriggling maggots that it seemed to rise and fall in undulating billows," James Newton Miller of West Virginia recalled. "From the edges of the swamp the ground rose, especially on the north side, which was quite steep."[60]

Looking down at the first mass of prisoners shuffling into the prison interior, more than one inmate realized with mounting horror that the guards' advance billing of the camp had been a gross lie of epic proportions, just as Goss had predicted. "As we entered the place a spectacle met our eyes that almost froze our blood with horror, and made our hearts fail within us," Robert Kellogg explained. "Before us were forms that had once been active and erect—*stalwart men*, now nothing but mere walking skeletons, covered with filth and vermin. Many of our men, in the heat and intensity of their feeling, exclaimed with earnestness, 'Can this be hell?'" The resemblance between the swarming mass of men and a mound of ants was not lost on several prisoners. "As we approach the place," Pvt. George A. Hitchcock wrote in his diary, "a cloud of smoke hangs over all, rising from innumerable fires, through which we discern a dense black moving mass of humanity that reminded me of a great disturbed ant hill." Entering the stockade later, Pennsylvanian Ezra Hoyt Ripple recalled that "when we looked down in the prison it resembled an immense anthill teeming with life" where "not a particle of vegetation could be seen, the surface trampled as hard as the floor of a brick yard, and resembling a half-burned brick in color."[61]

Stumbling into the prison on that rain-drenched May afternoon, Goss echoed the assessment of his fellow prisoners when he first caught sight of his new home. "As we waited, the great gates of the prison swung on their ponderous oaken hinges, and we were ushered into what seemed to us Hades itself. Strange, skeleton men, in tattered, faded blue—and not much of blue either, so obscured with dirt were their habiliments—gathered and crowded around us; their faces were so begrimed with pitch-pine smoke and dirt, that for a while we could not discern whether they were Negroes or white men." As bad as the Richmond prisons had been, Goss could tell that Andersonville was a far worse place. "All my former experience of prison life had not prepared me for such unmitigated misery as met me everywhere. Of those of our company who that day entered these prison gates, not one third passed beyond them again, except to their pitiful, hastily made, almost begrudged graves."[62]

SIX

Too Much Fuss over a Very Small Matter

"We cannot accuse any officer of ever having shot a prisoner," John Minnich observed, but he had little doubt that several sadistic guards "need not have been begged to do so." In his view, "it is one phase of our prison life not found in the Government records of Rock Island." Fellow inmate Charles Wright agreed. "In April, 1864, the sentinels on the parapet commenced firing at the prisoners and into the barracks, and this practice continued while I remained. I am ignorant as to the orders the sentinels received, but I know that the firing was indiscriminate, and apparently the mere caprice of the sentinels."[1]

Random acts of violence were an all-too-familiar feature of life in the Rock Island Barracks. As an ever-increasing stream of prisoners flowed into the prison and conditions deteriorated during 1864, both inmates and guards were subjected to enormous stresses and faced severe shortages. Prisoners grew desperate as they suffered the ill effects of scanty rations, crowded barracks, a lack of adequate clothing and supplies, epidemics of disease, and the overarching fear that accompanied their confinement. In the meantime, many of the best Union men were fighting on faraway battlefields, leaving guard duty to soldiers of lesser merit, primarily adolescent boys and old men. Many of the soldiers mustered into the 133rd Illinois Regiment were sixteen and seventeen years old. Alfred Orendorff, a captain in the unit, was only eighteen years old. Coupled with their youth, many prison sentries also received comparatively little training. As a result, they evinced less tolerance for infractions of the rules than did their absent brethren. Without the ameliorative influence of women or the self-control instilled through rigid army discipline and tradition, the sentries were poised to erupt into violence with little provocation.[2]

Soldiers in the 133rd Illinois Volunteer Infantry Regiment generally were adolescent boys with little training. Courtesy of the Leda R. Clark Collection, U.S. Army Military History Institute.

Minnich recalled an incident that illustrated the volatile temper of his captors. As winter ended and the weather improved, inmates often wiled away the hours playing outdoor sports. During a baseball game one day, a wild ball flew out of reach and struck a guard, Capt. John Hogendobler. Nicknamed "Hogdriver" by the prisoners, this ill-tempered fellow was a "Greybeard," an older officer serving with the Thirty-seventh Iowa Volunteer Regiment, one of the units comprising the prison garrison. Most of the Greybeards ranged in age from about forty-five up to their sixties. One man, Curtis King of Muscatine County, Iowa, was eighty years old. The infamous Greybeard Hogendobler had earned a well-deserved reputation as a consummate bully. He seldom missed an opportunity to assert his power over the inmates, and his acts of cruelty were limited only by his imagination. Woe to the man who incurred the wrath of the Hogdriver.[3]

On this occasion, John Minnich was that man. "I myself felt the stings of Hogendoble's [*sic*] tongue and the blow of his coward's fist because he was accidentally hit by our ball during a game, for which he would accept neither apology nor excuse," Minnich wrote of the incident. No manner of explanation could placate the Greybeard. Enraged, he shouted "every vile epithet that would come to his base mind, while trying to strike me in the face with his clinched fist and then threatening me with his pistol because I would not stand up and meekly take his blows." Minnich dared not strike back, for that would give Hogendobler the justification he needed to shoot the prisoner.[4]

The "Greybeards" of the Thirty-seventh Iowa Volunteer Regiment were older men between the ages of forty-five and sixty, although some soldiers were in their seventies. Courtesy of the U.S. Army Military History Institute.

"His foul epithets, with his revolver thrust almost against my face and a threat to blow my 'd—d brains out' if I did not stand up and take the blows aimed at my face, were more than I could quietly submit to," Minnich confessed. Looking into the muzzle of the pistol, "which just then seemed to have a bore as big as a Gatling gun," Minnich turned his head and took the full brunt of Hogendobler's blows on his ear.[5]

Finally, the embattled prisoner lost his temper, and against his better judgment he screamed at his tormentor. "Shoot, damn you! Shoot, you coward! I can't help myself. I apologized for the ball having struck you unintentionally, and you will accept neither apology nor excuse. Now shoot!"

Inexplicably, this comment seemed to soothe the savage beast. Hogendobler stopped and examined his prey. Virtually everyone in the prison yard looked on the scene with awe, anxious to witness the uncertain denouement. "He stared at me a bit after I had relieved myself, and then with another string of curses ordered me to follow him, which I did," Minnich recalled. "Not knowing his intentions, and at that particular moment, with my blood boiling, not much caring, he led the way outside to the guardhouse, and ordered that I be ornamented with a ball and chain 'for a month.' I was well satisfied to get off so cheaply. We had a trick of unlocking fetters at night, though ostensibly we were never without them."[6]

Despite the humiliation of this treatment, Minnich escaped with relatively minor punishment. In standing up to the bully, he probably prevented worse treatment. Not everyone was so fortunate. One day as Captain Graham, Hogendobler's friend and accomplice, passed through the barracks, he ordered the men to stand at attention as he inspected their quarters. One fellow was so weak and sickly that he could barely get to his feet. Somehow he climbed from his bunk and stood on wobbly legs, but Graham was dissatisfied with this effort. Minnich was not present, but he later heard about the incident from several acquaintances. In a fit of anger, the captain "seized the man by the collar, jerked him out of the ranks, struck him with his fist, forced him to the floor, and kicked him in the body and head, all the while cursing him with anything that came to his foul mouth."[7]

Other unconscionable episodes occurred almost daily. When he learned that prison administrators herded inmates beyond the stockade walls to cut trees, fell stumps, and perform other types of manual labor, Minnich was outraged at this "abuse of all military custom and authority." Work performed by the prisoners brought money into Union coffers, but the men laboring in the fields received no remuneration. At a time when Rock Island residents were desperate to purchase foodstuffs from the camp sutler, Minnich was incensed that such obvious inequities passed without reproach. He protested vociferously to all who would listen that the men must resist such patent abuses; yet the practice continued.[8]

His turn to set an example came soon after he arrived at the prison. "In March 1864, one raw, cold morning, I and nine others from my barrack were detailed for outside work," he wrote. "I went with the detail as far as the guardhouse outside, where we were halted, and axes, picks, and spades given us, and then we were ordered to move off around the corner of the prison wall." Even as the other men shuffled off to their labors, Minnich refused to move.

Observing the blatant disobedience to his order, the sergeant of the guard was brusque. "Well, why ain't you moving?"

When Minnich said that he had no intention of moving, the sergeant demanded an explanation. "We are prisoners of war, and you have no right to take us outside of the prison to do government work without pay," the obstinate inmate replied.

"So that's it, is it? Well, we'll call the lieutenant and see what he says."

The lieutenant, a barrel-chested fellow nicknamed "Big Ben," marched over to the prisoner after the sergeant informed him of the problem. He listened to the argument quietly and without interruption, although he grew red in the face before the tale was told. "Well, I'll have to report this to Colonel Johnson," he muttered at the conclusion, but he did not mete out a harsh punishment. Instead, he ordered the guards to escort the obstreperous captive back to the prison.[9]

Minnich twice defied authority and lived to recount his experiences, but his fellow prisoners thought he was pushing his luck. One amiable old-timer,

"Uncle" Jim Ford of Owenton, Kentucky, admonished his stubborn comrade for taking unnecessary risks and incurring the wrath of spiteful jailers. "Well, of course you're right; we all know it and feel the same way," he said, "but what can we do?" Retaliation was an ever-present threat, and it was not unheard of to see a fellow shot down in his tracks for relatively minor infractions of the rules.

Minnich answered his rhetorical question. "I advanced the point that if we all stood together and refused they would not dare do it; but that if we didn't assert our rights they would make us do the labor for nothing and charge the government for full wages and put the money in their pockets. And to this day I have always believed that was done."[10]

Despite the risks of protesting poor treatment, Minnich believed that the captives could protect themselves from retribution if they refused to yield on questions involving humane conditions and the military courtesies and rights that must be afforded to all soldiers captured on the battlefield. He repeatedly sounded a single refrain—"We are prisoners of war, and not convicts"—and argued that the only hope of surviving the ordeal at Rock Island was for the prisoners to band together and support each other.[11]

Bullying behavior directed toward weak or ill prisoners especially infuriated him. Although many officers and guards engaged in such antics, Minnich reserved special vituperation for Captain Bucher, "about as mean as men are made." Although the captain possessed "a fair exterior (he was a handsome fellow)," his good looks were merely "hiding the brute" lurking beneath the surface. Recalling an episode that occurred late in his tenure as a prisoner, Minnich wrote that Bucher was overseeing the transfer of men from one barrack to another when the guard spotted an inmate sitting next to the stove with a blanket draped over his shoulders.

"Here, you in there, come out here and fall in," he ordered.

The emaciated figure rose from his bed and stumbled to the door. Explaining that he was still recovering from "a spell of sickness" and thus was unable to fall into line, he asked for permission to stay in his bunk.

Bucher was livid. "Come out here, I tell you, or I'll pull you out!"

Sensing that a confrontation was in the offing, the prisoner reluctantly ambled toward the officer. Several men witnessing the scene called out that the fellow was not malingering. One look at his wasted body and the gaunt, pallid skin of his face told an observer that the prisoner was in poor health. Bucher was unmoved by these entreaties. "This only seemed to aggravate the case," Minnich remembered. "The Captain in a rage seized the poor fellow by the shoulder, whirled him around, pushed him forward, at the same time giving him a kick behind which, had it not been for falling against the man in front of him, would have thrown him forward on the ground."

As he had repeatedly demonstrated on previous occasions, Minnich showed his rebellious streak. "You damned brute," he yelled. "I knew the risk, but could not help it," he later explained. Each man watching the sordid affair was anxious to intervene "to strangle the beast," but he felt powerless to do so. Bucher glared at the assembled throng as if weighing the likelihood that they might rush him en masse before he could summon help. Turning his attention away from the wretched man struggling to stand, he issued an order to march and swiftly departed. "That was the last time that I can remember having seen Bucher," Minnich wrote.[12]

As bad as these incidents were, the shootings were infinitely worse. One of the most highly contested features of life in the Rock Island Barracks remains the question of how many inmates were shot down by guards, whether the shooters' actions were intentional, and if so, whether their motives were justified. Each prisoner knew he must not venture over the deadline near the stockade walls. Even strolling too close to the line was ill advised, for the sentries perched on the parapet might misinterpret the prisoner's intentions or else use the occasion to extract revenge with impunity. To test whether this rule was strictly enforced invited calamity, for the errant captive faced the risk of severe punishment or instant death from a Union Minié ball. Most levelheaded prisoners simply went about their lives and stayed far away from the forbidden area, but a hail of bullets cut down some hapless souls, nonetheless.[13]

Guards had orders to shoot prisoners who ventured past the Rock Island "deadline." Courtesy of the Illinois State Historical Library.

Gunfire became more common as the year 1864 drew to a close. Many Rock Island guards were so-called "hundred days men"—troops mustered into the army on a temporary basis to "fill the gaps" caused by attrition in the ranks—and as these unseasoned soldiers proliferated, discipline suffered precipitously. The sound of smoothbore muskets discharging at all hours of the day or night became routine. In some cases, at the changing of the guards, a sentry would deliberately fire his rifle to clear the barrel. This practice, while chilling to prisoners fearful of being shot, was not unique among Civil War soldiers; however, reckless young men could not always be counted on to exercise due diligence. Local residents sometimes complained that they were endangered by this indiscriminate gunplay. An editorial appearing in a local newspaper, the *Democrat,* in June 1864 complained that several men working in a quarry on the riverbank just outside of Davenport, Iowa, opposite the prison, "have been annoyed and seriously endangered by the discharge of fire by the guards of the rebel barracks on Rock Island, who have been in the habit of firing across the river." The editorial concluded by laying blame for this foolhardy behavior on "some of the hundred day's men, who like children with new toys are unduly anxious to test the merit of their rifles."[14]

When they learned of the situation, Union authorities moved to restrain the guards. Major Kingsbury, the officer in charge of the island arsenal, wrote a note to Colonel Johnson, the prison commandant, asking that Johnson curb the enthusiasm of the men under his command. "It has been reported to me that men engaged in quarrying stone for the United States on the other side of the river have been driven from their work by the firing of your men, and that their lives and those of the neighboring inhabitants endangered thereby," the major stated. "Will you please give such orders as will prevent a recurrence of such reckless conduct, and enable the workmen to resume their labors?" Johnson agreed to do what he could to eliminate such episodes in the future.[15]

The pledge to rein in this conduct was easy to promise, but difficult to fulfill. When asked to explain their actions, the guards said they were not only cleaning their rifles, but sometimes they were firing at a target on the east end of the island. Poor marksmen often missed the target completely, and these rounds were the source of many problems. An exasperated Johnson later wrote that the "carelessness of the Guard in discharging their pieces at the target has been the source of many complaints to these Headquarters, which have shown that if life has not been lost it was not for the want of opportunity."[16]

It was not unheard of for the guards to shoot themselves. One young soldier serving in the 133rd, William Sutton, inadvertently shot off two of his own fingers. An unlucky prankster named George Lowe was engaged in a bit of lighthearted mischief with the sentry who came to relieve him. As the two boys struggled with Lowe's rifle, they somehow got ensnarled in the strap that held his cartridge box, thereby cocking the gun. When Lowe tried to untangle his musket, it accidentally discharged and killed him. These activities would have been amusing had they not been so pathetically and needlessly tragic.[17]

The musket discharges—sometimes accidental, sometimes not—also endangered the prisoners. Minnich concluded that few accidents occurred among the "murderous lot" that manned the parapet. "Their firing into the barracks during the night became a matter of such common occurrence that men in the outer rows next to the deadline feared to sleep on the upper and middle bunks, and slept on the floor in many instances for safety."[18]

Using the sink—that is, the outdoor toilet adjacent to the barracks—was a hazardous enterprise, especially at night. After the war, Charles Wright recalled the experience. "Going to the sinks at night was a most dangerous undertaking, for they were now built on the ' deadline,' and lamps with reflectors were fastened to the plank fence—the sentinel above being unseen, while the man approaching the sink was in full view of the sentinel." If the inmate escaped a bullet, he could be assured of a humiliating adventure, nonetheless. "Frequently, they would halt a prisoner and make him take off his pants in the street, and then order him to come to the sink in his drawers (if he had any). I have heard the cocking of a gun presented at myself while going to the sink at night, but by jumping into an alley between the barracks I saved myself the exercise of walking to the sink in my drawers or from receiving the contents of the gun."[19]

Wright was fortunate; not everyone eluded the contents of the gun as easily as he. Samuel Frank of the Fifth Alabama Cavalry Regiment was shot dead after he left his barrack on the way to the sink on June 9. Later that same month, Bannister Cantrell of Company G, Eighteenth Georgia Regiment, and James W. Ricks of Company F, Fiftieth Georgia Regiment, were gunned down. According to Charles Wright, the men "were on detail working in the ditch, and had stopped to drink some fresh water just brought to them." Official records indicate that John P. McClanahan, formerly a private in Company D of the Ninth Tennessee Cavalry and a resident of Barrack 8 at the time, was shot dead by a guard on October 24, 1864, apparently during an escape attempt.[20]

According to historian Benton McAdams, one of the worst episodes occurred around June 24 or 25 when "the boys of the 133rd nearly committed a massacre." The incident is shrouded in mystery to this day because the prison administrators did not keep records of the event. Seventeen men from Barrack 78 were admitted to the prison hospital with gunshot wounds, but the reason for the shooting was not provided. When the *Argus* inquired about the event, Colonel Johnson and his staff denied that it had ever happened.[21]

Minnich's most vivid memory of a shooting inside the prison occurred during the hot summer of 1864, after the authorities had ordered the men to dig a ditch near one of the main streets to be used "for sanitary purposes." A single pump provided water for the entire prison, so men naturally clamored around the ditch waiting for their turn to retrieve fresh water. Minnich recalled that during the hottest part of the day "there would be as many as a hundred buckets in line on each side of the pump, each man waiting his turn to fill his bucket, and often relieving the almost exhausted pumpers by pumping their buckets full." It was no small wonder that this scene would lead to an outbreak of violence.[22]

One afternoon the crowd grew especially restless as the men operating the pump experienced a problem that forced a delay. When someone near the front of the line realized that the pump finally was working, he yelled, "Water!" Desperate to partake of the cool waters, twenty or so men frantically began pushing and shoving. Chaos erupted as the mass of bodies became entangled and as shouts bellowed from the group. Alerted to the melee, a vigilant guard standing on the parapet called out for the crowd to disperse. The sentries had been warned to be particularly watchful for prisoners attempting an escape in the wake of several incidents that had cast the prison administration in a negative light.[23]

Whether the guards knew the brouhaha was merely an exuberant push for water or thought it was something sinister has remained open to debate. Whatever the reason, at least one guard raised his gun and fired into the crowd. "Three went down," Minnich remembered. "One, the first, shot through the liver, died in two hours; the second, in front of him, was bored through the intestines from behind, the ball making its exit near the navel; and the third was caught near the waistband from the rear, the bullet perforating the body, cutting through the inner wall of his right pocket and dropping into that receptacle." One man died, and the other two were transported to the prison hospital.[24]

With the passing of the years and the lack of accurate record keeping, it is impossible to know how many captives died at the hands of their captors in the Rock Island Prison Barracks. The estimates range from a low of nine to a high of many score. Minnich and his fellow inmates would have their readers believe that the violence and cruelty were so frequent that such acts lost their shock value. "I noted some cases that came under my own observation, but by no means a complete list," Charles Wright wrote. Keeping such a list would have been a difficult task. "In fact, the prisoners became so accustomed to the firing from the parapet, that unless it occurred near his side of the prison, a man would take little notice of it."[25]

The only clear fact that emerges from camp records is that no Union officer or soldier was reprimanded, much less court-martialed, for shooting a prisoner. Camp administrators, including Colonel Johnson, the commandant, turned a blind eye to the situation unless it endangered nearby civilians. In one typical case, a shooting was excused with a comment by the prison authority investigating the matter that the unfortunate incident was an "indiscreet act of a raw soldier who had not sufficient judgment to perform his duty properly."[26]

Confederate prisoners who died in the Rock Island Prison were laid to rest in a nearby cemetery. Courtesy of the Rock Island Arsenal Museum.

As for the victims of the shootings, those men who survived a hail of bullets were carried to the prison hospital where they might or might not receive proper treatment. The less fortunate men were laid to rest in a special cemetery set aside for the prisoners who died at Rock Island. They were buried next to their comrades who had succumbed to disease, the frigid weather, or the horrors of war. Many remains are interred there to this day.

"One of the great instruments of death in the prison was the deadline," Warren Lee Goss wrote of the Andersonville Stockade, unconsciously echoing John Minnich's reflections on life in the Rock Island Prison. Consisting of a row of stakes driven into the ground with boards stretched across the top, the line was fixed between fifteen and twenty feet inside the stockade walls and Confederate sentinels guarded it assiduously. Each man who entered the camp understood that "any person who approached it, as many unconsciously did, and as in the crowd was unavoidable, was shot dead, with no warning whatever to admonish him that death was near."[27]

Prisoners were shot down if they ventured too close to the deadline in the Andersonville Stockade. Reprinted from *The Soldier's Story* by Warren Lee Goss.

Goss recalled a horrifying episode that occurred on his second day in the prison. "A poor one-legged cripple placed one hand on the deadline to support him while he got his crutch, which had fallen from his feeble grasp to the ground." Even a patently innocent transgression such as that one could not go unpunished. "In this position he was shot through the lungs, and laid near the deadline writhing in torments during most of the forenoon, until at last death came to his relief. None dared approach him to relieve his sufferings through fear of the same fate." Had any intrepid soul risked an approach during the hour the old man lay dying, the guard assuredly would have shot him down.[28]

Virtually every soldier who

survived his ordeal at Andersonville and wrote about it afterward recounted tales of shootings at the deadline. "We were particularly cautioned by those who had been there some time, to beware of the ' deadline,' about which we had heard upon the night of our arrival, and then believed to be untrue," Sgt. Robert Kellogg wrote. "We found it to be no fiction, however." Investigating conditions at Andersonville before the end of the war, the U.S. Sanitary Commission repeated the reports offered by camp alumni. "Twenty feet inside and parallel to the fence is a light railing, forming the 'deadline' beyond which the projection of a foot or finger is sure to bring the deadly bullet of the sentinel." Josiah Brownell reported the durable rumor that "sentries were always on a sharp lookout for a shot, as they had a furlough of 60 days for killing, 30 days for wounding, a man on the deadline."[29]

An insane or despondent prisoner wandering too close to the forbidden area was a surprisingly common occurrence. John McElroy remembered a German fellow who seemed to have slipped into lunacy. "As he went hobbling around with a vacuous grin upon his face, he spied an old piece of cloth lying on the ground inside the deadline. He stooped down and reached under for it. At that instant the guard fired. The charge of ball-and-buck entered the poor fellow's shoulder and tore through his body. He fell dead, still clutching the dirty rag that had cost him his life." Similarly, Ezra Hoyt Ripple from Pennsylvania remembered that "many poor fellows, desperate and crazed, deliberately went to their deaths this way." Reflecting on the despair of the inmates, Charles Smith mused that "there were some cases of insanity, some of which came to their death by crossing the deadline, when they were immediately shot. Sometimes we thought they were not so very crazy after all."[30]

As word drifted back to the North about the brutal conditions in Andersonville, the deadline became infamous. A fascinated, horrified public read sensationalized accounts of shootings by wicked guards who fired at hapless prisoners as though hunting game in the wilds of the nearby pine forest. The origins of the deadline, while perhaps apocryphal, sometimes are traced to a comment uttered by Gen. Howell Cobb, a well-known Confederate officer from Georgia who visited the prison not long after it was constructed. In an address to the assembled soldiers designed to inspire them, he urged the old men and adolescent boys to perform their duties diligently. Emphasizing the importance of preventing escapes, the general posed a rhetorical question that challenged the men to be vigilant in guarding the deadline. "Would you turn this horde of Lincoln's hirelings on the sacred soil of Georgia?" he asked. A month later, General Winder, commissary general of the prisons, issued an order holding a guard personally responsible for escapes that occurred during his watch.[31]

Goss had heard the stories of Rebel sentries anxious to avoid blame for escapes and eager to receive furloughs when they killed offending inmates. "Scarcely a night or day passed but the sharp crack of a rifle told of the murder of another defenseless victim," he wrote. "Men becoming tired of life committed suicide in this manner. They had but to get under the deadline, or lean upon it, and their fate was sealed in death." He recalled a New York soldier who had lost his cooking utensils and was forced to eat his food raw. As starvation slowly set in, this withered old stick figure grew weary of begging for food. "He announced his determination to die, and getting over the deadline, was shot through the heart." Considering his predicament, it may have been a blessing that he took this short, rapid path to destruction. "I doubt not he saved himself by such a course much trouble and pain, anticipating by only a few weeks a death he must eventually have suffered."[32]

Aside from shooting prisoners who crossed the line, Confederate authorities seldom entered the camp to punish inmates. Nonetheless, they developed a system for disciplining escaped prisoners who were recaptured. Captain Wirz had a set of stocks built near his headquarters, and errant prisoners would spend hours or even days writhing in agony there. Being fitted with a ball and chain, hanging by the thumbs, and "riding the mule"—sitting on a sawhorse until a man's legs were rendered immobile—were not unheard-of punishments. However, compared to the shootings at the deadline or episodes of violence among the prisoners themselves, these torturous practices were used sparingly at Andersonville.[33]

Even more heartbreaking than the violence inflicted by guards were incidents of crime and brutality among the prisoners. Petty offenses such as theft and property destruction were hardly surprising in light of the crowded conditions and the desperate plight of the men, but the level and organized nature of the violence were deeply disturbing. An individual first entering the stockade had to protect himself or he would immediately fall victim to crime and violent altercations unimaginable to someone unfamiliar with a life in captivity. New inhabitants of the prison immediately sought out their "like-minded" brethren; thus, men tried to congregate with other members of their regiment whenever possible. In some instances, kinship ties were more important than military units. The Irish mingled with the Irish, the New York men lived with their fellows from the Empire State, and so forth. What little safety that could be had was found in numbers.[34]

Confederate authorities employed a variety of punishments to discipline errant prisoners. Reprinted from *Five Hundred Days in Rebel Prisons* by Charles Fosdick.

At its apex, Andersonville would have been the fifth largest city in the Confederacy had its population been tallied in a census. Like many cities teeming with diverse ethnic neighborhoods, residents of the stockade had divided themselves into different sections. The sections often competed with each other for food and other resources, especially proximity to water sources and the distribution of rations. The stakes were high—literally determining whether men lived or died—and so it was little wonder that inmates lashed out against each other to obtain the benefits that often accrue when the strong prey on the weak.[35]

If prisoners caught their comrades stealing or committing other crimes, they seldom appealed to camp authorities for assistance. It probably would have been pointless to do so, for the prison administrators had neither the requisite number of men nor the inclination to intervene in the internal questions of camp life. Instead, the inmates meted out their own brand of street justice, with mercy an unlikely option. Inmate John Ransom recalled, "a man caught stealing from one of his comrades [was] stabbed with a knife and killed." Goss and other prisoners found this kind of swift, heavy-handed punishment appropriate given the severity of the crime: "Stealing blankets from boys unaccustomed to hardships was downright murder," and therefore it "became an evil, at last that must be checked." John McElroy agreed. "The administration of justice was reduced to its simplest terms. If a fellow did wrong he was pounded—if there was anybody capable of doing it. If not, he went free."[36]

Thefts were not the only crimes perpetrated by one group of prisoners on another at Andersonville. Many former inmates recalled beatings and murders in abundance. "Stealing and fighting were of common occurrence, and quite a number of murders were committed," Sgt. Daniel Kelley remembered. "About sixty of the most abandoned characters had organized a gang to plunder the men of all they possessed which was of value." If a victim were lucky and complied without complaint, he might be stripped of his valuables and left in peace. Resistance was futile, and ruffians did not look kindly on opposition. "If they were refused, knives and clubs were freely used to meet their demands, and frequently men lost their lives by endeavoring to resist," Kelley wrote. Sam Boggs remembered that gangs "were now adding to the horrors of the nights by their murders and robberies." James Newton Miller surmised that "these were a band of thieves, robbers and murderers, mostly from New York City, who had probably enlisted as bounty jumpers or substitutes, had been captured, and now in prison banded themselves together to continue their old occupation."[37]

Eventually, a de facto prison police force, deemed the "Regulators," emerged to ensure a semblance of law within the stockade. "Big Peter" Aubrey—a corporal from Company G of the Second Massachusetts Regiment of Heavy Artillery—became the head of this ragtag group of law enforcers. Unlike some of his fellow prisoners, Goss admired Big Peter's firm approach to law and order, harsh as it seemed upon occasion. "Pete was an uneducated Canadian," he recalled, "a man of gigantic stature and great physical strength, of an indomitable will, great good nature, and with innate ideas of justice, in the carrying out of which, he was as inflexible as iron. A blow from his fist was like that from a sledgehammer, and from first to last he maintained so great a supremacy in camp, that no description of the prison at that time would be complete without a sketch of him." Prisoners like Charles Smith also appreciated the activities of the Regulators because the "raiding" crimes "made it necessary to have an organized police force, men, officers and court, which met every morning to try any and all cases coming before it."[38]

Not everyone was as charitable toward Big Peter or the Regulators as Goss and Smith were in their memoirs. Because the Regulators sometimes assisted the prison administration in uncovering escape plots and informed on prisoners engaged in villainous activities, it was difficult to determine whether they were friend or foe. When the August rains swept away portions of the stockade walls, some prisoners might have escaped had the Regulators not been on duty to prevent a mass defection. The Regulators saw themselves as a force to ensure that camp life ran smoothly and, in their view, duty sometimes required them to assist the Confederates as well as the prisoners.[39]

Whatever their detractors might say, the Regulators performed a useful service when they assisted in the effort to capture the worst gang in the stockade during the summer of 1864. A group of thugs calling itself the "Raiders" ruled the prison with an iron fist in the spring and early summer. Led by a tough hoodlum named William "Willie" Collins, a soldier from Company D, 88th Pennsylvania Regiment, the Raiders robbed, tortured, and murdered their fellow men. Collins adopted the moniker "Mosby" after the legendary Confederate partisan ranger John S. Mosby, and he assembled a group of ruthless "chieftains" to help him commit his crimes. Each chieftain styled his band of desperadoes after his own surname; thus, Charles Curtis of the 5th Rhode Island Artillery Regiment led "Curtis's Rangers," John Sarsfield of the 144th New York Regiment fronted "Sarsfield's Rangers," and Patrick Delaney of the 83rd Pennsylvania Regiment headed up "Delaney's Rangers." "Collins's Rangers," or more generally "Mosby's Rangers," became the most infamous gang at Andersonville.[40]

At the height of their power, in the spring and summer, the Raiders may have numbered as many as five hundred men, although most participants were merely opportunists who gravitated to the strongest force in the camp and would have deserted the Raiders if law and order were enforced. The group's modus operandi was to greet "fresh fish" when they first arrived in the stockade, grabbing any money, clothing, or other valuables before the new men could acclimate themselves to stockade life or form alliances. Sometimes pursuing a subtle approach, the Raiders might befriend a new man, take him under their wing and offer him a place to spend the night. Then, as the sun descended, they would pounce and beat the unlucky fellow with their fists until he surrendered everything of value, even the shirt off his back.[41]

Early in their tenure, the Raiders operated under the cover of darkness, but as time went on they grew bolder, prowling the grounds for fresh victims in broad daylight. The gangs dealt with resistance swiftly, brutally, and with no compunction for the injuries and deaths they caused. Tales of their ferocity abounded, and their reputation for barbarity grew with each telling. Proud of their mythic stature, they used whatever implements they could find, including knives, to terrorize their victims and add to their legend. Although it is difficult to know how many men died at the hands of the Raiders, the bodies began to stack up by the score as spring gave way to summer.[42]

Like everyone else in the stockade, Goss was alarmed at the audacity of these vicious miscreants. "About this time, the raiders, under the leadership of one Mosby, became exceedingly bold, attacked new comers in open daylight, robbing them of blankets, watches, money, and other property of value. Rumors of frightful import were circulated through the camp of men murdered for their blankets and money. After this, more men were missing at the morning roll-call, of whom there could be no reasonable account given."[43]

This sorry state of affairs continued until the other prisoners banded together to stop the Raiders and bring them to justice. Sgt. Leroy Key of the Sixteenth Illinois Cavalry Regiment, a twenty-four-year-old soldier of uncommon strength, vigor, and moral courage, led the effort. At six feet two inches tall, this former Mississippian began organizing companies of thirty men from among the Regulators and preparing them for a preemptory strike. He understood that brutal men must be dealt with in brutal fashion, and so Key concocted a plan to overpower the Raiders with superior numbers.[44]

As he trained his men to fight, word of his efforts circulated throughout the camp. John McElroy remembered the reaction. "In spite of Key's efforts at secrecy, information as to his scheme reached the Raiders. It was debated at their headquarters, and decided there that Key must be killed. Three men were selected to do this work." On the afternoon of June 28, the men, led by Charles Curtis, cornered Sergeant Key alone in an out-of-the-way part of the stockade. How Key managed to escape with his life is a subject of some conjecture and dispute. McElroy wrote that Key, realizing his precarious position, brandished a pistol at his would-be assailants, thereby inducing them to call off their attack. At least one later historian has disagreed with this embellished account, concluding that Key talked his way out of trouble by assuring Curtis that Key's men were not seeking to undercut Curtis's Irish gang, but merely organizing to defend themselves against the more brazen Raiders. In any event, Key walked away from the confrontation unscathed, but more convinced than ever that he and his band must swiftly act if they were to defeat the thugs.[45]

On the following day, June 29, a series of crucial events commenced which eventually led to the undoing of the Raiders. It began, as pivotal events often do, with a seemingly routine occurrence—the beating of a prisoner. This brave man, a newcomer named Dowd, was severely thrashed when he refused to surrender his valuables to the Raiders. Left for dead, the bloody victim somehow got to his feet and staggered over to the main gate to speak to a guard. On another occasion, he might have been left to fend for himself in what was essentially an internal matter; however, on this day a sympathetic guard listened to the prisoner's account and took action. Entering the prison with Dowd, a Confederate detail marched through the ranks rounding up the offenders as the victim pointed them out. When he was fingered, an enraged John Sarsfield vowed to "cut out Dowd's heart and throw it in his face." Despite the threat, the roundup continued unabated.[46]

Dowd's success in procuring assistance from the Confederate authorities may have been due in no small measure to Sergeant Key's efforts. Unknown to Dowd, Key had met with Captain Wirz that same morning and asked that the Rebels intercede to stop the Raiders' brutalities. According to surviving accounts, the commandant initially scoffed at the request; however, when Dowd appeared at the gate bloody and obviously brutalized, Wirz relented. In one of his few popular acts as commandant, he even allowed the prisoners to hold a trial for the bandits and, after their conviction, provided lumber for the construction of the gallows.[47]

Vowing to stop the Raiders was one thing, but isolating guilty parties with precision proved to be a more daunting matter. Excitement reverberated through the stockade, and the hunt commenced. Very soon the Raiders learned a lesson in the fragility of alliances. Their comrades disassociated themselves from the band as soon as it became clear that the balance of power had shifted. "Very soon the camp was in an uproar," prisoner Eugene Forbes confided in his diary, "for the men came into the arrangement, and the raiders were hunted from one end of the camp to the other." Robert Kellogg vividly remembered how the Raiders were caught. "The Rebel Quartermaster, rebel sergeants and guard, went into the prison, and, piloted by a notorious character known as 'Limber Jim,' and his comrades, they soon ferreted out the infamous scoundrels." "Right finally prevailed," Ezra Hoyt Ripple later wrote, "and six of the most desperate and prominent members of the 'Raiders,' as they were called, were captured and turned over to the rebel authorities for safekeeping, while the 'Regulators' empanelled a jury and tried them."[48]

When he was informed that the prisoners wished to try the alleged offenders, General Winder issued General Order No. 57 on June 30 to authorize the action. Instead of a tribunal consisting of Confederate military officers, the Raiders would receive a genuine trial by a jury of their peers selected from among the prison population. All the rules of testimony and evidence would apply. Twenty-four potential jurors were chosen from a pool of new arrivals to reduce bias, and from there, the list was narrowed to twelve men. To ensure that they would not be lobbied to mete out harsh punishments, the jury was removed from the stockade during the trial. A fellow from the Eighth Missouri—strapping, six foot one inch "Big Pete" McCullough—stepped into the role of judge advocate and presented his case against the defendants with the skill befitting a seasoned trial attorney. When no prisoners volunteered to undertake the unenviable task of defending the Raiders, a Confederate guard was assigned to serve as counsel for the accused.[49]

One by one, the defendants were herded before the tribunal while a parade of witnesses testified as to beatings, robberies, and murders committed by the men on trial. Investigators had found all sorts of booty buried beneath their tents and "shebangs"—knives, watches, money, and the personal effects of many long-dead and wounded victims. Even the remains of one man were discovered beneath a Raider tent. Facing such overwhelming evidence, a conviction was all but a foregone conclusion.[50]

Like everyone imprisoned in the stockade at the time, Warren Lee Goss followed the proceedings with great interest. "The trial lasted through a number of weeks," he recalled. "Competent men were appointed to defend the prisoners by the authorities. An able lawyer, an officer of the rebel guard, conducted the defense, afterwards stating to me that he had no doubt of the guilt of those who suffered punishment. The prosecution was conducted by men selected from among the prisoners. Six of these men were pronounced by a jury guilty of murder."[51]

The half-dozen men condemned to die were well known among their fellow prisoners. Willie "Mosby" Collins; Charles Curtis; John Sullivan (Curtis's faithful right-hand man); Patrick Delaney; John Sarsfield; and a young naval officer, Andrew Muir, were sentenced to be hanged on July 11, 1864. Eighteen others received lesser sentences, although Leroy Key, Big Peter, and members of the Regulators who had taken seriously the biblical promise of an "eye for an eye" augmented their punishments with whippings and beatings.[52]

The authorities brought wood into the stockade after the jury handed down its verdict, and work began on a scaffold in full view of the condemned men, who spent their days imprisoned in stocks as they awaited justice. After General Winder approved the executions on July 10, the stage was set to close the strangest chapter in the history of the Andersonville Stockade. Around four o'clock in the afternoon of the following day, the six prisoners were ushered to the gallows. Captain Wirz and Father Peter Whelan, a priest who had ministered to the Raiders in their last hours, looked on the scene from a distance, but they honored their vow not to interfere.[53]

True to their natures, the Raiders were not content to go gently into that good night. Displaying his remarkable cunning one final time, Charles Curtis pulled free from his jailers and dashed for the creek, calling out "this cannot be" as he tried to escape. In a dramatic scene, he hurled himself through the mud, straining to disappear into a sea of humanity just beyond the water. He may have had a dagger with which he slashed some of the Regulators as they gave chase, although accounts differ on this point. They all agree, however, that a mass of prisoners fell onto the fleeing villain and pounded him into submission. Although in times past he might have counted on colleagues to come to his aid, no one assisted him on that day. Back they dragged him through the mud and refuse, back through the contaminated water of the stream, back up the stairs to keep his appointment with the hangman's noose.[54]

Several doomed men, having undergone profound transformations during their twilight days, uttered pathetic little speeches about the injustice of the sentence, the illegitimacy of the tribunal, and the dehumanizing effects of capital punishment. Curtis was defiant to the end, urging the executioners "not to be talking about it all day" because they were "making too much fuss over a very small matter." Muir took the opposite tack, saying he was but "a poor little Irish chap" who had been misled into committing horrible depredations by "evil associates." The crowd watched, unmoved. Someone called out that no matter what they said they were all guilty and deserved to die.[55]

When the remarks had ended, the executioners slipped meal sacks over the offenders' heads and kicked the props from beneath their feet. Five men instantly fell to their deaths. In a bizarre coincidence, the rope around Collins's neck snapped, and he tumbled to the ground. Everyone froze. Some of the more superstitious fellows in the crowd muttered that it was a sign of Collins's innocence—a trial by ordeal gone awry. Before a groundswell of sympathy could build, Key and other Regulators rushed forward, hoisted the big man from the ground, and led him back up the stairs where a fresh rope was fastened around his neck.[56]

After experiencing this unexpected reprieve, the heretofore silent Collins lost all pretense of dignity. Blubbering like a frightened child, he begged for mercy. In another time and place, he might have received a measure of sympathy; as it was, most of the prisoners had lived in fear of him and his gang. Collins's death would marginally improve their already bleak circumstances. No one stepped forward on his behalf. Barely a minute passed between his first and second trips to the gallows. The rope did not break again.[57]

In July 1864, the Raiders were tried, convicted, and executed by their fellow inmates for crimes committed inside the Andersonville Stockade. Reprinted from *Life and Death in Rebel Prisons* by Robert H. Kellogg.

The lifeless sacks of human flesh hung from the scaffold for more than fifteen minutes. No one who witnessed the bodies swaying from those ropes that day ever forgot the sight. Twenty-six thousand men fell silent for one of the few times in the history of the Andersonville Stockade when the groans, screams, and cries of a suffering mass did not drown out the ambient noises of the nearby pine forest. As the eerie moment passed and the noises resumed, life returned to the normal rhythms and routines of a Confederate prison stockade. The executioners cut down the Raiders' bodies and left the remains for the Confederates to handle. All over the camp, inmates wandered back to their groups and continued the daily struggle to survive the rigors of a life in captivity. The episode passed from the front pages of their minds to the back pages of myth.[58]

SEVEN

The Grave Question of Escape

Escape: No other word captures the joy, the exhilaration, the hopes, and the fears of a prisoner of war quite as accurately. For some inmates, it is the beginning and end of their lexicon. It is all they dream of from the moment they rise until the moment they retire. They will draw their last breath in the effort, for it is better to die as a man than live as a skeleton, passively watching each day slide by with little hope of a better fate.

A man stood with his comrades if he hoped to survive the rigors of a life in confinement. Recognizing this elemental reality, many inmates of the Rock Island Barracks formed a secret society, 7 C K, or the "Seven Confederate Knights." Sporting a seven-pointed star bearing the motto "*Dulce et decorum est pro patria mori*" (it is sweet and becoming to die for one's country), the members of the order pledged to "suffer death rather than swear allegiance to effect a release from prison."[1]

The captives believed they must do something to stem the tide of defections from the Confederate cause during the harsh winter of 1863–64. The crisis of faith began on January 16, 1864, when a Union naval officer, John D. Harty, arrived at the barracks and made a startling offer. Any inmate who wished to swear an oath of allegiance to the United States government would be immediately released from the stockade and his deprivations would end. The results were astonishing to behold—far beyond what Harty and Union authorities had expected. More than 660 men swore the oath and left the prison by the end of the first week. By the end of the summer, more than 1,000 Rock Island men had turned their backs on the Southern Confederacy.[2]

These "newly made Union men" were removed from the bull pen and housed in eighteen barracks separated from the general population. Their new quarters were sardonically dubbed the "calf pen," and they stayed in this area until they could be mustered into the service of the United States. Although some converts took the oath merely to improve the odds of escaping, many former prisoners went on to serve in the Union army. Their actions—opportunistic in a best case scenario, treacherous in the worst case—did not go unnoticed within the ranks. "Never since the Son of Man was tempted by the Devil, was dishonor more cunningly devised or temptingly displayed," one prisoner concluded. Observing his former comrades in arms as they raised their hands to swear allegiance to the enemy, one man could hardly contain his anger and disappointment. "This is the saddest day of all the days of my prison life," Lafayette Rogan wrote in his diary. "Fifteen men deserted us and take up arms against our cause. Oh, how depraved the present generation are become. Self, home, parents, dear wife, and children are abandoned for the sake of a few oz. of meat and bread—God forgive."[3]

"Newly made Union men" swore an oath of allegiance to the U.S. government in the Rock Island Prison, thereby turning their backs on the Confederate cause. Courtesy of the Illinois State Historical Library.

The 7 C K was organized to hold fast against desertions by persuading true believers that a united brotherhood supported them in their hour of need. They might lack nutritious food, adequate clothing, and the comforts of home, but they could count on unflagging camaraderie to see them through the travails of prison life. By some accounts, almost three thousand men eventually joined the order before the prisoners were liberated in June and July 1865.[4]

The secret society served another purpose as well. "I distinctly remember that after the organization of the 'Seven Confederate Knights' the success of a 'sortie' by the prisoners was discussed in my presence," John Minnich later confessed. Escape plans were hardly an innovative feature of prison life, but 7 C K improved the chances of organizing a credible effort. Minnich recalled that "it was then argued that with between eight thousand and nine thousand men our chances of making a successful break would be good, provided we could rely on all to stand together." Solidarity was easier said than done, as the men soon discovered. "But doubts were expressed as to the feasibility of perfecting the plans, owing to the large number of weak-kneed and spies among us. Suddenly, the guards were doubled, and orders were issued forbidding the prisoners from assembling in groups of more than 'two' on any of the streets and avenues. Then we knew that the spies had got in their work and there was in consequence a greater severity on the part of our jailers toward us."[5]

Despite such setbacks, the prisoners would not be dissuaded from planning their escapes. The human mind is continually inventive, and the inmates time and again proved themselves resourceful. One young fellow, George Kern of Bourbon County, Kentucky, became a legend because of his unorthodox escape. Standing in the stockade one evening as dusk descended, he observed the camp surgeon passing along the roadway in a horse and buggy. With no advance planning, Kern decided on the spot to hitch a ride. He caught a friend's attention and pointed to the carriage. "I believe I can make my escape with that buggy," he said with as much bravado as he could muster, "and if I do, you can have my clothes."

To his friend's considerable astonishment, Kern dashed out behind the surgeon and bent low, keeping pace with the carriage. In the fading light, the small, boyish figure was difficult to detect as he rolled beneath the buggy wheels, grabbing hold of the undercarriage and hoisting himself up off the ground. To his great good fortune, the prison guards were lax in performing their duty that night. They were disinclined to check beneath the buggy as it slowly rolled through the gate and beyond the walls of the prison.[6]

Kern's actions after this dramatic episode remain a source of dispute to this day. Confederate sympathizer Kate Perry later bragged that Kern came to her house seeking aid and comfort. "Late one evening the bell rang," she reminisced to Confederate veterans in her autumn years. "A young boy came in—an escaped prisoner! We got him in." She confirmed his identity as George Kern, an escaped inmate, and learned that he was fifteen years old. His small stature and girlish appearance suggested the means by which he might escape. "I had my emergency fund, and we concluded that, as he was small and slender, we would dress him as a girl. This we did down to every detail. Hoops were worn; he hated them. I prepared a pretty little hand basket and placed within it a box of face powder, comb, brush, and all such adjuncts to the toilet, together with extra collars, cuffs, and handkerchiefs. He was to impersonate a shy country girl. Poor boy! How sad he was when he bade us farewell!"[7]

The tale was terrific, filled with the excitement and drama that boded well for entertaining veterans in the twilight of their lives. As is often the case with war remembrances, however, the truth was far more prosaic. Kern escaped from the Rock Island Barracks, just as he said, but he did not seek out Kate Perry. Instead, he found another Confederate sympathizer who gave him a man's suit of clothes and fifty dollars for travel expenses. In yet another act of unmitigated audacity, Kern waited at the train station for a ride, invisible to passersby because he looked far too young to be a soldier in either army.[8]

Another improvised scheme succeeded because it relied on the gullibility of an inattentive guard. Inmates J. B. Hendricks and J. E. Tucker were working on the roof of a small building outside the stockade walls with another prisoner whom they did not know. As the inmates were returning to the stockade under guard, the first prisoner remembered that he had left his tools behind. He asked the Union sentry to accompany him back to the work site. Incredibly, the guard marched off with his prisoner, leaving Hendricks and Tucker standing alone outside the stockade walls. Amazed at their good fortune, the two men made good their escape. "The Guard is now in confinement and will be brought before the General Court-Martial in session at this post for such gross neglect of duty and carelessness," the camp commandant, Colonel Johnson, wrote in a subsequent letter to Commissary General Hoffman.[9]

Other thrilling stories of escapes may have been manufactured, at least in part, in the decades following the war when veterans recalled their unparalleled heroism to entertain paying audiences and readers. Dr. Thomas F. Berry of Oklahoma claimed to have escaped from eight different Union prisons and slipped away from his captors another five times while in transit. A master of hyperbole and gross distortion, the good doctor recalled suffering sixteen wounds during his exploits in Confederate service as well as incurring five wounds while serving overseas. In an article that appeared in *Confederate Veteran* in 1912, he claimed to have absconded twice from Rock Island, including once in November 1863. According to Berry, he was caught while hiding in Cincinnati, Ohio, and returned to Rock Island. This incident was curious because Berry was not listed as one of the first prisoners arriving that November. Perhaps the passage of time had obscured his memory so that he was confused about the date. Camp records indicate that he escaped from Rock Island on December 4, 1864, and was never recaptured. He apparently crawled through the camp's sewer system and swam the Mississippi River.[10]

These notable opportunities were the exception to the rule; throughout the life of the prison, successful escapes were rare. Credible efforts usually required meticulous advance planning—never an easy chore for desperate men—as well as a liberal dose of good luck. One story of a well-planned and flawlessly executed scheme, which may have been at least partially fabricated, involved B. M. "Ben" Hord, a Confederate soldier from Nashville. According to his own account, Hord formulated an ingenious plan to walk out of the front gate disguised as a Union soldier. After he acquired a stolen cap, blouse, and coat, he fashioned them into a passable uniform. To complete his costume, he also carved a pistol from a piece of pine board. As a detail of guards was leaving the camp one afternoon, Hord simply blended into the crowd and disappeared. Later, after he was recaptured, he claimed to have been held in the Rock Island dungeon, where he supposedly witnessed one prisoner kill another and saw a black Union soldier go insane, shooting down several inmates, including one poor soul who was mortally wounded. Although some of the incidents that Hord recounted could be verified through other accounts, including the story of the insane black soldier, the existence of a dungeon on Rock Island was never corroborated.[11]

For every story of a dramatic, successful escape, many more anecdotes recounted the consequences of foiled attempts. One such tale involved an outside group initially calling itself the Order of American Knights, later rechristened the Sons of Liberty, in honor of the patriotic group of colonial revolutionaries that fought against Great Britain before the American Revolution. These Northern men who sympathized with the Southern Confederacy hatched a series of ambitious schemes to disrupt life in the Union by seizing the federal and state arsenals in Indianapolis, Columbus, and Springfield before joining forces with the Confederate army. Part of their plan was to liberate the prisoners at Rock Island and lead them into Kentucky and

Missouri. Had the group chosen a less intricate enterprise, it might have achieved a measure of success. As it was, the plan was leaked to Union authorities, and the conspirators were rounded up and imprisoned before they could take decisive action.[12]

If 7 C K and the rest of the Rock Island prisoners hoped to taste freedom before the end of the war, they could not depend on outside forces for assistance. Left to formulate their own plans, the fellows considered their options and decided that tunneling under the stockade walls was the preferred method. As soon as men took up residency on the island, almost every barrack sported tunnels of greater or lesser length. Whispered rumors of a nearly completed underground cavern circulated through the camp faster than a smallpox epidemic. The progress of a tunnel and the relative contribution of each man in a barrack were sources of pride among men who had few pleasant topics of conversation.[13]

Minnich recalled his own participation in a tunneling scheme. "Sometime during the summer of 1864 it became whispered in the camp that a tunnel was in process of completion under Barrack No. – on the south side, and that it would be finished the same night and that any who might feel disposed to seek freedom by the underground route were welcome to make the trial." Finding the prospect of escape exciting, Minnich was determined to be among the intrepid fellows who scampered through the hole in search of freedom. Unfortunately for the inmates, the tunnel engineers miscalculated the distance under the walls and came up short. Then the worst possible event occurred—it was little more than happenstance, a quirk of fate—namely, a Union sentry serendipitously intervened. "Sometime during the day a bluecoat, nosing about no doubt for the very purpose of detecting 'rat holes' by the fence, put his foot in it, the thin crust giving way under his weight." The prisoners dared not use the tunnel afterward for fear that the guards might set a trap. "Not a rat showed himself to be caught," Minnich recalled. "That was one of the few tunnels not 'given away' from the inside. But it had some comicalities attached."[14]

One "comicality" was the prisoners' varied levels of preparation for the trip through the tunnel. Crossing the avenue around eleven o'clock on the same evening that the tunnel had been uncovered, Minnich was surprised to see dozens of men—probably more than a hundred—crouched and hiding in the shadows, awaiting a signal that it was safe to slip into the tunnel. The men either had not learned of the guard's discovery or they were so anxious to escape they could not bring themselves to stand down from the doomed enterprise. In any event, Minnich was amused at "the 'get-up' of some of the would-be absconders. Some came just as they stood in their clothes, while others were rigged out in various degrees of 'heavy marching order.' One had all his camp equipage slung to him—blanket, saucepan, tin cup, and all. How they expected to get through the tunnel and make their way through a hostile country in full regalia is more than any one can figure out. It was grotesque, to say the least."[15]

A less grotesque attempt occurred on June 14, 1864. Ten hardy souls slipped through a tunnel they had dug under Barrack No. 42 and emerged on the far side of the south wall. The effort might have succeeded, but an eagle-eyed sentry spotted the last two men as they emerged from the hole in the earth. He sounded the alarm, and the chase commenced. Union soldiers spilled from the guards' barracks like ants pouring from a recently disturbed mound; within minutes, they had captured three escapees. In the meantime, one desperate, luckless fellow threw himself into the Mississippi and drowned while trying to swim the four-hundred-foot expanse of the river. Six men were more fortunate; they crossed the rapids and climbed onto a high ridge overlooking the area. Their pursuers were tenacious, however, following them onto the ridge and capturing four men without further complications. Of the original ten inmates, two made good their escape.[16]

Escapes generally occurred during the summer, but a winter endeavor was not out of the question. David Sears, a mill owner who lived near the Rock Island Prison, remembered that four men had tunneled under the stockade walls during the winter of 1863–64. The prisoners soon found that getting past the walls was a minor problem compared with fording the freezing waters of the Mississippi River. After searching in vain for some time, they eventually found a place where the water was only four feet deep and the rapids were not strong enough to sweep them down river. They emerged near Sears's mill, only to be spotted by a mill worker, who raised the alarm. The mill crew came running, armed with whatever weapons they could find. As Sears recounted the episode, his men "expected to find bold thieves but were astonished to see four cold and wet prisoners who immediately offered to surrender, and were taken into the mill. They were perishing from the cold and were glad of the opportunity to warm themselves at the big stove. Ice had begun to form on their clothing."[17]

Escapes usually were foiled because Union authorities had recruited spies from among the prisoners; thus, plots were uncovered before men could get beyond the stockade walls. One such plot Minnich remembered was an occasion when three "diggers" were laboring to extend their tunnel beyond the deadline, and they found their route blocked by a large rock that had been deliberately lodged in their path. "In some way the news was conveyed outside, and the diggers were rounded up (there were three of them) and were made to do a 'pas de marche' for nearly half a day in a broiling heat under the cloudless midday sun on the side of the barrack next to the fence, and the sentries were given orders to shoot any of them who for a moment failed to 'mark time.'"[18]

Minnich eventually realized that a prisoner serving as a Union spy—a "spotter"—was responsible for informing the authorities of the tunneling operation. "But the 'spotter' in this adventure was in turn 'spotted,' and only prompt action on the part of the [jailers] saved him from stretching a rope made of the inner bark of cottonwood. He was taken out, and I never saw him again." Had the spy not been removed from the barracks, he would have been disciplined—or worse. Minnich was convinced of the fellow's guilt. "He had never been seen conferring with the guards in daytime, but I had seen him conversing in a low tone with an officer at night near a tree on the main avenue. I came upon the pair suddenly from the rear on my way to my barrack, and they were both plainly startled." After that day, the inmates kept a watchful eye on the spotter until he disappeared from the prison.[19]

Despite his proximity to the tunneling, Minnich never found the right opportunity to escape from the Rock Island Barracks. In fact, only forty-one men were confirmed to have escaped from the prison during its operation. Like

Escape was the dream of every inmate, North and South.
Courtesy of Rod Gragg.

most inmates, it was never far from Minnich's mind. When the prisoners closed their eyes, they could dream of escape. Under the walls, over the walls, through subtle acts of subterfuge—it made no difference. A man denied his freedom never relinquishes the memory of his life and the world beyond the confines of his prison. He never stops longing for an escape from his present reality.[20]

The men of Andersonville also dreamed of escaping from their abominable conditions. From his first day in the stockade, Warren Lee Goss joined any plot that seemed reasonably feasible. "A great portion of my time from May to the last day of June was spent in unavailing attempts at escape by means of tunnels," he recalled. "I was engaged in six, which were discovered by the prison authorities before their completion." The problem was not in the planning or implementation of the tunneling schemes, but it was too difficult to keep such endeavors secret from camp spies. Union prisoners had been promised extra rations by their Confederate captors for any information that would stymie escape attempts. Although far from sanguine about his chances to engineer a successful tunnel, Goss understood that the spies possessed a strong incentive to cooperate with the authorities. "If you narrow down a man's purpose to sustaining his body—let his be a continual struggle for a foothold on life, with uncertainty as to its results—give a man, in fact, crime with bread, on the one hand, and on the other, integrity and truth with death—the thousand recollections of the old home, with the arms of a dear mother or wife or children that once encircled his neck—all these recollections bid him to live. Consequently, it was difficult to trust men with secrets which might be sold for bread."[21]

Spies were not the only impediments to escape attempts. Digging in the muddy embankment was difficult because the ground had been so thoroughly beaten down in efforts to search for well water and for small caverns to protect the men from the elements, that the work to find escape routes was fraught with peril. Adequate tools were hard to find. The tunnel might collapse before it was completed, trapping the men underground and smothering them without hope of rescue. If the diggers were caught in the act, as they often were, they could expect a beating, to be sentenced to wear a ball and chain, the loss of rations, or to be shot down without further inquiry.[22]

Recognizing the propensity of prisoners to dig tunnels despite the hazards, the Confederates were eternally vigilant in entering the stockade and searching for holes carved in the ground. Even Captain Wirz marched through the camp, with his ever-present pistol at his side, looking for evidence of the inmates' tunnels. He seemed to take offense at the effrontery of the Union captives, as though their efforts to break free were personal insults. "Py tam," he screeched through clenched teeth as he confronted a man caught tunneling. His thick German accent made his words almost incomprehensible when he was infuriated. "Vy don't some of you Yankees get out? Mine togs are getting 'ungry to pite you!"[23]

The threat of using dogs to pursue escaping prisoners was hardly an idle comment. The Andersonville authorities kept a pack of hounds just outside the stockade walls ready to give chase through the swamps and woodlands surrounding the camp. Many postwar writers thrilled their readers with accounts—some probably embellished—of trudging through dense forests with vicious bloodhounds in hot pursuit. If the dogs caught up with a fugitive before the sentries could intervene to apprehend the poor fellow, the resulting injuries could be severe.[24]

Confederate authorities at Andersonville relied on dogs to track escaped prisoners. Reprinted from *Life and Death in Rebel Prisons* by Robert H. Kellogg.

Goss knew the risks of tunneling, and he gradually came to believe that other means of escape must be employed if he hoped to succeed. "I had been engaged in so many tunnels which were failures, that I began to regard them as an unprofitable speculation, yielding no prospects of a desirable nature," he wrote. He was determined to explore other options. As luck would have it, he did not have to wait long. Early one afternoon during the summer, as he was taken from the camp to collect wood, Goss was startled to see how lackadaisical the guards were in watching the prisoners. An idea took root. "I commenced picking up sticks, and thus gradually worked my way beyond them."[25]

He faced a decision. He could dash through the woods at that moment, pushing himself ever deeper into the swamps and fields of southwest Georgia. He was alone in enemy territory with no food, water, or provisions of any kind. If his luck held, he might put several miles between himself and the Rebels before the guards could raise the alarm. However, before nightfall the dogs would be turned loose at the spot where he last had been seen gathering sticks. They would come after him, sniffing his scent, relentless in their pursuit. These indefatigable engines of destruction would not stop until they sank their razor-sharp teeth into his flesh.

Even if he managed to avoid capture, he could not envision a time when he would be safe. He had heard rumors of General Sherman's progress into north Georgia, but he had no idea where the troops were stationed and how he might find them. It was one thing to run for freedom when he was in the company of his comrades, for they could sustain each other. If he were alone, the odds did not favor a successful escape.

Goss had almost given up on the adventure when he discovered that he was not alone after all. "I looked around, and saw at a distance several of my companions, who had taken the hint, following me, picking up sticks in the same manner." Emboldened by their presence, he waited until the men drew near. "We got together, and, without saying a word, by mutual consent, dropped our wood, and ran like mad creatures through the woods for several miles."[26]

Night fell, and still they were free. Despite his fears of capture, Goss began to feel encouraged that he and his newfound friends might yet join up with invading Union troops. In his months of captivity—first, in the Richmond prisons and now in the Andersonville Stockade—he had never been so close to accomplishing his own goals. In prison a man quickly learned to entrust his fate to others—enemy sentries, Confederate authorities, fellow prisoners, Union exchange agents, or the cruel hand of fate. For the first time in many months, Goss seemed to be the master of his own destiny, at least for the moment.

The men lay down to sleep, but a driving rain left them drenched and cold in the morning light. Even worse, they heard the faraway but unmistakable sounds of dogs barking and baying. The Rebels had picked up their trail, but the prisoners did not have the strength to flee. The result was inevitable.

That same morning, "we were captured by bloodhounds while clinging to trees, and, more frightened at the dogs than hurt by them, were carried back to the prison, where we reluctantly took up our quarters again, after receiving a damning from the accomplished 'commander of the prison.'"[27]

Goss learned a valuable lesson from this experience. He might engineer a successful prison break, but it required far more preparation and thought than most inmates realized. Tunneling under the walls or dashing for freedom through the woods without a detailed, calculated plan invited disaster. He and his comrades had been lucky to emerge from the brush with their lives, but next time they might not be so fortunate.

In the weeks ahead, he set his considerable intellect to solving the logistical problems of an escape. He talked with his comrades, asking questions about their previous attempts and why they had failed. He immersed himself in the mechanics of tunneling, digging, and the subtle art of trickery. Slowly and methodically, he developed a primer on prison escapes. Shuffling through the desolate environment, lost in contemplation, Goss was the embodiment of the Enlightenment man. Any problem could be solved and any obstacle surmounted if he poured his time and attention into learning from past mistakes and crafting a satisfactory plan for the future.

Without warning, he stumbled upon an opportunity he had not previously considered. "While looking around the prison one day, hoping and wishing for something to 'turn up' by which I might solve the grave question of escape, I observed an old well, partially dug, from ten to twelve feet from the deadline, which had been finally abandoned after digging over thirty feet without obtaining water." Despite his disdain for tunnel work, Goss realized that he might taste success from digging a well, which the Confederate authorities allowed. If the well were expanded into a tunnel, he might yet escape undetected. After discussing the plan with a "trusty, enterprising fellow," Goss and his confidant began their excavations.[28]

The duo made swift progress because they did not fear reprisals from their jailers. As long as the work was viewed as well digging and not tunneling, they could come and go with relative impunity. Thus, the men achieved feats that surreptitious diggers could only dream about. One night, they lowered themselves into the hole and spent the hours carving eight feet of mud and sticks from the earth. Ever the efficient overseer, Goss expanded the venture and brought in crews to continue digging in shifts, thereby ensuring that fresh men would labor with verve. "Gradually we increased our numbers until we had twenty men at work, all of whom we knew could be trusted, as they belonged mostly to our battalion. We organized four reliefs, each of which were to dig in the tunnel two hours during the night."[29]

The hole eventually stretched fifty feet, extending the shaft more than thirty feet beyond the stockade walls. Goss had learned his lessons well. Many diggers, foolishly assuming that all they needed to do was to burrow up under the timbers, emerged in plain sight of the guards. Avoiding detection was the paramount consideration for Goss and his comrades, and this meant that they must emerge well beyond the guard towers. Realizing that patience was a virtue that might be amply rewarded, he insisted that the digging continue well past the point where his predecessors would have pushed up through the ground outside the prison.

They waited for an especially dark, rainy night when the sentries might be less vigilant than usual. Carrying their canteens and tin cups, they tossed a rope down into the dark well and slid to the bottom. Each man crawled on his hands and knees, single file, through the pitch-black hole. They had not yet extended the opening upwards, and so the fellows in the lead used their cups to scoop the remaining six feet of dirt from their path. "This had to be performed with great care, first, for fear of being discovered, and second, there was danger of being smothered by the falling earth."[30]

Goss assumed the "honor" of sticking his head through the open hole to inspect the surroundings. To his dismay, he saw an outer picket less than twelve feet away, hunched over a fire. Had it not been for the sounds of the rain slapping the vegetation and the crackling flames of the fire, the guard might have heard the digging and, upon investigating, noticed the movement of the earth. As it was, his back was turned to the scene, and so the escapees slipped from the tunnel. It was a heart-stopping series of minutes as each man pulled himself out of the hole, got to his feet, bent forward, and scurried into nearby underbrush. "Once, when a twig broke," Goss remembered, "he made a motion to look up, and I thought we were 'gone up'; but he merely stirred his fire and resumed his crouching position. As the last man came out, and, at a safe distance, we stood in whispered consultation, the hourly cry of the guard, 'Twelve o'clock, and all is well,' went round the stockade."[31]

They were free, and undetected. Although they faced grim conditions ahead, each fellow was heartened by the initial success of the enterprise. They divided up into groups of five and set out in different directions. Goss had left little to chance. He had considered each route carefully, going so far as to sketch out maps showing the physical features he believed to be present. "After considering all the different points where I might reach our lines, I concluded there were less difficulties in the way of reaching Sherman's forces at Marietta than any other," he later explained.[32]

The problem, of course, was the distance. He and his band would have to traverse more than 120 miles of hostile territory with no assistance but their own wits and whatever accoutrements they could carry. Still, they had few alternatives but to persevere. Revealing his plans to the men, they "looked upon me as a Moses, who was to lead them to the promised land." Before he could wallow in the glow of such high praise, Goss was mortified to hear the far-off sounds of dogs approaching.[33]

It would be a bitter ending to a great adventure, but they were not ready to surrender. "Not a moment was to be lost," he wrote. The men threw themselves into the swampy waters that led to the Flint River. Although they were already exhausted, they stumbled through the mud and brush. When they found themselves on the banks of the Flint, the men discovered logs sufficiently large to be used as makeshift boats. Under the cover of night, they pushed the logs into the river, jumped on board, and floated with the current. Swollen by torrential rains, the Flint swiftly wound its way beyond the Andersonville Stockade toward parts unknown. Goss was uncertain if the meandering river took them closer to their destination or farther away, but with the hounds close behind, any place was better than their present location. Holding fast to the logs, they hunkered down and made good time throughout the night. Daylight revealed far different terrain. Whatever else happened, they were pleased to realize that the sounds of the dogs had faded with the coming light.[34]

Cold and ravenous, they divided a single johnnycake they had squirreled away from their meager prison fare, but the paltry rations did little to alleviate hunger pangs. Goss had secured a compass, which guided them through the swamps that day, but it did not assuage their fears. Although they knew where they were headed, they did not know what obstacles lay between them and Sherman's troops. One man somehow had procured a butcher knife, but it would not save them from bullets or a pack of vicious dogs. To prepare for troubled times ahead, each man found a large stick that could be used as a club, if necessary.[35]

"Night came upon us, dark and rainy, and found us still travelling through the dark forest and wet swamps of the country," Goss wrote of that long-ago time. Just after midnight, as they tripped through the foliage, exhausted from their long ordeal, the band caught sight of a campfire in the distance. Crouching behind a clump of trees, they whispered to each other, mulling over their predicament. They longed for the warmth of a fire and the hardy camaraderie of Union soldiers, perhaps the smell of bacon sizzling in a frying pan, the taste of greasy meat on their chapped lips. The fire promised these things—and more. But they could not indulge in romantic self-delusion; such luxuries were for free men standing on free soil. The campfire was most likely a portent of dangers to come.

Even as they debated their next course of action, Goss heard a sound not far from where they kneeled. To his surprise, it emanated from within a nearby log. "I sprang to my feet, with my club poised ready to strike—perhaps it was a bear! I challenged the log with the common expression among soldiers, 'Are you Fed or Reb?' 'Yankee,' came the reply; and emerging from the log, which for the first time I observed was hollow, came a human form, which, after shaking itself like a water spaniel, asked, in tones strangely familiar, 'Well, boys, what next'?"[36]

Immediately suspicious, Goss left nothing to chance. "Going to tie your hands, old fellow," he said, "until daylight shows enough of you to see if you look honest."

Surprisingly, the fellow laughed at this threat. "Well, well! Why, don't you know Tonkinson?"[37]

Goss and his men were astonished. Tonkinson had been among the original group of diggers that escaped the preceding night. After he and his five men had departed, they had floated down the Flint River on logs just as Goss and his comrades had done, although Tonkinson had become separated from his band. By a remarkable coincidence, he had settled into the hollow log not long before Goss and company stumbled onto the scene.

When they recovered from the shock of seeing their old colleague, the escapees welcomed him to their group and invited him to consult with them on their next course of action. The men faced a dilemma. They might easily skirt around the campfire and continue their trek deep into the swamps without fear of detection, yet the fellows were hungry, cold, and lost in the woods. A conservative course left them in their present state of abject misery. The fire promised warmth, food, and assistance—if it belonged to a person or persons sympathetic to the Union cause. After a brief but spirited discussion, they agreed that they must reconnoiter the landscape to determine whether the strangers gathered around the fire were friend or foe.[38]

One by one, they crept through the reeds ever closer to the circle of light. A lone Confederate sentry sat with his gun cradled in his lap, squinting into the darkness as he warmed himself by the fire. One of the escapees slipped close enough to reach out and strangle the guard, but he thought better of it when other voices drifted out from nearby tents. Because the ex-prisoners could not determine how many men were in the camp, they backed away from a confrontation. Weak with fatigue from lack of food and sleep, and unarmed save for a single butcher knife and their homemade clubs, they were no match for well-conditioned men bearing guns.

Bitterly disappointed, they trudged blindly through the marshy land, groping for purchase and dazed by their privation. Intermittent rain slapped their faces as they concentrated on putting as many miles as possible between themselves and the men in the tents. "About three o'clock in the morning it stopped raining, and we lay down together under a tree, to get such rest as we best could," Goss recalled. They lay in the mud, miserable and cold, almost too hungry and weak to continue the journey. Yet, as before, somehow, they got to their feet at first daylight and resumed the pathetic march to wherever luck or fate might propel them.[39]

Except for a few berries they picked from a bush, they ate nothing all day. They might have perished in the swamps had they not trapped a young deer the next afternoon. "We killed a little yearling heifer, one holding her by her horns while the other cut her throat with our sheath-knife." They quickly carved the skin into strips that could be fashioned into crude haversacks. "We had no matches, or other method of kindling a fire, and of course ate our meat raw, with what little salt we had to season it."[40]

The meat nourished them, but they were hardly rejuvenated. In the ensuing days, the men lost track of time. How far they wandered under the unrelenting sun was anybody's guess. Each day they struggled to find enough food and fresh water to sustain them. The days blurred together except for one notable incident. One afternoon the escapees stumbled into a clearing among the trees where a group of black men had assembled. Fearful that the group might raise a hue and cry, Goss and his comrades turned to flee.

"Don't be afraid, massa white man," a voice called out.

The fugitives halted, turning back toward the blacks. Goss stepped forward and spoke to a white-haired man who seemed to be the leader. "Uncle," he said, "I suppose you know what kind of fellows we are."

Rolling his eyes, the old man responded. "Well, I reckon."

"We are hungry, and want something to eat sadly."

"Well," the black man said, "you does look mighty kind o' lean. Step into de bushes while I peers round to see if we've got some hoe-cake."[41]

Although they knew it was dangerous to relax their guard, Goss and his band of ragged ex-prisoners were too weak to care. They collapsed in a heap and waited for the blacks either to bring them food or turn them over to the Rebels. Either way, their ordeal would soon conclude. Fortunately, the old man and his group returned with the promised hoecakes.

After Goss and his comrades had wolfed down the food and rested for a few minutes, they once again considered their plight. One fact was clear: They could not stay there for long, despite their desire to relax and enjoy the hospitality of their unexpected hosts. Their presence imperiled both groups of men. If the Confederates captured Goss and his fellows in the company of black men—whether the latter were free men or escaped slaves—the consequences for everyone would be dire.

In an effort to thank his host, Goss addressed the white-haired man one final time. "Well, uncle," he said, "I suppose you know that Uncle Abe is coming down this way to set you all free when he gets the rebs licked."

"Yes, yes," the old man replied. "I'se believe the day of jubilee is comin'; but 'pears to me, it's a long time; looks like it wouldn't come in my time."[42]

"Bidding him God speed, we went on our way with lighter hearts at the thought that there were friends in the midst of our enemies," Goss wrote. But lighter hearts inevitably gave way to emptier stomachs. On what seemed to be their eighth day of freedom, the men had exhausted their supplies and were afraid that starvation would soon overtake them. Tripping into a clump of raspberry bushes, they had just set to work picking berries when each man heard a terrifying sound in the distance.[43]

Dogs—lots of dogs, judging by the noise—howled and barked as though they had caught the scent of some trapped or wounded animal. The escapees had discussed what they should do if the Rebels were in hot pursuit. Now it was time to fulfill their compact. They knew if they stayed together, the entire band would be captured. If they separated, at least one or more fellows might elude the jailers. Without another word, they scattered in all directions; it was every man for himself.[44]

"I jumped into a little brook which ran along through the low land, which was not wide enough to amount to much, as my clothes brushed the bushes on either side," Goss recalled. The plan was to run through brooks and streams to mask the scent, but it was not possible on the present terrain. He knew he could not outrun the hounds, so Goss took refuge in an oak tree, clinging to the branches like a lifeline, climbing as high as he could. Hand over hand, he climbed, sucking air into his lungs in short, tortured gasps as he ascended.

Somewhere along the way he dropped his club, but he was oblivious to everything save finding sanctuary. Far below, he heard the dogs circling the tree, baying as they sniffed the ground. He was sure he had been spotted, and soon the Confederate soldiers would appear, ordering him down from the safety of the oak. If he refused to comply, he would be shot like a treed animal, and down he would come to rest on a bed of reeds and mud.[45]

He waited for the inevitable conclusion, but it never came. Miraculously, the beasts continued on their way without incident. Goss had escaped detection. He might have been heartened by the prospect, but a sickening noise drifted up from the ground, squelching whatever good cheer he otherwise felt. "I sat in the tree, and heard them when they captured my comrades," he remembered. Minutes later, the sounds of struggling faded in the distance, and he was left alone with his hopes and fears.[46]

"Here I was," he wrote in his memoirs. "I had been without sufficient sleep for eight nights and days, almost continually drenched with rain. My hip was badly swollen with travelling; my feet bleeding, and clothes, by constant intercourse with brambles and cane-brake of the swamps, hung in picturesque tatters around me." The outlook was bleak, but he was still a free man, and that was something.[47]

His freedom had been purchased at a terrible price, and it was still far from assured. He could not stay perched in the oak forever; he must resume his trek or he would die in the swamps and the struggle would have been for nothing. When he was confident that the dogs and Rebels had gone, Goss slid down the tree and "congratulated myself warmly on being rather smarter than the rest of my crowd." Despite this momentary celebratory feeling, he could ill afford to wallow in self-congratulations for long. After consulting the compass, he discerned that he was headed in the direction of the Chattahoochee River near West Point, a town not far from Atlanta. Satisfied that he was following a proper route, he set out toward the river, hoping to ride its currents to safety as he had done earlier on the waters of the Flint.[48]

Much to his chagrin, Goss had underestimated the tenacity of the Confederates. "I had not gone more than two miles before I heard the dogs on my track bellowing and yelling like wolves." From the noise, he could tell they were rapidly gaining ground. He had to prepare himself for the inevitable confrontation. Looking around, he did not see another tree to climb and his club was long gone. Fortunately, he found an old wooden fence, dilapidated from age and neglect, collapsed on the ground. Kneeling, he wrenched a stake from the pile of leftover wood and jumped atop the old fence. As he did so, he heard a ferocious sound in the underbrush. Moments later, the first dog lunged at the fence and was on him, tearing at his wrist.[49]

He turned, swinging the stake with as much force as he could muster. The wood connected with the lead dog's head, and the animal uttered a satisfying "prolonged yell," retreating away from the fence. In a matter of seconds, the pack had surrounded the desperate man, alternately baring their teeth and baying to the heavens. It was impossible to keep them all in sight at the same time, so Goss jerked his head back and forth, brandishing the club all the while.

A strange man called out, "Let go them thar dogs, you Yank, and get off the fence."

Surprisingly, Goss laughed, refusing to move until the man called off the dogs. Pointing a rusty pistol toward the escaped prisoner, the fellow considered this request. "Well," he said at last, "I reckon yer kind er tuckered out, and I'll gin yer a little spell at breathin.'" The dogs immediately fell back at his command.[50]

Goss climbed down from the old fence and surrendered. His great adventure had ended at the hands of a bounty hunter. The man said the Confederates had hired him to track down escaped slaves and prisoners for thirty dollars a piece, a sizable sum in a depressed economy. He and a group of men had been tracking the escapees since the first day of their breakout. The rains and marshy ground had delayed the chase, but they were indefatigable in their efforts, taking pride in their rate of success.[51]

Days later, after a long, grueling march back to the stockade, Goss found himself standing in front of the main gate. Captain Wirz charged from his office, noticeably upset. Trembling, he flung his good arm high in the air. "Ah, py Got!" he exclaimed in his thick German accent. "You is the tam Yankee who get away vunce before!" Turning to the bounty hunter, he said, "Vell, did you make de togs bite 'im goot?" When the hunter said no, Wirz seemed angrier than ever. "Vell, you must next time."[52]

Back he went into the prison—back to his monotonous life of scarcity and suffering, back to the horrors of the Andersonville Prison pen. Goss achieved a measure of notoriety for his exploits, and men from all parts of the stockade gathered to hear his tales of life on the run. He learned that eight of his comrades had been captured not long after they emerged from the tunnel, four made it more than twenty miles, but the rest were never heard from again. No one could say with authority whether they died in the swampy land beyond the walls or escaped to a better life, although rumors and legends arose to explain their fate.[53]

In his absence, conditions in the camp had deteriorated as ever more prisoners arrived in droves from distant battlefields. The death rate skyrocketed, and desperation settled over the population like a suffocating shroud. "In this manner they dropped off all over the prison," Goss recalled. "One day you would see a man cooking his food; the next day he would be dead." As soon as a poor man expired and his clothes and possessions had been stripped from his person, his carcass would be stacked with the others for removal to the nearby graveyard.[54]

The Andersonville graveyard was the final resting-place for many inmates who could not survive deteriorating conditions in the camp. Reprinted from *The Soldier's Story* by Warren Lee Goss.

It is little wonder that Goss remained unrepentant. He continually roamed the stockade grounds, always searching for a new plot, a new band of men conniving to recapture their freedom, or a lone fellow who wished to hear him wax eloquent on the subject of escapes. During the life of the camp many prisoners briefly tasted freedom, but only 329 successful escapes could be confirmed. Goss was not among them, despite his best efforts. Instead, he was forced to focus his attention on eking out his survival even as life in the Andersonville Prison posed one relentless challenge after another.[55]

EIGHT

That Most Terrible of Afflictions—Hunger

Starvation was a constant element of life and death in Civil War prisons. Some inmates came to regard this companion as a newfound friend, an invisible comrade with whom they might pass their hours of boredom and delirium. Like virtually all prison survivors, John Minnich and Warren Lee Goss recalled their daily struggle for sustenance as among the worst challenges of a life in captivity. They never forgot the sights and sounds of flesh-colored skeletons crying out for a morsel of bread in their last, desperate hours.

Minnich arrived at Rock Island in February 1864, and was appalled at what he found. From his perch in Barrack 47, he bore witness to scenes he could never have imagined during his days in the ranks as a Confederate soldier. Everywhere, emaciated men shuffled through the prison. These remnants of humanity suffered from innumerable maladies, especially scurvy, a disease caused by a dearth of fresh meat, fruits, and vegetables.

Sometimes the rations were adequate, in Minnich's view, "but sometimes, and often, green with age and odorous to a degree. Months of this salt diet and lye corn bread, and then scurvy became epidemic—hundreds of cases, and nothing wherewith to combat the disease. Men walked around with mouths so sore that they could not eat, and their teeth actually dropping out with the attempt; others with limbs green and distorted."[1]

Treatment for contagious diseases required medical attention and the administration of medicines and vaccines that were not readily available, but scurvy could have been combated with a change in diet. Yet, incredibly, a scurvy epidemic swept through the Rock Island Barracks, as Minnich observed.

It might have been worse if it had been left to prison authorities to take action, but nearby citizens intervened to alleviate the suffering. In many instances, they merely wanted to extend a helping hand to fellow human beings and ease the ill effects of disease and impoverishment. The good folks from neighboring communities sent boxes of food and clothing to the inmates and asked nothing in return in rare cases of "Christian magnanimity."

Unfortunately, not all citizens' contributions could be attributed to pure motives. Some men and women wanted to glimpse the prisoners out of insatiable curiosity, and still others thought they owned the island and had a right to come and go as they pleased. Union guards were constantly aggravated at the appearance of local denizens bearing gifts of food and clothing for prisoners much as a modern person might feed animals at a local zoo. The most insidious motives, at least from the perspective of prison administrators, were Confederate sympathizers who sought to help the prisoners for political reasons. Kate E. Perry was a prime example of the latter.[2]

"I began my work by writing to all my friends in Kentucky and everywhere else, asking for speedy aid," she recalled. "I wanted clothing and tobacco, the soldier's solace, but clothing especially. Soon box after box of clothing and edibles began coming in. The prisoners knew what I was doing, and were constantly writing through headquarters for aid." She was not alone in this endeavor; other citizens also made donations, and the inmates appreciated the efforts just as Perry indicated. Although she later developed an underground mail and smuggling service that required the prison administration to ban her from entering the camp, this Northern woman with Southern sympathies earned the affectionate nickname "Faithful" among the Rock Island captives.[3]

Minnich praised the good people of the surrounding communities, whatever their motivations. "All honor to them! I do know that each man afflicted with scurvy was given raw Irish potatoes to eat as a curative, and was told that those potatoes had been subscribed by citizens of Rock Island City; and further, that with the coming of the potatoes to the sick the scurvy began to lose its grip and was finally extinguished." With the passage of time, he could not say how long scurvy had run rampant through the population, but it was long enough to leave him with a lingering impression of his captors' inhumanity. Scurvy would not have decimated the prisoners' ranks had the Union jailers been more attentive to the plight of their captives. "How long it prevailed, I cannot remember, as I was myself under the weather (though not from scurvy) a goodly part of the time, and took no note of time or events."[4]

Like many prisoners on both sides, Minnich's day-to-day existence consisted of scrambling to find enough food to sustain him through the day. The rations, although not generous or especially enjoyable to eat, initially were sufficient to sustain life. "We had no complaint to make of the rations issued us either as to quantity or quality," prisoner E. Polk Johnson recalled years later. "Until June 1st, 1864, no reasonable complaint could be made in regard to the food furnished the prisoners," Charles Wright remarked. "From the foregoing some may say that we were not so bad off for rations after all," Minnich wrote. "I will admit it might have been worse, but will not admit that it should have been as bad as it was."[5]

Recognizing that conditions were marginally tolerable, the prisoners nonetheless faced hunger during each day they spent in captivity. The problem was a matter of simple arithmetic and caloric intake coupled with the lonely, depressing conditions of incarceration, which meant that all prisoners experienced severe deprivation of one sort or another. Minnich mulled over the situation in his memoir. "Take a lot of men with healthy appetites who are accustomed to at least one square meal in a week, reveling in good health, and confine them with restricted limits, cut off from all outside associations, and limit them to a loaf of bread which baked could be pressed into a pint cup by hand and not be over full (I saw that done in my barrack, No. 47) and twelve ounces gross weight of beef or equal weight of mess beef or eight ounces weight

This pleasant drawing is misleading. Life inside the Rock Island Prison was far from idyllic. Hunger was a constant companion, beginning especially in the summer of 1864. Courtesy of the Rock Island Arsenal Museum.

of bacon, a quart of dry hominy every ten days for six months on a stretch without a break, and then say that they should not feel that most terrible of afflictions—hunger! I know what it means, and I saw others who felt it even more than myself, as well as some who did not seem to feel it at all."[6]

Despite the efforts of Perry and other local residents, the inmates simply did not get enough to eat after the late spring of 1864. Those men who could afford to augment their meager rations turned to the camp sutler for relief. Virtually every Civil War prison and army camp played host to these usurious merchants. In exchange for paying a tax to prison administrators—in effect, an override on profits—local entrepreneurs were admitted into the camp to hawk their wares. In the spirit of American capitalism, anything save liquor, firearms, or tools made for digging could be had for a price. Sutlers prowled the camps selling cider, milk, butter, eggs, canned fruit, boots, blankets, tobacco, and similar items.[7]

From the perspective of a later age, an observer might recoil at the cruelty of allowing sutlers to pass through prison camps—with the permission of prison officials, no less—to tempt men who were dying of starvation but might not have the funds necessary to purchase a small slice of salvation. At the time, however, such reservations were few and seldom spoken. Colonel Hoffman officially outlawed the use of sutlers, fearing that these men of commerce might offer their loyalties up for purchase and thus could become agents of the Confederacy by using their access to the camp to pass messages, money, and contraband of war. Despite an official proclamation from the faraway War Department, Union officers on duty at Rock Island deliberately ignored the manifesto by allowing an unofficial sutler, Albert C. Dart, to engage in his activities unimpeded. Hoffman eventually backed away from his edict, but the question of rations and the use of sutlers remained a source of mounting irritation in all Civil War prisons.[8]

Dart served as the unofficial sutler for most of the life of the Rock Island camp. Although a local merchant, John Burgh, had been the original barracks sutler, Dart finagled his way into the prison at the exclusion of any would-be rivals. He was audacious, preferring to drive a wagon loaded with goods directly onto the prison grounds in lieu of the more passive practice of waiting for soldiers to approach the sutler's building outside the stockade walls. He had grasped a fundamental lesson of American commerce—never wait for the customer to come to the store; bring the store to the customer. With his faithful bulldog padding behind the wagon, Dart made his rounds, bargaining with the prisoners, selling his load of syrup, lard, smoked beef, meat, fish, cornmeal, lemons, and apples before leaving the grounds.[9]

Sutler Albert C. Dart (second from left, standing in front of the wagon) sold food and household goods in the Rock Island Prison. Reprinted from *Rock Island: In Peace and in War* by B. F. Tillinghast.

Although opportunistic, at least Dart was honest with his customers. The men of the Rock Island Prison looked upon him with a certain begrudging appreciation for his goods and services; he was the safety net between them and starvation. That feeling changed, however, when he reappeared in the camp after a long absence. Hoffman and the War Department cut the prisoners' rations and once again prohibited sutlers from entering the camp in August 1864 as retaliation for atrocities committed in Confederate prisons. The first stories of Andersonville, Belle Isle, and other infamous camps had begun to filter into the North, and Union authorities were under pressure to respond with little concern for the hardships imposed on their prisoners. On this pretext, Hoffman diverted some monies that would have been used to buy rations into a special fund that he theoretically established for future purchases of fruits and vegetables to stave off scurvy among the prisoners. In reality little, if any, of that money was ever used for its intended purpose. When the war ended, Hoffman proudly presented the U.S. government with $1.8 million that had been appropriated but never used for prison administration, a fact that contributed to his well-deserved reputation for frugality.[10]

When Albert Dart finally reemerged in the camp on Christmas Eve 1864, he was determined to allow market forces to increase his profit. He informed the outraged prisoners who only moments before had heralded his arrival with good cheer that his prices had increased substantially in the interim between his visits. A quarter-barrel of flour in one of the nearby towns sold for $2.50, but Dart insisted on receiving $4.00 for the same commodity inside the stockade. Predictably, the response of the inmates to this unwelcome news was a cacophony of shouted protests and righteous indignation. It was one thing to take advantage of desperate men; it was another to leave them destitute in the process. They stormed away from his wagon en masse, refusing to give in to this unconscionable usury from a man who already turned a nice profit from his usual markup.[11]

It was a defining moment in the life of the camp, and everyone present knew it. If any prisoners broke ranks and purchased flour at the inflated price, the sutler would have won the day. If they stayed together as a group, this *de facto* trade union might yet compel the merchant to lower his price to a more reasonable level. "Dart communed with himself for a bit, then turned slowly toward the lower gate, and drove out, followed by hundreds of hungry eyes," Minnich remembered. "But not one single man asked him to stop. A principle was at stake."[12]

Principle or not, Dart's departure did not feed hungry men. Until the sutler returned, the inmates were forced to hunt for alternate sources of food. Rat hunting remained an ever-popular sport, and the fellows got to be experts at cornering their prey. "Rats were eagerly hunted, and in our barrack all points of egress from under our barrack were carefully blocked, leaving only one exit beneath each window, and then men would station themselves at the window with a 'gig'; and if a rat stuck his head out, the gig would descend like a flash of lightning, and—well, sometimes overeagerness caused the hunter to miss, and then no rat stew for him."[13]

Whenever possible, the men of Rock Island preferred bigger game. Minnich confessed that he took part in two dog abductions during his tenure in the prison. The second affair was especially gratifying because it involved Albert Dart. "I helped 'hide' two dogs—one an old long-eared hound, the other Dart's faithful and ever-watchful bulldog, whose round head did duty afterwards as a football, and in that capacity traveled over a large part of the prison, finally by an awkward kick being sent across the deadline, where none dared venture." Such was life in that prison stockade on the banks of the Mississippi River, that a man could write of the hunt for rats and dogs with pride in his ingenuity in surviving sickness and hunger for one more day.[14]

Like inmates at the Rock Island Prison, Andersonville prisoners found that fighting scurvy was their paramount concern because the disease was so commonplace. "Its symptoms were swelling and discoloration of the limbs, ulceration of the gums, and followed by lassitude and depression. I have seen prisoners take out their teeth and replace them, so badly was the mouth affected," inmate James Newton Miller reported. "It usually manifested itself first in the mouth," John McElroy recalled. "The breath became unbearably fetid; the gums swelled until they protruded, livid and disgusting, beyond the lips. The teeth became so loose that they frequently fell out, and the sufferer would have to pick them up and set them back in their sockets. The gums had a fashion of breaking away in large chunks, which would be swallowed or spit out." Warren Lee Goss agreed with his comrades' graphic depiction of this dread disease. "Thousands of prisoners were so affected with scurvy, caused by want of vegetables, or of nutritious food, that their limbs were ready to drop from their bodies," he remembered. "I have often seen maggots scooped out by the handful from the sores of those thus afflicted."[15]

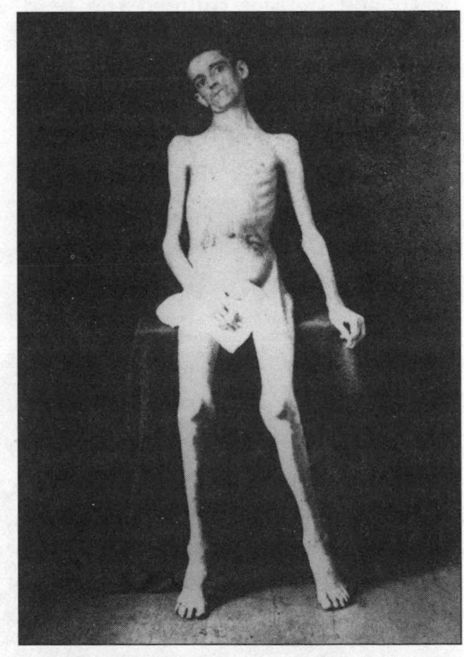

Starvation was a constant companion in Civil War prisons. Photographs of starving, emaciated "flesh-covered skeletons" emerging from Confederate prisons horrified the Northern public late in the war. Courtesy of the Library of Congress.

What made these cases so tragic was the needless suffering caused by the lack of sufficient rations. Despite the prisoners' appeals for help, their guards merely looked on dispassionately. In Goss's opinion, "persons wasted to mere skeletons by starvation and disease, unable to help themselves, died by inches the most terrible of deaths, with not a particle of medicine, or a hand lifted by those in charge of the prison for their relief."[16]

This assessment seemed to demonstrate the Rebels' monstrous disposition, but the story was a bit more complicated than Goss knew or was prepared to accept. The ever-increasing number of newly captured soldiers streaming into the stockade overwhelmed both the inmates and their captors. With few provisions on hand to feed or attend to the men, Captain Wirz and his crew were hard put to improve conditions inside the stockade walls. The arrival of Goss and his comrades on May 1 only exacerbated matters, pushing the number of prisoners beyond twelve thousand. Originally designed to warehouse between eight thousand and ten thousand men in barracks, the stockade population was continually increased after each military campaign netted more prisoners of war. In July, the Confederates expanded the size of the holding pen by ten acres to a total of twenty-six and a half acres, which the authorities estimated was sufficient to keep ten thousand men imprisoned. The expansion, although helpful, was not nearly enough room to meet the burgeoning demand. At its most crowded, during the summer of 1864, before death and transfer thinned the herd, between twenty-nine thousand and thirty-three thousand men languished in the Andersonville Stockade. Instead of housing ten thousand men on the entire site, the camp held more than eleven hundred prisoners per acre.[17]

This famous photograph of the Andersonville inmates, taken by A. J. Riddle in August 1864, shows the squalid, crowded conditions that greeted prisoners like Goss when they arrived at Camp Sumter. Courtesy of the National Archives.

As impossible as it may have seemed, the inmates somehow adapted to their surroundings. "We soon became conversant with the ways and means of the prison," Goss explained. "There is a certain flexibility of character in men that adapts itself with readiness to their circumstances." Without this ability to live in conditions of severe deprivation, a man might give up and surrender to death. Goss had learned the tricks of survival during his earlier stint in the Richmond prisons. "While some pass their time in useless repinings, others set themselves resolutely at work, like Robinson Crusoe, to develop the resources of their surroundings into all the comforts they can force them to yield." Just as he had demonstrated at Belle Isle, Goss was determined to be among the resolute "others."[18]

His efforts to survive required numerous calculations coupled with deliberative judgment—difficult activities even under ideal circumstances. A case in point was Goss's decision to forego the privileges and responsibilities of his rank. The men were divided up into groups of ninety to receive rations. Sergeants represented each group, and a chief sergeant represented three groups, or 270 inmates. Every twenty-four hours, the chief sergeant advanced to the main gate to draw rations and distribute them to the men under his command. Each sergeant was rewarded for fulfilling his administrative duties by receiving an extra ration. Despite this benefit, Goss resigned his position in the hierarchy. His motive was hardly altruistic; he recognized that the burden of distributing rations to starving men far outweighed the benefit of receiving a few extra morsels of food. "When men are cut down to very low rations, they are not always discriminating in attaching blame to the proper source, which made the place all the more difficult to fill with credit," he explained. "This I early foresaw, and, therefore, left the position to some one anxious to fill it."[19]

Instead of involving himself in the thankless chore of distributing rations, Goss bartered with his fellow prisoners, agreeing to lend men the two-quart pail he had acquired in exchange for a bit of food. He roamed the camp, offering up the pail and his skills as a cook to augment the paltry rations he received from the Confederates. As he had demonstrated during his earlier incarceration, he possessed a knack for business. The plan to garner food through his commercial ventures was much more successful—and far less controversial—than resorting to rank to procure an extra ration. His acumen did not ensure his survival, but it certainly improved the odds.[20]

Despite the improvement of his own circumstances, Goss could not shut out the sights and sounds of the suffering around him. He often longed to reach out to sick and dying men to better their condition, but he had to place his own welfare first. "The terrible truth was, that in prison one could not attempt to relieve the misery of others more miserable than himself, without placing himself in greater peril." Good Samaritans were seldom found, but when they were, "the bitter cup of misery [was] pressed to their own lips."[21]

One story especially disturbed him. Pvt. Peter Dunn from Goss's company suffered the misfortune of losing his tin cup shortly after he entered the prison. He then lost his blanket. The items may have been stolen—no one knew for sure—but without them his chances for survival were practically nil. Facing his own shortages and struggling to survive each day, Goss could not bring himself to intervene. No one else came to the boy's aid, either. As the days slipped by, Dunn was no longer lucid. "Gradually, as he wasted away, his mind wandered, and in imagination he was the possessor of those luxuries which the imagination will fasten upon when the body feels the keenest pangs of hunger," Goss recalled.

Shuffling through the camp, Dunn would speak to onlookers, offering them his pity, unaware of where reality ended and illusion began. "This is a dreadful place for the boys—isn't it? I don't enjoy myself when I have anything good to eat; there are so many around me who look hungry." He caught sight of Goss. "You look hungry, too, Sarge."

In brief moments of lucidity, Dunn bowed his head and acknowledged his desperate predicament. "Oh dear! I'm hungry myself, a good deal." Those moments were rare. Instead, this starving man, little more than a flesh-covered skeleton, wandered through the camp, all the while pitying the men who did not enjoy the feast he imagined that he had eaten.

"Poor, poor Peter! He soon died a lingering death from the effects of starvation and exposure," Goss later wrote. "In the lucid moments that preceded death, he said, as I stood over his poor famine-pinched form, 'I'm dreadful cold and hungry, Sarge.' Then again relapsed into a state of wandering, with the names of 'Mary' and 'Mother' on his lips; and the last faint action of life, when he could no longer speak, was to point his finger to his pallid, gasping lips, in mute entreaty for food!"[22]

Another heartbreaking case involved Charles E. Bent, a young drummer boy from Goss's company. He was "a fine lad, with as big a heart in his small body as ever throbbed in the breast of a man." The frail, shy boy normally preferred to keep his thoughts and opinions to himself. One afternoon Goss noticed that Bent was not wearing the ring he usually sported on his finger. Fearing that the diminutive young man had been robbed, Goss asked about it. "When I was out just now," the boy patiently explained, "my sister came and took it, and gave it to an angel." The next evening, Bent died without having regained his senses. "His pain and sorrow were ended, and heartless men no longer could torture him with hunger and cruelty," Goss wrote as a simple epitaph.[23]

Charles E. Bent, a drummer boy in Goss's company, explained that his sister took Bent's ring and gave it to an angel. Reprinted from *The Soldier's Story* by Warren Lee Goss.

Insane men who rambled incoherently as they died were bad enough, but sometimes it was worse when a fellow was clearheaded. Suffering from the lingering effects of typhoid, another drummer boy, C. H. A. Moore, wasted away in the stockade, but he was sane and understood exactly what would happen. His prematurely aged husk soon would be pronounced dead. Afterward, the corpse would be carried to the deadline and stacked with the others, like cordwood, until slaves entered the compound and hoisted them onto a mule wagon to be carried over to their final resting place, a mass grave just outside the stockade walls.[24]

Goss knelt by the dying boy's body and tried to soothe him, but to no avail. He was beyond consolation. Death was nearby, anxiously waiting, and the young man knew it. "His face bore an unchanged, listless expression, which, I have noticed in prison, betokened the loss of hope. He spoke of home and his mother, but his words were all in the same key, monotonous and weary, with a stony, unmoved expression of countenance." The end came in a soft hour of the evening when no one save Goss noticed that another young man had passed from the scene.[25]

These men and their deaths haunted him. Goss watched them shrivel and die before his eyes, but he could do nothing to alleviate their sickness and suffering without imperiling his own precarious situation. Sometimes he felt on the verge of insanity himself, as though staring down from a precipice into a valley of madness. Even a man of tremendous faith had to question why God appeared to have turned His back on scenes of such unimaginable suffering. Surely human beings deserved solace in their darkest hours.[26]

NINE

Sickness and Death Were Inevitable Accompaniments

Disease was the great killer of the Civil War; twice as many soldiers died from illness than perished on the battlefield. It was an era when doctors and medical personnel understood little of the dangers of bacteria and infection. Horror stories of surgeons who sawed off a gangrenous limb, wiped the blade on a gown or rag, and immediately moved to the next patient were all too common, as were tales of filthy, unsanitary conditions in army hospitals. It was little wonder that wounded soldiers often preferred to take their chances fighting a disease or injury in the privacy of their tents than to place themselves under the care of army "quacks."[1]

Communicable diseases ran rampant through army camps and prisons. In retrospect, this phenomenon is understandable. Many soldiers, especially those who hailed from rural communities, had grown up isolated from diverse populations. As a result, they had not been exposed to childhood diseases that especially inflicted urban dwellers who came into frequent contact with large numbers of people. With little or no immunity to the variety of diseases prevalent in nineteenth-century America, soldiers who marched off to war often were struck down in their first months of service with measles, mumps, tonsillitis, and other common illnesses. Although these maladies generally did not kill the men, they did incapacitate them for weeks at a time, leaving them weak and ineffectual in combat for many months afterward.[2]

Soldiers who survived bouts with common childhood diseases faced a menu of far more severe illnesses, many of which were caused by poor sanitary practices. Rapidly changing weather, damp clothing, polluted water, unsanitary waste disposal, and the generally poor health and dietary habits of soldiers created rich breeding grounds for a number of killer diseases, most notably diarrhea brought on by dysentery, but also typhoid, malaria, yellow fever, and pneumonia. Venereal disease and scurvy rounded out the list of common and potentially debilitating or deadly diseases. Several Civil War campaigns succeeded or failed depending on how many men could be moved from the sick list to active duty.[3]

For all the problems associated with diseases on the battlefield and in army camps, these killers were infinitely worse inside the prisons. Unlike men who were free to move about and change their clothes and physical location, captives had little choice but to wallow in their own filth, particularly when they lived in close proximity in crowded barracks. They often wore the same rags for months at a time with no opportunity to bathe in clean water. Far worse, they had no other option but to consume contaminated food and water on a regular basis. Diseases swept through the prisoners' ranks with astonishing speed, mowing men down like a scythe cutting through a wheat field.[4]

Crowded barracks often allowed contagious diseases such as smallpox to infect prisoners before an epidemic could be identified. Courtesy of Rod Gragg.

Smallpox was the most fearsome of all the dread diseases in conditions of confinement. Caused by a virus, this "prowling spotted beast" began with an infection of the mucous lining of the nose and throat. From there, it invaded the rest of the body, initially producing flu-like symptoms: nausea, vomiting, headache, backache, and a fever as high as 104 degrees Fahrenheit. Severe abdominal pain and disorientation often set in, followed by the appearance of a distinctive pattern of symptoms, notably a series of small red spots on the tongue and in the mouth. The spots developed into sores, broke open, and spread the virus throughout the mouth and throat, causing the infected person to become contagious. About the time that the sores broke open in the mouth, a rash appeared on the skin and eventually erupted into large bumps filled with an opaque fluid. These pus-filled bumps known as pustules—sharply raised, round, and firm to the touch, a clear sign of smallpox—were the size of BB pellets. If the victim survived the high fever, the pustules formed a crust and then a scab. By the end of the second week, all the sores had scabbed over and the scabs eventually fell off the skin, leaving a series of distinctive, pitted scars on the infected body. These scars signified a smallpox survivor.[5]

Smallpox was the ideal biological agent in crowded prisons. It was transferred through the air in tiny droplets expelled orally from an infected person, especially through coughing and sneezing, although talking could transmit the disease as well. Sometimes it was spread from person to person through blankets, linens, and clothing. With a relatively long incubation period—full-blown symptoms generally did not appear until twelve to fourteen days after the first exposure—the virus had ample time to spread without detection. Moreover, it could survive in the open air for up to twenty-four hours, even in winter conditions. If one man entered a prison after having been infected, he potentially could contaminate every inmate in the prison before anyone realized that the men were at risk.[6]

Smallpox infection at such close quarters often was a death sentence. The mortality rate was commonly thought to be about 30 percent, but much depended on the age and general health of the victim. The virulent "sledgehammer" form of the disease may have claimed the lives of 60 to 80 percent of the infected population. For prisoners, who seldom enjoyed good health or plentiful rations, any form of smallpox was a cause for great anxiety; few men who entered a prison hospital or pesthouse after showing signs of the disease emerged to live another day.[7]

In light of the squalid, overcrowded conditions of confinement, smallpox appeared in the Rock Island Barracks only a few weeks after the first shipment of prisoners arrived. To make matters worse, the alignment of the buildings was so close that it did not take much contact for the disease to travel from one barrack to another with almost lightning speed. The outbreak could have been avoided, or at least substantially mitigated, had the jailers been more vigilant in attending to the prisoners' needs. In 1796, a British physician, Edward Jenner, had discovered an effective vaccine. The publication of his

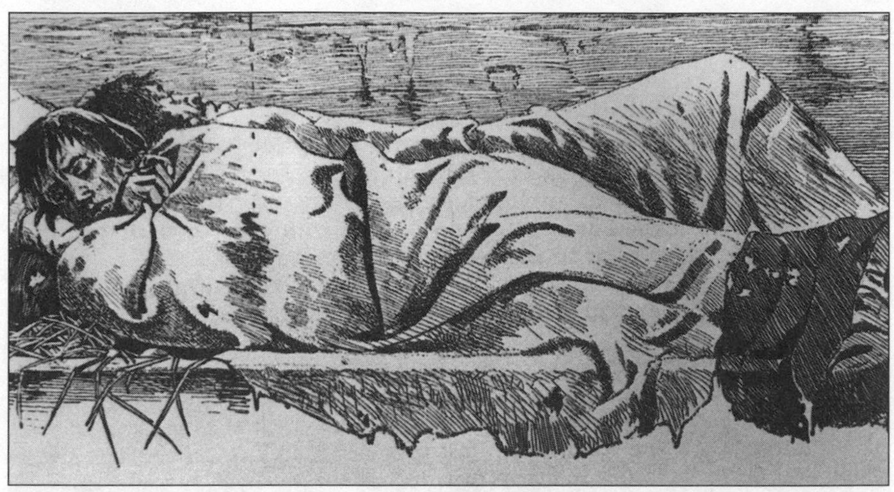

Smallpox often was transferred from one prisoner to another through shared blankets and bedding. Courtesy of Rod Gragg.

paper "The Inquiry" two years later was extremely controversial, causing some critics to characterize Jenner's vaccine as worse than the disease. Earlier efforts to eradicate smallpox had caused as much pain and suffering as they had relieved. By the beginning of the Civil War, however, physicians on both sides of the Atlantic recognized that Jenner's vaccine generally was effective. Nonetheless, understanding the efficacy of the vaccine and administering it to vulnerable populations were altogether different matters.[8]

The first Confederate soldiers confined at Rock Island had been infected with smallpox while they were interned temporarily in a prison camp in Louisville, Kentucky. Owing to the relatively short time between the prisoners' incarceration in Louisville and their arrival at Rock Island, the outbreak was not detected immediately. It was only on December 6, 1863, about three weeks after the first men entered the barracks, that the distinctive red spots became visible. Unfortunately, the prison administrators were still scrambling to complete camp construction, and they had few supplies on hand to combat the disease. Consequently, they did little to alleviate the suffering of the inmates.

"The authorities were not prepared for the appearance of this fearful disease—the hospitals not being finished," prisoner Charles Wright observed. "The infected and healthy men were in the same barrack. The disease spread so rapidly there was no room in the buildings outside the prison, and certain barracks within the enclosure were set apart for smallpox hospitals." Although the camp surgeon Dr. J. J. Temple and his assistants T. J. Iles and Marcellus

Moxley eventually tried to vaccinate the inmates, it was too little, too late. "The death rate at this time was alarming. On the 9th of March 1864, twenty-nine men had died in the hospital from my barrack, which did not have its full complement of men," Wright explained. He estimated that the disease killed 25 percent of the inmates in his building.[9]

After the first prisoners arrived, Union authorities finally constructed a hospital for the inmates at Rock Island. Courtesy of the Rock Island Arsenal Museum.

Alarmed at the appearance of the disease, Asst. Surg. Gen. A. M. Clark inspected the prison in February, finding thirty-eight confirmed smallpox cases. No pesthouses had been constructed to quarantine men suffering from contagious diseases, so Clark segregated the infected men in barracks located in the southwest corner of the stockade. In the meantime, he ordered the construction of pesthouses to handle future cases. Despite these efforts, it was too late for many Rock Island prisoners already sharing quarters with smallpox-infected inmates. Ninety-four men had perished by the end of December. A month later, the total stood at 231, and it rose to 346 in February. In July 1865, when the prison closed, 1,960 prisoners and 171 Union guards had died from smallpox and other diseases.[10]

The epidemic did not escape the attention of the Union authorities in the commissary general's office. When he learned of the situation, Surg. Charles S. Tripler, medical director of the Northern Department, called for a special report detailing "the causes of this mortality." In a report to the acting surgeon general on March 4, 1864, William Watson, the surgeon who replaced the inexperienced Moxley at Rock Island, attempted to address this question in detail.

Absolving the camp administrators from blame, Watson concluded that "everything has been done by the medical officers, and all their efforts had been promptly seconded by Col. A. J. Johnson, commanding the post, to check the spread of smallpox and mitigate the severity of other diseases." Despite these efforts, during his inspection of the newly created pesthouses, in Watson's words, "I found a great want of cleanliness among the patients and attendants, which is disappearing under stringent regulations requiring the regular use of bath tubs and the labors of a permanent detail as laundrymen." Watson remarked that the real culprit in the smallpox epidemic was the uninformed prison population, "where the impression seemed to prevail that it was injurious to wash, which resulted in an accumulation of filth that, in connection with the disease, suspended entirely the functions of the skin, producing congestion in cases that might have progressed without unpleasant symptoms."[11]

Holding prisoners responsible for their own suffering because of a lack of cleanliness and the squalor of their conditions is akin to blaming the victim for the perpetration of a crime. Nonetheless, the establishment of pesthouses did much to stem the spread of disease in the Rock Island Prison. By the time John Minnich arrived in February 1864, the smallpox epidemic had been contained. He faced many challenges owing to the lack of rations and the proximity of disease, but he escaped the worst of the ailments that afflicted Civil War prisoners.[12]

Rock Island was not the only Civil War prison to experience widespread epidemics. Smallpox and other contagious diseases also ran rampant in the Andersonville Stockade. "There being no sanitary regulations in camp, and no proper medical provisions, sickness and death were inevitable accompaniments to our imprisonment," Warren Lee Goss wrote after the war. As was the case at Rock Island, smallpox swept through the ranks. In March 1864, less than a month after the camp opened, Confederate authorities were shocked to learn that two inmates transferred in from the Richmond prisons were infected with the virus. Moving the two men into the prison hospital was no guarantee that an epidemic could be avoided because the hospital was inside the stockade. With Confederate sentries in daily contact with prisoners, the authorities' fear that the disease might spread to the local population was palpable and real.[13]

The jailers found a solution when they removed the infected men from the prison population and isolated them in the woods outside the stockade walls. Chief surgeon Isaiah White somehow located an old surgeon—immunized from smallpox, in all likelihood—to care for the victims. This quick-thinking action no doubt contained the smallpox epidemic before it got out of hand. As an added precaution, prison surgeons moved through the stockade vaccinating men who did not have vaccine scars.[14]

Crowded conditions inside the walls of the Andersonville Stockade contributed to the spread of the disease and the high mortality rate in the prison. Reprinted from *The Soldier's Story* by Warren Lee Goss.

Unfortunately for the prisoners, the vaccinations created almost as many problems as they prevented. Many of the men were suffering from scurvy when they were inoculated. Consequently, when the smallpox vaccination entered their immune systems, it created pustules that rapidly became ulcerated. Left untreated, the ulcers became gangrenous, which sometimes required surgeons to amputate rotten, blackened limbs. To prisoners watching the scene, this series of vaccinations and amputations was incontrovertible evidence that the barbaric Confederate authorities had undertaken a deliberate campaign to poison the inmates. Many postwar tales of Andersonville accusing the Confederates of plotting to exterminate prisoners can be traced to this series of seminal events.[15]

The rapid spread of disease and the apparent cruelty of the Southern authorities severely tested the religious faith of the captives. Had it not been for the appearance of the Providence Spring in August 1864, Andersonville survivors would have found little cause for continued belief in Christian mercy and charity. For those men inclined to believe in a loving God, the unexpected appearance of fresh water could only be the result of divine intervention.[16]

The spring water appeared—as if from the hand of God—at a time when it was most needed. July and August were irrepressibly hot and humid; men perished in droves as they broiled under the fierce summer sun. Goss remembered this period of life in Andersonville as a mixture of insufferable heat mixed with blessed relief. "Extreme heat, during July and August, was often followed by days dark with intermittent showers. On one occasion, the ground was rendered so hot by the intense rays of the sun as to blister my feet by mere contact." When the rains came, men emerged from the holes they dug in the ground to escape the sun and desperately tried to capture water in their cups and cooking utensils. Their reactions varied. "Some laughed, others cried as if mad, while still others crouched in the rain, or saw the whole scene unmoved, as if gazing on a panorama with which they had no concern."[17]

More prisoners might have died were it not for the thunderstorms that arose on some cloudy afternoons, pelting the men with much-needed rain and fresh water. Yet even the showers were a mixed blessing. Inmates struggling to fight disease were drenched with water and cold with chills; they found little comfort in the driving rain. The torrential water rushing through the camp also invaded the spaces that men had carved into the ground to protect them from the elements. What few possessions they owned were pushed out of their homemade "shebangs," only to slip along the newly carved gullies toward the lowest part of the camp.[18]

Other men, parched and thirsty, were delighted at the prospect of gulping down uncontaminated water. Despite the flooding, they greeted the rain with glee, for they could fill their cups and canteens to their hearts' delight. The stream that ran through the stockade had been polluted for so long that only rainwater was sufficient to stave off extreme thirst. A few hand-dug wells also provided a measure of relief, but too many men had no source of fresh water before the summer storms appeared.[19]

The rains continued, on and off, for the first ten days of August. On August 9, flooding caused portions of the stockade walls to break off, driving General Winder and the Confederate authorities into a panic. "Never in my life have I spent so anxious a time," Winder reported after the timbers had been restored and the threat of thousands of fleeing Union prisoners scouring the countryside had been eliminated. "If we had not had a large Negro force working on the defenses I think it would have been impossible to have saved the place." As it was, the Confederates and a group of impressed slaves labored for sixty hours

Portions of the stockade walls at Andersonville broke loose when torrential rain fell in August 1864. Reprinted from *Life and Death in Rebel Prisons* by Robert H. Kellogg.

before the walls were secure. During that time, the Regulators—the inmates' police force—had to restore order with help from the guards, who, fearful of a mass riot, turned their artillery pieces on the prisoners.[20]

The "heaviest thunderstorm of the season," as inmate George A. Hitchcock described the August 9 tumult, pushed an underground spring through the earth halfway up the northern slope on the western side of the prison pen, like a sign from God. The prisoners rushed from all quarters to enjoy the pure waters, some of which flowed beyond the deadline. "Hurry up, hand me the boot-leg bucket," prisoner Sam Boggs heard a fellow captive exclaim as he stumbled toward the new water source. "There is a spring of just bully good water bursted out, up by the 'dead-line' north of the creek, and there is a big crowd there, but I think I can get some of the water."[21]

Virtually every prisoner in the camp recalled the scene when the Providence Spring first appeared, and they attributed it to the work of a loving Creator. "It was said that one of these [lightning] bolts struck an old pine stump, and as the spring burst forth from the foot of this stump that it was the result of the lightning stroke," Ezra Hoyt Ripple wrote. "Possibly God may have chosen to bring the water by this agency. All the same, whether by this or the word of His power, He brought it and that was enough for us."

Many men proclaimed it a "providential dispensation." John McElroy wrote that the spring "poured out its grateful flood of pure, sweet water in an apparently exhaustless quantity. To the many who looked in wonder upon it, it seemed as truly a heaven-wrought miracle as when Moses's enchanted rod smote the perched rock in Sinai's desert waste, and the living waters gushed forth." Realizing that the appearance of the water was less miraculous than it might have appeared, prisoner James Newton Miller wrote that "it is no wonder we called it 'providence spring,' though it was only the uncovering of a former spring which had been covered over by the washing of sand and soil."[22]

Unlike some of his comrades, the downpour disturbed Goss. "The force of the rain, running down the hillside, continually upset me, by undermining the sand beneath my feet, until at last losing my blanket and philosophy, miserable and grotesque as others, I went rushing and pitching after my tin pail and blanket, caught up and carried away by the torrent." Despite his frustration with the rain, he understood the symbolic significance of the Providence Spring. "One great good resulted from this freshet," he wrote. "On the hillside where the stockade had been broken away, a spring was discovered, which supplied an abundance of pure water to the prisoners, in contrast with the filthy stream which had been our only supply during the summer."[23]

During four and a half long months, Goss endured the daily tribulations of surviving his Andersonville captivity. Compared with some of the weaker men, he was blessed with a strong constitution, an iron will, and an unconquerable hope that help was on the horizon. He and his comrades repeatedly heard stories that an exchange was in the offing or that Union Gen. William T. Sherman and his men were making their way into Georgia. "Prisoners coming in from Sherman's army brought news of a raid under Stoneman and Cook," he wrote. "When Stoneman was raiding toward us, with evident intentions of releasing the prisoners—which I have since ascertained to be true—our hearts beat high with hope." Hope was a thin reed—hardly enough to sustain the inmates indefinitely—but as the summer months stretched toward autumn, it would have to do, for hope was all they had.[24]

TEN

Crazy with the Idea of Freedom and Home

September 1864 brought profound changes to Goss's and Minnich's lives in their respective prisons. Reflecting the increasingly desperate situation in the South as Union armies tightened their stranglehold on the Confederacy, Warren Lee Goss's jailers decided to move the Andersonville prisoners in order to avoid General Sherman's march across Georgia. Meanwhile, in the Rock Island Prison, John Minnich faced a crisis unique to Confederates: the appearance of Negro soldiers as sentinels.

One day late in September, Minnich and his fellow inmates gazed up at the walls of the Rock Island Prison and discovered, much to their shock and dismay, black faces staring down at them. A unit of "contrabands"—black Union soldiers—had been assigned to garrison the camp. Prison records show that soldiers of the 108th Regiment, U.S. Colored Infantry, reported to their new post on September 24.[1]

Recruited from Kentucky during the spring of 1864, a little more than a year after President Lincoln's final Emancipation Proclamation went into effect and two years after the Militia Act authorized blacks to serve as soldiers, the unit was commanded by Lt. Col. John Bishop. Bishop was a white officer who originally enlisted in the Sixty-eighth Illinois Regiment, where he won promotion to the rank of lieutenant. Realizing that the 68th Illinois would never win him fame and glory—it was a three-month regiment and never entered combat—he applied for a colonel's rank with the 108th and won the position in due course. The regiment was composed of former slaves and a few freedmen, hardly the type of unit that would engage in glorious military campaigns, but at least Bishop could boast of his jump in rank as sufficient inducement to take the helm of a colored infantry regiment.[2]

Colonel John Bishop commanded the 108th Regiment, U.S. Colored Troops, when the unit arrived at the Rock Island Prison for garrison duty in September 1864. Courtesy of the Dave Newberger Collection, U.S. Army Military History Institute.

The 108th replaced the departing 133rd Illinois at Rock Island. As bad as the boys of the 133rd had been—and they had been an abysmal, poorly trained, loosely disciplined lot—at least those trigger-happy teenagers were white. The great fear of many Confederates, even transplanted Yankees like Minnich, was that blacks would rise up and destroy the way of life built by white Southerners over past generations. To look up at the walls of the prison and see armed black men was almost more than the Confederates could bear. Inmate Lafayette Rogan expressed the indignation felt by many of his comrades when he wrote that "8,000 Southern men to day are guarded by their slaves who have been armed by the tyrant." Watching a black man patrolling the prison perimeter, Minnich remembered "the impress of his brutal features stamped ineffaceably on my memory—a squat-built Negro as black as any ever painted by nature's brush, low forehead, deep-set eyes, and the elongated jaw of the gorilla, a face denoting at once the low grade of mentality characteristic of the lowest type of the Negro—a mere brute." The local newspaperman J. B. Danforth, a Southern sympathizer and Colonel Johnson's nemesis, was more restrained in his prose, but almost as appalled at the arrival of the 108th as the prisoners had been. "On Saturday morning," he observed, "980 'Free Americans of African Descent,' with their servants, arrived here from Louisville, carrying muskets and dressed in the uniform of the United States."[3]

The black soldiers who climbed the walls at Rock Island were well aware of the reversal of fortunes. In some cases, they were looking down on men who once had been their masters. David Sears, a local mill owner, was delivering flour to the camp one day when a prisoner told him that he recognized a few of his former slaves patrolling the wall. Sears noted the inmate's frustration because "it was more than he could stand to be guarded by his own niggers." Seething with resentment toward their captors, the Rock Island prisoners became more restless than ever. Plotting escapes and planning mischievous schemes were the only outlets for their anger, and they were determined to demonstrate their fury in no uncertain terms.[4]

The reactions of the Southern prisoners and Copperheads to the appearance of black soldiers were completely in line with the attitudes and policies propagated by Confederate leaders. A major reason for the collapse of the Dix-Hill Exchange Cartel was the stalemate between Union and Confederate negotiators on the thorny question of how captured black soldiers should be treated. Comments uttered by many Confederate political and military leaders, especially President Jefferson Davis and Gen. P. G. T. Beauregard, left little doubt that blacks employed in any military capacity beyond mere day laborers was anathema to the South.[5]

It is no small irony that the young men serving in the 108th Colored Infantry faced almost as much antipathy from their white comrades in arms as they did from the prisoners. Segregated from other Union soldiers in the barracks, they slept, ate, talked, and fulfilled their duties in a world unto itself. The fifty black soldiers who died at the prison were interred in a section of the island cemetery separate from the white guards who perished there. Jim Crow's name was unknown at the time, but his fierce determination to separate white men from the "coloreds" was no less evident. As was the case with virtually all of the 180,000 blacks who donned the uniform of a Union soldier, the men of the 108th were assigned more than their share of the unappealing grunt work endemic to military life. Garrison duty and battalions that performed manual labor generally were considered to be the worst positions in the army, so it was little wonder that a regiment from the U.S. Colored Infantry eventually turned up at the Rock Island Prison.[6]

The citizens of Davenport, Iowa, also were inhospitable to black soldiers. On several occasions, residents noted with distaste the presence of these strange, unwelcome men on the streets of their town. A typical article featuring crude, demeaning remarks appeared in the Davenport *Democrat* in January 1865. "A Dark Transaction," the headline read. "Two darkies having trespassed on the laws by stealing and riotous conduct in this city, thereby getting themselves locked up in jail; a squad of their dark brethren, some forty strong, who stand guard for a living, on the island, managed to escape from their quarters last evening and came to Davenport with arms in their hands and wool erect, for the purpose of rescuing their brethren, or to perish in the attempt." Continuing with the unnecessarily colorful prose, the article observed that "these 'black boys in blue' are getting to think less of 'white trash' than ever. It seems as though there was a screw loose on the island, else so many would not have been allowed to come over here at once to startle the usual peaceful citizens of Davenport into such fearful commotion." Concerned that violence might break out between his troops and the easily startled Iowans, Colonel Bishop prohibited his men from visiting Davenport in their off-duty hours until May 1865, when he rescinded the order shortly before the unit permanently departed.[7]

At least their appearance on the Illinois side of the river was greeted with marginally less hostility than it was in Iowa. Because Illinois residents often competed with their counterparts across the Mississippi, it was probably inevitable that this rivalry would carry over into the reception afforded the men of the 108th. Thus, when the regiment departed for Vicksburg late in May, an editorial in the Illinois-based *Argus* begrudgingly observed that the "colored soldiers, as a general thing, have conducted themselves with great propriety, since they were stationed here." This comment was high praise, indeed, considering Danforth's initial reaction to the troops as well as the animosity usually associated with the appearance of the black guards at Rock Island.[8]

Not only was their arrival heralded with no small measure of trepidation and anger by most observers, Union and Confederate, but the trek from Louisville also left the regiment at less than full strength. Sixty men reported sick and three were shuffled off to the guardhouse as soon as the unit arrived. Within a short time, the sick list swelled to nearly two hundred men. An old farmer who had picked up with the 108th, Isaac McMerkin, was in such a sad state that he died the day after he made it to the prison. In keeping with its strict policy toward black soldiers, the U.S. government charged McMerkin's widow $17.50 for the musket and equipment he lost when he died.[9]

An unfortunate but unsurprising part of the prisoners' schemes to torment their new guards was their effort to stone the black men perched on the parapet. Guard reports indicate that prisoners flung rocks at the sentries mostly during the long nights when it was almost impossible to get a bead on the culprits. Minnich claimed that such incidents were much discussed but never initiated. "I learned at the time about the rocking affair proposed, but never put into execution," he wrote forty-four years later. "A report once came to our barrack that some hot, reckless prisoner proposed that 'we ought to gather rocks and in the night knock the niggers off the wall,' but wiser counsels prevailed, and the matter was dropped. Nothing of the kind was ever carried out to my knowledge."[10]

The 108th Regiment, U.S. Colored Troops, patrolled the walls of the Rock Island Prison, much to the consternation of many white prisoners. Courtesy of the Illinois State Historical Library.

Whatever the truth of the matter, clearly the black soldiers and white prisoners regarded one another with thinly veiled and sometimes not-so-thinly-veiled hostility. In time, the guards of the 108th proved almost as willing to shoot prisoners as their predecessors had been. One incident stood out in the minds of many inmates. As discussed in Chapter 6, on the evening of October 24, 1864, James P. McClanahan of Company D, Ninth Tennessee Cavalry, a prisoner confined to Barrack No. 8, bribed a private in the 108th to allow him to slip under the north wall. As he was attempting to escape according to his plan, McClanahan caught the eye of Pvt. Peter Cowherd, C Company, of the 108th. Cowherd raised his rifle, took aim, and shot McClanahan dead. Whether Cowherd was ignorant of the bribe and only performing his duty as a Union soldier or whether he chose to betray the prisoner after money had changed hands was not clear. A commission composed of several Union officers exonerated the guard, although to the incensed white prisoners it was but another example of the deliberate cruelty of their jailers.[11]

According to Minnich, "I do remember that some were good fellows, confining themselves to a strict discharge of their duty without any display of undue harshness." Nonetheless, in his view, black sentries who adhered to appropriate military procedures were exceptions to the rule. A typical example of their gratuitous brutality occurred not long after the soldiers of the 108th first appeared on the parapet. As the weather grew colder and the prisoners searched in vain for coal or other sources of fuel with which to fire their stoves, a prisoner from Barrack No. 30 ventured close to the deadline to collect kindling. "I was on the avenue between 43 and 44, nearer 43, and saw this man walk through the snow to a tree standing near the edge of the ditch," Minnich recalled. He wasn't alone in observing the scene; a black sentry spied the prisoner as well. As the hapless inmate stooped to retrieve branches that had fallen or been hacked from the tree, "this same Negro, arriving at the end of his beat at the ditch, without warrant, authority, or cause, and in the most brutal manner possible, ordered the man to drop those limbs. I can hear him yet: 'You damned Rebel, drop dem lim's.'"[12]

Incredibly, the prisoner ignored this admonition and went on collecting wood as though no one had spoken. He may have been "clearly within his known rights," in Minnich's view, but the guard grew furious at the prisoner's feigned indifference. "The nigger repeated: 'Drop dem lim's, I say!' The man kept on, not heeding the order. Within a couple of paces of the steps, the nigger raised his rifle, took deliberate aim, and pulled the trigger. Shot through the spine, the poor fellow fell forward on his face in the snow motionless."[13]

Perhaps the most notorious incident that occurred between black soldiers of the 108th and white prisoners at Rock Island involved a man whom inmate Ben Hord indecorously labeled a "crazy nigger." He was William Boyd, a twenty-six-year-old farmer who had enlisted in the unit in Kentucky. He might have passed through history as another faceless, nameless black man fighting for his freedom and dignity, but Boyd distinguished himself by acting in such a manner that he was confined to the Rock Island guardhouse. At first, his odd behavior was taken as the kind of inappropriate conduct punishable by a court-martial. Sometime after he was ushered into the guardhouse, however, his superiors noted that he was "deranged." Hord, hardly a detached observer, claimed that Boyd had "gone suddenly crazy on post" and fired indiscriminately into the squad, mortally wounding one man and injuring others. This blatantly repulsive act and the resultant diagnosis should have been enough to disqualify Boyd from further active duty, but it was not. After settling down and adopting a serene outward appearance, Boyd secured his release to resume his duties on the wall. He occasionally relapsed and found himself back in the guardhouse, but days later the horrified prisoners would spot him again patrolling the perimeter.[14]

Boyd might have continued this weird Jekyll-Hyde existence had the regimental surgeon, Pearl Martin, not intervened. After reviewing the case and meeting with the "deranged" guard, Martin recommended that Boyd be committed to a hospital for insane soldiers in Washington, D.C. "I have carefully examined the said William Boyd of Capt. Benton Tuttle's company and find him incapable of performing the duties of a soldier because of insanity," he wrote. Someone along the chain of command agreed with Martin's assessment, and Boyd left the Rock Island Prison Barracks shortly thereafter. Once again, the Union military displayed its remarkable penchant for absurdity by preparing a bill for several pieces of equipment—a belt, a scabbard, and two bayonets—that Boyd had lost during the time he served at Rock Island. Insanity was no excuse for misplacing army-issued paraphernalia.[15]

The question of how white prisoners should react to the presence of black sentinels at Rock Island plagued John Minnich and his fellow inmates throughout the remainder of their time in captivity. The men fretted over the indignities showered upon their Southern heritage, but they were powerless to prevent the soldiers of the 108th from patrolling the walls. It was one among many hardships endured by the proud men of the South.[16]

Rock Island prisoners suffered enormously, yet at least the relative stability of the camp administration—black guards notwithstanding—allowed for a measure of predictability in prison life as well as an orderly, consistent progression of events. Even Commandant Johnson's and Commissary General Hoffman's extreme parsimony and the periodic acts of cruelty perpetrated by Union sentries could be endured by inmates armed with grit and determination. Prisoners interned in the Andersonville Stockade—indeed, in many Confederate prisons—faced a much more uncertain future in 1864. External events taxed the administrative capabilities of the South in a manner never experienced in the more prosperous North, leading to chaos and confusion in Southern prisons.[17]

As summer gave way to autumn and August dissolved into September, the Confederacy found itself in an increasingly desperate situation. The economy was in shambles, suffering from hyperinflation that almost completely devalued Confederate currency. Soldiers deserted in record numbers. Equipment—rifles, horses, uniforms, shoes, foodstuffs—was practically nonexistent. Worse still, after three and a half years of fighting, the Southern landscape was scarred by artillery fire, rotting corpses, and charred, burned-out husks that once had been stately mansions and buildings of commerce. Despite this dismal state of affairs, the bloodshed dragged on interminably. As long as Gen. Robert E. Lee's Army of Northern Virginia remained relatively intact, the Confederates refused to yield.[18]

In an effort to force the South to capitulate, Gen. Ulysses S. Grant developed a strategy aimed at dividing and conquering the Confederacy. As part of his plan, Grant dispatched his most trusted lieutenant, Gen. William Tecumseh Sherman, to pierce the heart of the Confederacy in Tennessee and Georgia, thereafter advancing toward Atlanta, an important rail and communications center. The objective was to squeeze the Rebels into submission by disrupting the vital link between Georgia and the states of the upper South. Moreover, the Tennessee-Georgia campaign might prevent Confederate Gen. Joseph E. Johnston's army from combining forces with the Army of Northern Virginia and thereby prolonging the war.[19]

Union Gen. William T. Sherman's march through Georgia caused Confederate authorities to move the prisoners from Andersonville to other prisons in September 1864. Courtesy of the National Archives Collection, U.S. Army Military History Institute.

Many inmates suffering in Southern prisons heard tales of Sherman's exploits and his slow, steady progress through the Confederate interior. They plaintively noted in their diaries that "Uncle Billy" was the Great Liberator who would charge the Gates of Hell at the Andersonville Stockade to release his oppressed people and smite their enemies. The prisoners' tone of hopefulness intertwined with righteous anger reflected a fiery, Old Testament vengeance that sustained many a man through his darkest hour. Sherman seemed to be well on his way toward fulfilling their hopes and dreams of liberation when he marched into Atlanta on September 2, 1864. In capturing that key city, he also did much to assure President Lincoln's victory in the fall presidential election.[20]

Unfortunately for the prisoners, this hoped-for Moses failed to reach Andersonville, despite dispatching a contingent of troops to explore the possibility.[21] The Confederate high command, anxiously watching Sherman's advance, did not know his plans after Atlanta capitulated. Fearing that he would send forces to free the Andersonville prisoners, Maj. Gen. Samuel Jones, Confederate commander of the Military Department of South Carolina, Georgia, and Florida, ordered that the men held in all Georgia prisons must be moved to a more secure location away from Sherman's likely path. As a result, the jailers temporarily moved prisoners to Charleston, South Carolina, far removed from southwest Georgia.[22]

In September 1864, Maj. Gen. Samuel Jones ordered his men to move Union prisoners held in Georgia to escape Sherman's advance through the countryside. Courtesy of the Museum of the Confederacy.

Warren Lee Goss remembered the subterfuge that accompanied the move. "Rumors of exchange continued to pervade the prison. Men, crazy with the idea of freedom and home, wandered up and down the prison, clinging to every rumor, like drowning men to straws." Judging by the hurried activities of the prison administrators, all signs seemed to point toward a mass exodus from the stockade. Finally, after what seemed an eternity, orders arrived. "We were told that there was a Federal transport fleet off Savannah, waiting for us. To all in prison this seemed the dawn of freedom, and the most incredulous believed."[23]

Early in September the inmates were marched from Andersonville to a nearby train and crowded into boxcars. Fearing they might be shipped into Alabama and deeper into the wilds of the Confederacy, the prisoners were heartened to see Macon, Georgia, after a hard day of travel in the poorly ventilated cars. At least they were headed in the right direction. Anxious for news of Union activities, Goss found a fellow who claimed with authority that the days of the Southern Confederacy were numbered. "A Negro informed us that 'Captain Sherman' had taken Atlanta, and was making for Macon as 'tight as he can come,'" he recalled. Displaying a remarkable prescience, Goss mused that this bit of information made their journey "look like removing us to a place of security rather than an exchange."[24]

The prison train eventually rolled into Charleston just before sundown. Ordered from the boxcars, the men shuffled through the city streets as best they could. Goss marveled at the terrible destruction that greeted their arrival. All around lay the ruins and rubble of a once stately antebellum city. "It was no figure of speech, but a reality, that grass was growing in the streets of the proud but doomed city which first raised its hand against the Federal government," he wrote.[25]

At the conclusion of their march, the men found themselves in a temporary prison at the Charleston racecourse, a large open field similar to a modern fairground. Surrounded by guards, the field had been used on several occasions to augment prisons elsewhere in the area, especially facilities at Castle Pinckney in Charleston Harbor, the city jail, and nearby Roper Hospital. "The situation was pleasant," Goss remembered. "The green grass, to which our sight had been unused for many weary months, met the eye with refreshing pleasantness."[26]

Goss and his fellow survivors may have been pleased with their new prison compared to the Andersonville Stockade, but the Confederates were frantic. The racecourse was so overcrowded that sentries could not adequately oversee them and sufficient rations could not be found. On September 12, General Jones wrote to Confederate Secretary of War James A. Seddon to explain that new accommodations must be secured immediately. "The safety of this place and Savannah demands that the prisoners be removed," he concluded. Unwilling or unable to wait for further instructions, General Jones wrote to Secretary Seddon again that same day. "It is absolutely essential to send some prisoners from this place. I have ordered an officer to Florence, S.C., to construct [a] stockade for them."[27]

The rural crossroads known as Florence was eleven years away from becoming an incorporated town when South Carolina seceded from the Union in 1860. Little more than a railroad depot tucked into a large pine forest in the northeastern corner of the state, the hamlet was barely a dot on the map. Viewing the area five years later, Sidney Andrews, a Northern newspaper correspondent, described it as "a name rather than a place; or, say, a point at which three railroads centre, rather than a town." Andrews's description was apt, for Florence began as the intersection of three railroad lines during the antebellum period, and slowly grew into a town after the end of the Civil War.[28]

Decades later, Bessie A. Gregg of the Maxcy Gregg Chapter of the United Daughters of the Confederacy described the town during the War Between the States. "In the days of the Confederacy, Fair Florence was not the bustling, progressive, business woman of three score years that she is today." In those troubled times, the town could not boast "of paved streets, magnificent schools, fine hospitals, and beautiful churches" as she could in the twentieth century. Instead, Florence was akin to "a shy little farmer girl dressed in cotton, and living among virgin pines, perhaps in old Gamble's Hotel," a centerpiece of the area. "Were it up North it would be a business center, but there seems little doing here," inmate John W. Northrop explained. "Things look deserted; woods on every side; clearings near the tracks adorned with decaying brush and stumps. I am told that the country near is noted for savage gangs of marauders who have been known to fight to the death when attempts by civil authorities have been made to break them up." Prisoner Charles Fosdick was far less charitable than Northrop. "It was an old, dilapidated town, with but few houses, and in the whole place was not one respectable dwelling."[29]

Florence may have been a small, unimpressive place, but Fosdick was mistaken in calling it an old town. It arose from humble roots not long before the prisoners arrived in 1864. During the 1840s, railroad officials chartered the Wilmington and Manchester line to allow transportation between Wilmington, North Carolina, and portions of South Carolina, especially Charleston. Later, two companies—the Cheraw and Darlington Railroad in 1849 and North Eastern Railroad Company in 1851—constructed lines "from the city of Charleston to such point on or near the Wilmington and Manchester Railroad west of the Great Pee Dee River as may be selected." The site they chose was located near the Mars Bluff community ten miles from the small town of Darlington. As president of the company that constructed the Wilmington and Manchester line, Gen. William Wallace Harllee enjoyed the distinction of naming the new intersection. He proposed that it be christened in honor of his young daughter, Florence Henning Harllee.[30]

In 1853, the Cheraw and Darlington Railroad made its first run into the area called Florence, although the town that grew up around the railroad was not incorporated until 1871, and Florence County was not created until 1888. As a result of these inauspicious origins, Florence was a planned community specifically designed to service the needs of railroad passengers and personnel; thus, a machine shop, a hotel, and several mercantile stores grew up around the train depot. On the eve of secession, six hundred people called Florence home.[31]

General Jones selected the crossroads as the location of a new prison for several reasons. First, the Pee Dee area of South Carolina had been relatively insulated from the war even as late as 1864. Moreover, because Florence was far enough removed from major towns and thoroughfares, Sherman posed no immediate threat. The proposed prison was not situated near an urban area, so prisoners could not endanger many local residents. For that matter, nearby inhabitants who might harbor Union sympathies could not give aid and comfort to the inmates without attracting undue attention. The intersection of three railroad lines also made it comparatively easy and convenient to transfer prisoners to the new camp.[32]

As the first order of business, General Jones instructed a young lawyer turned military officer from Darlington, Maj. Frederick F. Warley, to begin constructing the new stockade. Coupled with his selection of Florence as the prison site, Jones made an excellent choice in tapping Warley for this taxing assignment. Although he was still only in his early thirties, Warley was a prominent member of the community. (Florence still features a street named after this long-dead military and civic leader.) Admitted to the bar in the state's lower courts in May 1852, when he was only twenty-two years old, Warley practiced law in the area until his sudden death at the age of forty-six. On June 28, 1859, as secessionist fever infected the area, he took a slight detour from his legal career by establishing a military company, the "Darlington Guards," and assuming the rank of captain.[33]

In January 1861, with a roster of one hundred enlisted men and fourteen officers, the company traveled to Charleston on orders from South Carolina Gov. Francis Pickens. The unit arrived just as Citadel cadets fired on the *Star of the West*, the civilian ship that President James Buchanan sent to relieve Federal soldiers garrisoned at Fort Sumter in Charleston Harbor. The Guards stayed until the Union commander, Maj. Robert Anderson, surrendered to the newly created Confederate States Army in April. Afterward, the war in the eastern theater moved to Virginia and began in earnest as the Lincoln administration assembled an army to oppose secession. Rather than travel north to fight, Captain Warley stayed in South Carolina and disbanded the unit. Men who had served under him in the Guards joined other units—especially the newly created Pee Dee Rifles and the Pee Dee Light Artillery—and fought for the Southern Confederacy in the ensuing four years. They struggled and died in places that later became famous in the annals of American military history: Sharpsburg (Antietam), Fredericksburg, Chancellorsville, Gettysburg, and Spotsylvania, among others.[34]

Warley began his post-Guards service to the Confederacy by commanding an artillery unit at Battery Wagner near Charleston. As a result of his actions there, he was promoted to the rank of major. Later, after being severely wounded, he was placed into a boat to be carried ashore for medical treatment. Unfortunately for the major, the boat was captured and he was sent to the Union prison camp at Fort Delaware, despite the severity of his wounds. Warley had only recently been exchanged when he received the order from General Jones. His wounds were debilitating, and he did not feel up to the strain of constructing a stockade for the overflow of prisoners; nonetheless, his orders were clear and unequivocal. On the same day that General Jones wrote to Secretary Seddon, Warley's men began cutting pine trees and constructing the new prison.[35]

The construction plan was conceptually simple, as it had to be. Time was short and money was limited. Laborers pulled down pine trees and cut them into long, cylindrical poles to serve as walls. Afterward, they dug a ditch five feet deep and seven feet wide around the site. This effort provided additional security because the ditch could not be crossed without considerable difficulty.

This drawing of the Florence Stockade, first published in 1890, shows the prison interior as well as Confederate quarters outside the walls. Reprinted from *Prisoners of War and Military Prisons* by Asa B. Isham, Henry M. Davidson, and Henry B. Furness.

After excavating the hole, the laborers established a perimeter a short distance away, marking the spot where the interior walls would be built. As they placed logs on the inside perimeter, they also packed dirt from the ditch against the logs to allow guards to walk along the edge of the stockade and thereby patrol all parts of the prison.[36]

Despite the urgency of building a new stockade, Major Warley did not possess adequate resources to complete his assignment in the allotted time. On September 17, only five days after he began constructing the new camp, the first prisoners arrived by train. Secretary Seddon had received General Jones's correspondence and acted on it immediately by ordering sixty-five hundred captives shipped to Florence. Because the stockade walls were not yet completed, the first prisoners were taken from the train and marched into an open cornfield. Old men and teenage boys sporting only double shotguns and squirrel rifles guarded them until the prisoners could be herded into the partially completed enclosure.[37]

Demonstrating admirable ingenuity, the major scrambled to complete the prison by visiting local plantations and impressing about a thousand slaves to join his men in laboring on the stockade walls. Despite his resourcefulness, Warley received disturbing reports that the prisoners held in the cornfield were milling about in a state of near mutiny. Moreover, General Jones sent a telegram to the major informing him that fifteen hundred additional prisoners would arrive in Florence shortly and, even worse, the guards accompanying them would have to leave immediately. In his weakened condition, Warley almost collapsed from the weight of this heavy burden.[38]

Desperate to resolve the increasingly volatile situation, Warley replied to General Jones that an adequate force of guards must be dispatched to Florence or the prisoners could not be held.[39] General Jones promised to send a company of regular troops and two pieces of artillery to Florence, but Warley knew he could not wait for outside men and matériel to alleviate his situation. Once again demonstrating a commendable ability to improvise, he commandeered three locomotives and sent them along with several recruitment officers to the nearby towns of Sumter, Marion, and Darlington to round up guards for the camp. The recruitment officers corralled approximately a hundred soldiers and residents to serve as sentries—some willing volunteers, others reluctant draftees—and the immediate crisis subsided. Also, on the same day that he asked General Jones for additional assistance, Warley transferred most of the prisoners from the cornfield into the partially completed stockade as the slaves and his men worked to finish walling in the enclosure.[40]

When construction was completed toward the end of September, the camp was approximately 1,400 feet long and 725 feet wide, making it a 23 ½-acre rectangular, open field bounded by upright logs driven into the earth. The Confederates later expanded the enclosure to 27 acres. During the initial construction, they hammered pine logs approximately 20 feet long into the ground at a uniform level. Subsequent accounts listed the height variously at 12, 15, and 16 feet, although the latter seems to be the most often cited measurement. A cannon was mounted on a platform at each corner in case the prisoners rioted. As in other prisons, North and South, a " deadline," or no-man's-land, extended 10 to 12 feet inside the stockade, and guards were authorized to shoot any prisoners who crossed the line for any reason. A creek comprising part of the Four-Mile Branch (sometimes referred to as the Pie, or Pye, Branch Creek), flanked by a swamp, snaked through the site.

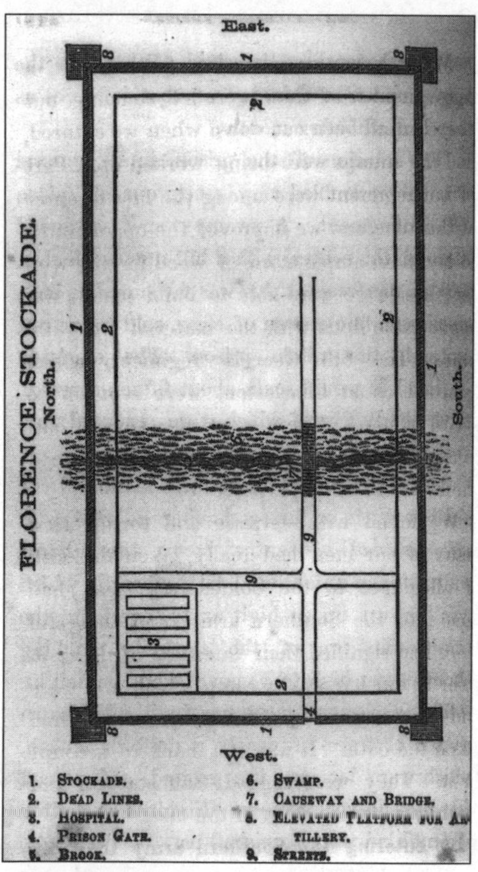

The layout of the Florence Stockade was eerily reminiscent of Andersonville. Reprinted from *Life and Death in Rebel Prisons* by Robert H. Kellogg.

The main gate was built into the west wall and opened to reveal an interior road. The road ran the length of the prison from west to east and crossed over another road that ran from north to south. The main road passed over the creek and the swamp before dead-ending at the eastern wall. The stockade hospital, consisting of five huts covered with pine bough roofs, was located in the northwest corner of the camp. Prisoners squatted on both sides of the swamp and fashioned their own shelter, as best they could, from blankets, shirts, and other garments.[41]

As Major Warley completed construction on the new stockade, his troubles were far from over. Aside from the obvious lack of resources, the confusing

Confederate chain of command proved particularly difficult to overcome. Gen. William M. Gardner was responsible for prisons east of the Mississippi River, but he was not informed that prisoners had been sent from the Andersonville Stockade to Florence until October, almost a full month after the first trainload arrived. In the meantime, Gen. William Joseph Hardee, who replaced General Jones as commander of the Military Department of South Carolina, Georgia, and Florida in the weeks following the fall of Atlanta, exacerbated matters by undercutting General Gardner's authority. Nicknamed "Old Reliable" because of his indefatigable attention to duty and his rigid demeanor, General Hardee was convinced that he exercised authority over the Florence prison by virtue of his position, despite General Gardner's command over prisons in the eastern theater. In October, when both Gardner and Hardee ordered their subordinates to inspect the Florence prison, Hardee countermanded Gardner's order by instructing camp administrators to disregard any instructions they received from Gardner.[42]

On October 10, after he learned of the existence of the Florence prison and the refusal to obey his orders, General Gardner wrote to General Cooper, adjutant and inspector general of Confederate forces. In his correspondence, Gardner asked to "be relieved from the duties devolved upon me by Special Orders, No. 175." Citing prior war injuries, which required him to "resume my crutches," the general also hinted at problems in the military chain of command. "Movements are made without my knowledge," he reported. "I am not and have not been able to impart information on condition of prisoners if called upon by the Government. I learned by paper referred to me by the Secretary of War two days ago that there were a large number of prisoners at Florence, S.C. I had

Gen. William M. Gardner was responsible for overseeing Confederate prisons in September 1864, but he did not learn of the existence of the Florence Stockade for almost a month. Courtesy of the Museum of the Confederacy.

Gen. William J. Hardee engaged in a dispute with General Gardner regarding the Confederate chain of command and who most appropriately should exercise control over the administration of the Florence Stockade. Courtesy of the Museum of the Confederacy.

received no previous intimation that prisoners had been sent there." Gardner made a similar comment in correspondence he sent two days later to South Carolina Gov. Milledge L. Bonham explaining why a prison camp had been built in Columbia. "As to the prison at Florence," he concluded, "I know nothing of it. The prisoners are sent there without my knowledge and have never been reported to me."[43]

As this bureaucratic squabble between generals intensified, Major Warley decided he had endured all he could stand in fulfilling his unpleasant, wearying task. He could argue, like General Gardner, that festering war wounds prevented him from rendering further competent service. Even before completing construction on the stockade, he asked to be relieved of his command, and his request was honored. Although it wasn't until October 10 that Lt. Col. John F. Iverson of the Fifth Georgia Volunteer Infantry Regiment assumed command of the prison interior, the major stepped aside in mid-September. In the meantime, Col. George P. Harrison Jr. of the Thirty-second Georgia Volunteer Infantry Regiment arrived on the scene and became the highest ranking officer at the Florence Stockade beginning on September 20. Owing to the structure of the Confederate chain of command, Harrison did not exercise official responsibility for the administrative duties of overseeing the camp interior. That duty fell to Lieutenant Colonel Iverson in October.[44]

Colonel Harrison's arrival in Florence coincided with the apex of the political infighting between General Gardner and General Hardee. As the latest commissioned officer to arrive at the prison, the colonel wisely stood aside while the jurisdictional dispute continued. In yet another apparent maneuver to undermine Gardner's position, Hardee sent Insp. Gen. W. D. Pickett to observe conditions inside the stockade. Pickett reported on October 12 that

12,362 prisoners were incarcerated there, including 860 men in the hospital and 20 men out on parole. An additional 807 Union soldiers had sworn an oath of allegiance to the Confederacy and enlisted in the Confederate army.[45]

Col. (later General) George P. Harrison Jr. briefly served as the highest-ranking officer at the Florence Stockade. Courtesy of the Museum of the Confederacy. Copy photography by Katherine Wetzel.

Pickett was blunt in his assessment of the abominable conditions in the stockade. "The condition of these prisoners has not been much misrepresented," he observed. "The great majority of them look emaciated and sickly and are full of vermin, and filthy in the extreme. Three-fourths of them are without blankets and almost without clothing. Few have a change of underclothing. As a consequence, there is a great deal of suffering these cool nights and much additional sickness must follow. Most of them have erected temporary shelters, which will protect them to some extent from rain and dew until better shelters can be constructed. The principal diseases are scurvy and diarrhea, which carry off from twenty to fifty per day. The present sick-list is 785. The hospitals are made of the boughs of trees, are of temporary character, and will afford very little protection from rain. There has been very great want of medical attention; there is only one medical officer assigned them, whereas I am told ten are required for that number of men."[46]

Pickett recommended that "Federal authorities should be informed of the condition of their men" so they could provide much-needed supplies. He noted, too, that five thousand suits were housed in Charleston for the prisoners, but they had not yet received them. Nine additional surgeons were needed to provide the necessary medical attention. Additional cooking utensils and permanent shelters also would greatly improve matters. To that end, Pickett reported that "I have instructed Colonel Harrison to construct shelters out of clapboards."[47]

Three days later, on October 15, General Hardee responded by reporting that "additional surgeons are now at Florence," although he did not specify the number. He also promised that "everything in my power will be done to alleviate the condition of Yankees in my possession," although, again, he did not elaborate on specific plans. Hardee also did not refer to General Gardner's responsibility for administering the camp.[48]

Even as Hardee received Pickett's report, Gardner sent Capt. John H. Rutherford, assistant adjutant general, to inspect the prison. Rather than be drawn into the dispute between Gardner and Hardee, Colonel Harrison allowed Rutherford to inspect the stockade without interference. In a report dated November 5, 1864, Rutherford found many of the same conditions existing at Florence that Pickett mentioned in his report. "Prisoners have as shelter only such as they may have constructed for themselves," he wrote. In addition, "small huts, built partly of wood and dirt, of every variety and form, some over holes in the ground, with little dirt chimneys—some comfortable, and others very uncomfortable—constituted the interior of the prison. The prison hospital, improperly so-called, is situated inside of the stockade, and is simply separated from the rest of the prison by a pole fence. It would require a close examination to discover any more comfort in the hospital than in regular prison, the only shelter being such rude huts as have already been described."[49]

Although the reports drafted by Pickett and Rutherford differed in their details, they both noted the terrible conditions prevalent at Florence. As the Confederacy struggled to exist despite repeated failures on the battlefield and economic reversals at home, the leadership simply did not possess adequate resources to house and feed Union prisoners. In the words of Prof. G. Wayne King of Francis Marion University, "The result was that the prisoners were over-inspected and under-nourished." The numbers tell the story graphically. In October 1864, 12,362 prisoners populated the stockade. By November, the number had fallen to 11,424, and in January 1865 it had slipped to 7,538. While some of these decreases were due to special exchanges of sick and wounded prisoners, many were the result of deaths among the prison population.[50]

This new stockade was no better than its predecessor at Andersonville, but the arriving prisoners did not know what to expect as their train slipped through the South Carolina woods during that last autumn of the Southern Confederacy. It was a pitch-black night and rain pelted Warren Lee Goss and his comrades as they arrived in Florence. Without delay, they were ushered from the boxcars and marched into an open cornfield. Water and mud permeated the grounds; the prisoners scarcely found a suitable place to sleep. They collapsed in the mud and pulled their ragged coats and gum blankets over their heads to keep out the floodwaters. Inmates sneezed and coughed as they struggled to outlast the torrential downpour. It was an ugly, desperate test of endurance for men who were almost at the limits of endurance. The prisoners were saved only when the tempest gradually tapered off during the early hours of the next day.[51]

In the morning, the men were roused from an uneasy sleep and herded a third of a mile to the gates of the Florence prison pen. Like the men who preceded him, Goss was dismayed at the sight. "At last a 'stockade' similar to that of Andersonville loomed up before us," he wrote. "The prison, like that of Andersonville, was situated on two hill-sides, with a branch of muddy water running through the centre, embracing, in all, about twenty acres." Virtually every man who entered those walls as a prisoner shared Goss's sense of shock and despair upon realizing that the horrors of confinement had not yet ended. Prisoner Morgan Dowling described Florence as an extension of other Confederate prisons. "Here the old scenes of Belle Isle and Andersonville were reenacted, starvation, sickness, disease and suffering upon every side." John Harrold echoed the sentiments of his comrades. "Many of us hoped that our stay at Florence would be short, and consoled ourselves with the belief that our journey to that place was but preliminary to a speedy exchange; but time served to banish this delusion. It would be a difficult task to picture the despair which now overwhelmed me." Another inmate, Albert C. Leonard, agreed. "The wise Solomon has said that, 'Hope deterred maketh the heart sick,' and there was never a truer utterance, as was proven on this occasion, for despair taking the place of expectation turned our joy to sorrow and hundreds of deaths were the result."[52]

ELEVEN

It's Twelve O'clock and All Is Well, and Old Jeff Davis Is Gone to Hell!

Death, like the Grim Reaper of popular tales, watched over all activities in Civil War prisons, waiting, biding his time, secure in the knowledge that soon he would have company. As 1864 crept to a close and 1865 dawned, the diseases, deprivations, and misery of the prisoners only intensified. The end of the war was close at hand, but the suffering of the inmates was far from over. Many hapless souls would find release not in liberation from their prisons, but through the finality of death. In those closing days, John Wesley Minnich and Warren Lee Goss witnessed some of the worst episodes of the war.

Rock Island prisoners passed the time during their final months of incarceration in a poisoned atmosphere, forever on the lookout for ways they might extract vengeance from the black sentries who dared to look down on them from the parapet. Life behind the walls assumed a kind of monotony punctuated by periodic episodes of excitement when a fellow prisoner was shot down by the guards or punished for an infraction of the rules. The days blurred as Minnich and his comrades struggled to stay alive and healthy.[1]

As spring rolled around for the second year of his imprisonment, Minnich heard rumors of a Confederate defeat in the East. He was disheartened by the news but powerless to do anything other than grieve for the loss of his beloved Southern Confederacy. "We would have papers passed to us now and then which would tell of some great Union success," he recalled. "Richmond had at last fallen, Lee and Johnston had surrendered, Lincoln had been assassinated, and the unfortunate Wirz was in a dungeon. All these came in rapid succession. Then indeed were the dark days to come. Worse than all else, the knowledge that we were crushed to the earth at last, all power of resistance gone, and uncertain of our own ultimate fate was our bitterest potion."[2]

Like many Confederates, Minnich was worried that his captors would look upon the prisoners with contempt and exterminate them in retaliation for Lincoln's murder. Retribution was not beyond the realm of possibility. As if to confirm this fear, the guards grew restless; gunfire directed into the barracks seemed to intensify during that spring. Like everyone, Minnich wondered if the end would come early one morning—perhaps at roll call—when the inmates could be cut down in a group and disposed of with ruthless efficiency.

Inmates in the Rock Island Prison are shown here lining up for roll call. Courtesy of the Illinois State Historical Library.

He remembered one sordid event involving the same black soldier that earlier had reminded him of a brutish gorilla. "One warm day in spring toward evening a crowd had gathered at the lower end of 44 as usual to hold a confab with the inmates of the 'Calf Pen' and in many instances exchange rough 'compliments.'" These verbal duels between the loyal Confederates who remained incarcerated in the prison pen and the "galvanized Yankees" who had turned their backs on the South and sworn an oath of allegiance to the United States government were especially perilous. Sentries looked on the scene ready to shoot down any prisoners who moved to harm their former confederates by stepping over the deadline. "They were treading forbidden ground, and they knew they were making themselves liable," Minnich acknowledged.[3]

The ending, although tragic, was predictable. One young fellow, a Missourian—merely an onlooker to the developing melee—stood with his arms folded, leaning against a tree, silently observing the chaos. When the black sentry called out for the prisoners to cease their verbal assaults on the "newly made Union men" and their physical assaults on the deadline, the onlooker did not react, apparently believing that the guard's orders did not apply to him.

Minnich watched the sentry as he marched back and forth along the top of the wall like a caged wolf, occasionally stopping to bark out an order. His voice, already shrill at the outset, seemed to grow ever more hysterical. This change in pitch and tone carried an implicit threat—a warning to all rational men that would be ignored only at their own peril. Anyone watching the scene should have noticed the potential danger.

"For God's sake, boys, move back from the line," Minnich cried out in desperation. Pointing to the soldier standing on the wall, he implored them to move away and not give the guard a reason to open fire. "You know that he shot one man without any cause at all, and I tell you he is going to shoot if you don't keep away."

Minnich's warning went unheeded until the guard spun around, scattering the crowd. That swift movement should have ended the matter, but the guard, now ready to fire his rifle, would not be denied his bloodlust. He "directed his whole attention to the young Missourian, who had not moved in all the while and was still leaning against the tree, with his arms crossed on his breast and with the faintest smile on his face, as of one slightly amused by the antics of a lot of children at play." The indifference of this bystander apparently enraged the guard. "I saw him raise his gun and pull the trigger and saw the bark of the tree rise with the concussion of the shock of the impact of the murderer's bullet," Minnich later recalled. "The poor fellow fell in a heap at the foot of the tree—dead, bored through the throat. Another home in which some one would vainly await the coming of a son, a brother, and mayhap a sweetheart."[4]

Minnich was outraged at this needless bloodletting. "Wanton shooting of prisoners and the unspeakable treachery of guards form about as black a chapter of crime as any ever recorded," he wrote. He could have understood the guard firing into the mass of men milling about near the deadline, but the young fellow leaning against the tree was an innocent spectator. "It was nothing more, nothing less than a cold-blooded murder, as were those which preceded it."[5]

Considering this cold, calculating act as the "last straw," the witnesses congregated, and an "indignation meeting was held." They resolved to approach Lt. Col. Andrew P. Caraher, provost marshal of the prison, and demand that he do something about the guard. Like Colonel Johnson, Caraher was a Union officer who came to Rock Island because his seemingly limitless future had been thwarted by the cruel hand of fate. He had started his military career as a captain in the Twenty-eighth Massachusetts—the so-called "Irish Brigade"—and he seemed bound for high rank. After winning a promotion to major, Caraher's ascent was cut short when shrapnel slammed into his head during the battle of Fredericksburg in December 1862. His survival was a miracle; Civil War medical practices were anything but effective and sanitary. A wound to any part of the body other than a limb—which could be hacked off in fairly short order—often resulted in death. Caraher was one of the lucky men to walk away from a head injury, although he suffered from perpetual dizziness and severely diminished vision as a result. Thereafter, the trajectory of a once-promising career could no longer be characterized as meteoric. Recognizing that his options were limited, Caraher accepted an assignment in the Veteran Reserve Corps and held several positions before he was transferred to the Rock Island Barracks in February 1864.[6]

Accounts of Caraher's conduct at the camp vary considerably. Because he was in charge of camp discipline and determining which soldiers should patrol the walls, many inmates viewed him as little better than the prison commandant. On this day, however, he proved to be receptive to the prisoners' complaints. Approached by twenty or so incensed men, he listened to their account "with a grave face" before responding.

"Colonel," the group spokesman said, "we have come to the limit of endurance. We are being shot like dogs at all hours of day and night, when we walk on the streets and when we are asleep in our bunks. And now here is another man murdered in broad daylight without the least show of excuse." Referring to past incidents involving the same guard, the spokesman continued his diatribe. "This nigger has killed two men without a shadow of reason, and now listen: This nigger must go out of this prison, *and stay out*." They were strong words coming from men held in captivity. "If ever he comes back into this prison, *we'll hang him*, understand that. And you have not got men enough outside to prevent it. If it comes to the point of being murdered like dogs, then you'll have to kill us all."

The group waited to see how Caraher would respond to this angry demand. After a moment, he agreed with the prisoners. "Well, men, you are right," he said. "I'll see that this man is taken out, and I promise you that he will not come in here again."

True to his word, Caraher transferred the offending guard to another station, and he was not seen again. The men were jubilant, for his absence promised a marginally brighter outlook in coming days. "The nigger was immediately relieved, and I never saw him again," Minnich wrote. "Also, I noticed and recall that there was much less shooting after that."[7]

The rogue guard's propensity to shoot prisoners probably was not triggered by Lincoln's assassination—or other external events, for that matter. Whatever motivated the man to act as capriciously as Minnich claimed was likely of a more local origin. After his removal, the prisoners settled down to wait for their release, transfer to another facility, or some other alternative that fate or their jailers chose to send their way.

The road leading to the Rock Island Prison was desolate. Courtesy of the Rock Island Arsenal Museum.

Outside the main gate of the prison, visible to men who ventured beyond the stockade on work detail, an empty, desolate road stretched as far as the eye could see toward some unknown horizon. It led away from the Rock Island Prison, away from the shootings and beatings and deprivations and indignities, away from the pressures and horrors of captivity—that much was certain—but what lay beyond the road was a matter of conjecture. With the Southern Confederacy brought to her knees, prostrate and violated, Minnich and his comrades knew only that the future seemed barren and bleak.[8]

Warren Lee Goss's future in the Florence Stockade as the war wound to a close also appeared bleak. From beginning to end, his experience in that most hellish of Confederate prisons was indelibly stamped on his psyche. He especially remembered the opening scene—his introduction to life in the South Carolina prison—when he witnessed the desperate plight of an old man who complained bitterly during the miserable train ride from Charleston to Florence.[9]

That first night after they arrived in the midst of a colossal rainstorm and lay down in a field to rest, the old fellow had shared a blanket with his son. Someone said the boy's name was Willard Robinson. In the morning, the elder Robinson found his son's body, waterlogged and stiff. Grief-stricken, the old man lay on the soggy ground beside his son and wept. Sickened by the sight, several prisoners approached a Rebel guard and asked for permission to bury Willard's body. The guard told them to fall back into the ranks. The prisoners asked if the boy's father might witness his son's burial, but this request, too, was denied. With no alternative, the father placed a handkerchief over young Willard's face, folded the corpse's hands, and turned to leave. He could not watch as the Confederates lifted his son's body and threw it up on the mule wagon for disposal.[10]

After witnessing this heartbreaking incident, the captives stumbled into the nearby stockade. It reminded them, eerily, of Andersonville. Sentries patrolled the walls, announcing the time with an irreverent rhetorical flourish that the inmates found as humorous as conditions would allow. "It's twelve o'clock and all is well, and old Jeff Davis is gone to hell!"[11]

Goss and four hastily acquired comrades set out to find a place to squat.

Inmates were marched into the Florence Stockade and counted off as they crossed a creek that ran through the interior of the prison. Courtesy of the Library of Congress.

The stockade was filled to capacity and beyond, but eventually, after much searching, they found a suitable site. Without fanfare, they fell to the earth and carved a hole three feet deep into the sloping hillside and drove three sticks into the ground. Stretching an army blanket over the sticks, they fashioned a makeshift tent to protect themselves from the elements. "In this grave-like place four human beings lodged, kept their 'traps,' and called it their home."[12]

During his months of captivity, Goss had suffered much as he passed through the most notorious prisons of the Confederacy. He was determined not to succumb to despair with the end possibly around the corner; consequently, he always sought to improve his conditions and maintain his health so that one day he might walk free and easy from the walls that surrounded him. To this end, he ventured forward a week or two after arriving at Florence and asked the camp authorities for permission to leave the stockade and search for materials to reinforce his tent. The jailers assented. After foraging through the nearby forestland under guard, he dragged as much of an untrimmed pine brush as he could pull into the stockade. He and his roommates stripped off the pine branches and placed them in the bottom of their shelter as a makeshift carpet. They also patched up the rear of their shebang with tree limbs. It was a far cry from comfortable quarters, but the new arrangement afforded them one of the better tents inside the stockade. As in the past, Goss used his powerful intellect and driving will to good effect.[13]

During his weeks at Florence, he avoided scurvy, the scourge of many a man, by rinsing his mouth with hardwood ashes and water. He wore no shoes, so the cold, frozen ground proved especially treacherous. To prevent frostbite, Goss often meandered through the camp at night. If he constantly moved his feet and toes, he believed he could save them from the cold winter months in the Florence prison. Exhausted from his night's work and the "sharp winds which mercilessly sought out every hole in my scanty wardrobe," he slept during the day.[14]

Bartering became a way of life, just as it had been in other prisons. It assumed a special urgency at Florence, for a man with no shoes could hardly wade through the swampy marshland to retrieve water from the creek and not have his feet freeze. Of course, he could hire a fellow to assist him in this all-important endeavor for a "chaw of tobacco." A man also might trade an article of clothing for a cooking utensil or vice versa. A morsel of food, a bit of thread, the remnants of a stump—all became valuable commodities in the radically altered world of prison life.[15]

Desperately short of rations, even by Andersonville standards, inmates

This drawing of the Florence Stockade, sketched by Union cartographer Robert Knox Sneden in December 1864, seemed lost to history until the Virginia Historical Society purchased a group of Sneden's watercolors in 1994. Courtesy of the Virginia Historical Society.

found other sources of nourishment. Rats became a constant companion. The animals could be both a blessing and a curse. Sometimes they were hunted, and sometimes they were the hunters. If they were captured, they provided a feast for numerous men starved for sustenance. If they eluded capture, they returned in the night to invade the shebangs and steal food, no matter how carefully concealed. On cold winter evenings, when the ground was hard and the air was chilly, they were known to burrow into tents to be near the warmth of bodies. If they stumbled upon an inmate with gangrenous limbs, they ripped at his flesh with a fervor that was remarkable to behold. Many a prisoner screamed out in the night because he had been scratched or bitten by rats. He might fend off one or two vermin, but a gang of rodents proved too powerful to combat. A man sick with a fever or rendered immobile by his wounds must take care to be guarded by his companions. If he were alone, even for a moment, he might be found in the morning with his flesh ripped from his carcass, his face forever frozen into a grotesque mask of horror.[16]

A prisoner named Drury once happened upon another prisoner, Jess, who was hunting rats in the daylight. "Now feller," Drury said, "you seem to be at them about all your time."

Jess considered the remark for a moment as he scratched his back. "Yes. It's a pooty even thing; me and these fellers take turns."

"How so?"

"I torment them all day, and they torment me all night!"

"In that remark, oh Jess, was condensed more vigorous truth than poetical license," Drury said before he wandered away. The men of Florence realized that a thin line separated the victors and the vanquished in their quest for survival.[17]

To improve the odds of surviving, the prisoners revived the police force and "Big Peter" Aubrey, the big, hulking prisoner who served as the chief at Andersonville, again assumed the helm. His duties as the self-proclaimed "chief of police" meant that he would help the men fend off rats in the night, if possible. He also provided the men with adequate shelter from the elements. Lawless mobs of ratlike men such as the Raiders at Andersonville were absent from Florence thanks in large part to Big Peter. The police force also oversaw the removal of dead bodies, a constant chore in any Civil War military prison. An inmate who could not care for himself could call on Big Peter's guards to provide a helping hand in exchange for future consideration. The police force's devotion to law and order and its ability to clean up filth in the stockade made Big Peter a valuable asset to the men.[18]

Unfortunately, an organization is only as good as its leaders. "'Big Pete,' becoming prostrated with a fever, a gigantic, ignorant brute, with neither good sense, good humor, nor the disposition to deal justly, which were characteristic of Peter, took his place as 'chief of police,' and under his misrule cowardly acts were perpetrated upon prisoners," Goss recalled. In a short time, the police force degenerated from savior to villain, becoming "a tool of the rebels for detecting the work on the tunnels." If the officers believed that an inmate had failed to follow the rules as the police dictated them, the chief instructed his men to administer punishments, generally by tying the offender to a whipping post and lashing him on the back with a whip known as a cat-o'-nine-tails. Prisoner M. V. B. Phillips remembered that the police administered whippings based on rumor and innuendo. "But little evidence of the guilt of parties was required," Phillips observed.[19]

The police chief was cruel and unforgiving. One day he spied Sergeant English, who had pressed charges against the chief at Andersonville. Anxious to exact vengeance, the "big brute," in Goss's words, concocted a trivial charge against the sergeant and instructed his men to bind the offender to the whipping post. Without trial or further inquiry, the "officers" grabbed the man, tied his wrists behind his back, and presented him to their boss. The chief did not offer even a pretense of expostulation; instead, he repeatedly pounded the sergeant in the face with his fists. Only the intervention of Lieutenant Barrett, the Rebel officer in charge of stockade discipline, saved Sergeant English from an even worse punishment. Not generally a man to interfere when torture was in the offing, the lieutenant insisted that Sergeant English must be tried before he was punished.[20]

Lieutenant Barrett, a sadistic guard in charge of the interior of the Florence Stockade, fired his pistol into a crowd of prisoners on at least one occasion. Courtesy of the Library of Congress.

Despite this singular episode of fair treatment, Barrett was the most universally hated and excoriated figure associated with the Florence Stockade. The word "wretch" often was used in discussing his behavior. Prisoner Robert Kellogg remembered that "the overseer of the prison was Lieutenant Barrett, of the Fifth Georgia Regiment, and anyone who was ever in that stockade, will always remember him. It seemed that a greater wretch never lived." John Urban characterized him as "one of the most cowardly and brutal wretches who ever lived." He recalled that "this Lieutenant Barrett frequently came into prison and fired a pistol over the heads of the prisoners, to see them dodge around to get away, and their fright appeared to give him intense delight." Sam Boggs recalled that "Barrett was the most brutal fool I ever met." John McElroy observed that "I never met a man who seemed to love cruelty for its own sake as well as Lieutenant Barrett." Even considering McElroy's penchant for hyperbole and his practice of condemning virtually every Rebel he encountered as the "worst ever," his description of Barrett's barbarity was noteworthy. Charles Fosdick wrote, "Old Satan himself was

Interior Commandant. He came to us in human form, but had none of the good qualities of the race. He was a very wry-faced man, with fiery red hair, and a more inhuman wretch it was never my misfortune to meet. This was Lieutenant Barrett. All who were in the different prisons of the South will agree with me that Barrett was the most cruel man we ever came in contact with." "Woe betide the luckless wretch who got into his pathway," James Newton Miller wrote. "Wirz was mad most of the time, but Barrett was always mad." Inmate John W. Northrop fancied himself a poet, penning a long, vituperative ode to the man he called the "scum of Georgia." A few verses captured his hatred:

> Barrett, keeper of this prison pen,
> Parades these starved, near naked men
> Before women invited as his guests;
> Curses and fires in their ranks,
> Bestows on them insults and pests,
> Venomously shows his apish pranks,
> All for torment, naught to please;
> Adds insults to their miseries.[21]

Goss echoed virtually every other inmate at Florence in his hatred for this sadistic Confederate. Although he had kind words to say for the camp commandant, Lieutenant Colonel Iverson, he found Barrett to be the embodiment of everything base and cruel in human nature. "He was a rough, green, conceited brute, who never spoke without blasphemy, and never gave a civil word, or did a kind deed for any prisoner—a man with as few of the elements of good in his nature as I ever knew." Goss could not understand how Iverson allowed a brute such as Barrett to remain on duty. The only explanation was a remark that the commandant once muttered under his breath. "Barrett is just rough enough to scare the Yankees, and make them stand round."[22]

Barrett's administration of the stockade interior ensured that the prisoners would not merely "stand round"; instead, they avoided him at all costs. Survival in the Florence Stockade thus became a game of eluding Rebel guards, the prison police force, and the ravages of rats and disease, not always in that order. In this way, the time passed monotonously, one day fading into another without much to distinguish it from its predecessor except perhaps for weather conditions. The one exception occurred early in November, when the Confederates announced their intention to stage a mock presidential election.[23]

As rumors circulated that the Confederacy might be near collapse, camp administrators searched for a means of improving morale. Goss and his fellow prisoners were suspicious when the guards offered to hold a mock presidential contest on election day, Tuesday, November 8, 1864. They rightly surmised that the Rebels hoped to show the prisoners' support for the Democratic nominee, George B. McClellan, the former Union general who had been much beloved by his men. McClellan, the "peace" candidate, promised a negotiated end to the conflict, which probably would include recognition of the Confederate States of America as a separate, sovereign nation. This perspective was in direct opposition to President Lincoln's policy, which vowed to prosecute the war until the bitter end. Seldom has an American election presented such distinct choices. The Confederates hoped that if McClellan won the straw poll in the camp, the results would demonstrate that even Union soldiers recognized the cruel and morally suspect position endorsed by the Lincoln administration. This recognition might bolster Southerners' spirits at a time when the Confederacy seemed especially imperiled.[24]

Voting commenced by allowing prisoners to place beans into two separate bags—appropriately enough, white beans for McClellan, black ones (although some prisoners remembered them as red) for Lincoln. It was not surprising that the election results were hotly contested inside the stockade. Camp guards and toughs from a New York regiment sought to intimidate the prisoners into voting for McClellan. Some prisoners recalled that promises of food and creature comforts were tools used to rig the outcome of the election. Almost fifty years later, a former Confederate guard, Walter D. Woods, recalled that Lincoln received only two thousand votes, while McClellan garnered support from the remaining ten thousand inmates.[25]

Prisoners' accounts recall an opposite result. Simon Dufur was not certain of the numbers, but he clearly remembered that "a large majority had voted for Abraham Lincoln." Amos Stearns concluded that although not every prisoner participated, Lincoln received about 1,200 votes to about 600 for McClellan. William C. Keys, an inmate from the Seventy-seventh Pennsylvania Infantry Regiment, wrote that the "voting commenced and continued 'till old Abe's bean bag contained nearly a quart while that of his opponent could boast but a meager handful. Then the McClellan men broke up the election and left in disgust." Eugene Forbes of Company B, Fourth Regiment, New Jersey Volunteers, reported that in his thousand men, McClellan received 100 votes and Lincoln received 900. Another prisoner, John Hoster, believed that Lincoln won by 641 votes out of 1,900 polled. Ezra Hoyt Ripple concluded that Lincoln received thousands of beans to only a few hundred for McClellan. He believed that McClellan might have received more votes if the election had been held at home, but the prisoners were loath to provide aid and comfort to the enemy. Goss remembered "the result of the ballot was about fifteen hundred for McClellan and six thousand for Lincoln."[26]

Aside from the momentary distraction of the election, November and December were hard months for Goss. Worn down and sickly, he felt almost as wretched as he had during his period of delirium when he first entered the Belle Isle Prison in 1862. He was worried that he might succumb to illness if his circumstances did not improve. Fortunately, he possessed a skill that would provide him with special privileges, thus greatly enhancing his chances for survival. He could write. This led to an offer of employment that did as much as anything to save his life.[27]

The offer came at exactly the right time. December was a cold, gloomy month. Chilly winds cut through the men during long, bitter nights. The ground was white with frost, and insanity had infected much of the population. Goss walked the prison, teeth chattering, and prayed for solace in his hour of need. He looked back on December as one of the worst months of his life. To the end of his days, he regarded it as a time when he was at his lowest point, a walking husk that might have welcomed a speedy, painless death. He thanked God with a full heart for deliverance from the chill of December 1864.[28]

A Rebel adjutant came into the camp one day looking for clerks to register new prisoners when they entered the stockade, and record the names of unfortunates who died there. Goss wrote his name and detachment on a slip of paper and handed it to the guard. Later, an orderly came looking for him. Goss could be useful to the Confederate colonel, the guard told him. They walked over to the commandant's quarters, which seemed comfortable, almost palatial, by the standards of the stockade. It was a log house containing a fireplace and two or three pine tables.

A youngish officer in a gray uniform greeted him. He motioned for the prisoner to sit. "My poor fellow, can you write?" Goss did not speak. Instead, he reached for a pen at one of the tables and wrote a sentence as well as his name and rank on a piece of paper.

The officer considered the writing. He shook his head. "Very good; that will do. Go into the prison and get your traps, and I will set you at work."

"I have no traps," he said.

The officer seemed surprised. "No cooking utensils?" When Goss said no, he had none, the officer shrugged. "Well, I'll feed you well out here."

By most accounts, Lt. Col. John F. Iverson was an even-handed and fair commandant of the Florence Stockade. In this drawing, he confronts a thief in the prison hospital. Courtesy of the Lackawanna Historical Society.

Goss was astonished to realize that this man was Lieutenant Colonel Iverson, the camp commandant. He knew the offer might well save his life, but he could not in good conscience accept it without conditions. "I cannot agree to do writing except for the prison."

The colonel frowned. His voice grew cold. "What difference does it make to you?"

Goss could never give aid and comfort to the enemy, but he said nothing. He would write the list of names that might aid his fellow prisoners, but he would never betray the Union cause. He would not be labeled a traitor, a turncoat, a "Copperhead."

Iverson sighed. He understood the inmate's dilemma. "Well, your Yankeeisms shall be respected," he muttered at last.[29]

With that comment, Goss began his new job as a clerk. He signed a parole of honor and came and went freely in his new position. That first night, he ate a generous supper of beef and white bread, but he was careful to limit the quantity for fear that he would fall ill. He slept in the adjutant's cabin before a fire and counted himself among the most fortunate of souls.[30]

The next morning, Adj. Sidney Cheatham of the Fifth Georgia Infantry gave Goss a shirt and pants from his own wardrobe. "I did have quite a lot of clothes when I came here," he said, "but I gave them all away to the bloody Yanks who were running around in thar—like yourself." He pointed to the stockade.[31]

Goss nodded and thanked his benefactor. He still had no shoes, but his condition was vastly improved from what it had been only days earlier. As a gesture of goodwill to his friends inside the stockade, Goss sent his former wardrobe back to them to be used for their comfort. With a full stomach and warm clothes on his back for the first time in many months, he was ready to compile the register of soldiers who had passed through the gates of the Florence Stockade.[32]

He calculated that from September through December 1864, approximately seventeen hundred Union inmates had perished in the camp. At any one time, by Goss's estimation, the stockade never held more than fifteen thousand prisoners, and frequently the number was as low as five thousand, depending on the mortality rate and the timing of new arrivals. Despite his best efforts, Goss could not identify many of the men who rested in unmarked graves. With a heavy heart, he recorded them as "unknowns" in his register. "What a burden of sorrows, disappointed hopes, and miseries were embodied in that word! Their names, their history all unknown; uncared for, they died. Some mother, wife, father, or sister mourns them, or vainly waits for their coming."[33]

From his position as a clerk, Goss saw many sad sights in the Florence Stockade. Like other Union memorialists, he noticed numerous cases of insanity among the prisoners. He recalled his horror at watching "the shivering, half-clad beings, wandering with plaintive moans and chattering teeth up and down the prison." Similarly, prisoner Sidney Williams observed, "there was a large number of men who, as the saying goes, had lost their grip, either through sickness or other causes." "The sickness, insanity, and deaths in the prison now were frightful, far exceeding the worst period of Andersonville while we were there," Ezra Hoyt Ripple mused. "The great mental strain and the extreme disappointment, together with the terrible suffering from hunger and exposure, was too much for many and the prison fever soon had many in its clutches. Few recovered from it. In the delirium of the fever, men would run wildly and blindly across the prison until utterly exhausted, they would fall down and die where they had fallen."[34]

John McElroy had seen insane men at Andersonville, but he believed they suffered from melancholia, an understandable condition under the circumstances. The long months of hardship and strain, and the disease and death that permeated the stockade, were far worse at Florence. Some men became so deranged they could not remember the names of their regiment, their officers, or their own identities. In McElroy's estimation, at least ten men were reduced to imbecility. They roamed the camp muttering words that no one could understand. Sometimes they screamed for no reason other than the ghosts in their heads. It was not uncommon for a man in such a condition to venture too close to the deadline and be shot down by watchful Confederate guards.[35]

As usual, Lieutenant Barrett delighted in tormenting those lost souls. McElroy recalled a typical sight in the Florence Stockade. The redheaded Rebel seemed to enjoy issuing orders to an insane man; his face lit up like a child celebrating an opulent Christmas. When the man would not or could not obey, Barrett struck him with a fierce blow that knocked the unfortunate prisoner to his knees. Without further provocation, the lieutenant kicked and beat the man, who curled into a fetal position on the ground to avoid the brunt of the assault. This sport was by no means unique. McElroy concluded that the officer must have derived immense satisfaction from deliberately causing the suffering of others; no other explanation readily accounted for the zeal with which Barrett practiced his craft.[36]

Many men had reached the limits of their endurance by the time they were imprisoned in the Florence Stockade. As a result, cases of insane prisoners wandering through the camp were all too common. Courtesy of the Lackawanna Historical Society.

McElroy was never the most reliable observer, but he recalled an incident that, if true, was one of the most chilling episodes that occurred in the Florence prison. He could not say whether insanity or extreme clarity of thought was responsible. The incident occurred because freezing winter nights left the emaciated, starving men exposed to the elements. It was not uncommon to find men with frostbitten fingers and toes, dragging themselves and their putrefied, gangrenous limbs across the expanse of the stockade.

McElroy claimed he was walking across the interior of the camp not long after he arrived when a solemn voice called to him. It was little more than a whisper. "S-a-y, sergeant! Won't you please take these shears and cut my toes off?" Something in the terrible pleading tone of that voice caught his attention. He stopped and turned, amazed. "What?"

Lying on the ground in front of him was an Indiana infantryman. He held up a pair of dull pruning shears. All the flesh from his toes had rotted off, leaving behind bones as clean as if they had been scraped. The tendons still held the bones in place, but they seemed to cause the man immense pain. "Just take these shears, won't you, and cut my toes off?"

"You'd better let one of the rebel doctors see this before you conclude to have them off," a shaken McElroy told the man. "Maybe they can be saved."

The infantryman was adamant. "No; damned if I'm going to have any of them rebel butchers fooling around me. I'd die first, and then I wouldn't. You can do it better than they can. It's just a little snip. Just try it."

McElroy hesitated. He shook his head. "I don't like to. I might lame you for life, and make you lots of trouble."

"Oh, bother! What business is that of yours? They're *my* toes, and I want 'em off. They hurt me so I can't sleep. Come, now, take the shears and cut 'em off."

Reluctantly, McElroy took the shears in hand and leaned over the man's toes. He had no stomach for the task, but war had taught him to face many things he never would have imagined in his earlier life. He swallowed hard. In a quick motion, he snipped tendons and bones, one after the other, until all ten toes lay in a heap at the bottom of the man's dugout. Grimacing, he picked them up and handed them to their rightful owner.

The infantryman examined them complacently. Something in his dull, glazed eyes and gaunt, tired face already appeared dead. "Well, I'm durned glad they're off," he said after a moment. "I won't be bothered with corns any more. I flatter myself."

McElroy never saw the man again. The infantryman probably died, for gangrene generally was the high ground of a precipitous slope that caused a man to slide down from his life on earth into the deep, dark hole of his final resting place in an unmarked grave. Any infirmity, no matter how slight at first, was a cause for alarm. Men who found themselves with small open cuts and sores one day awoke the next day to find them filled with pus and infected. Soon, the wound festered under the hot afternoon sun and crusted over during the cold, blustery nights. These men had no choice but to endure; they crawled into their holes and tried to find warmth, but sometimes in the night they succumbed to the cold or the rats. Their shivering bodies simply stopped working, like a pulley with a broken rope. In the morning, their thin, useless bodies—sans fingers, toes, arms, or legs—were stacked near the deadline for removal and disposal on the mule wagons that lined up in the front of the stockade walls each day.[37]

McElroy's tale may have been an embellished variation on the story of John W. January, a corporal in Company B of the Fourteenth Illinois Cavalry. Suffering from an acute case of gangrene, January took decisive action to excise the offending limbs. "Believing that my life depended on the removal of my feet, I secured an old pocket knife and cut through the decaying flesh and severed the tendons," he later explained. "The feet were unjointed, leaving the bones protruding without a covering of flesh for five inches."[38]

These were the kinds of tragic sights that Goss witnessed in the Florence Stockade as the year inched to a close. Yet, amidst all the horror and suffering, he occasionally bore witness to affecting scenes of surprising tenderness. Late one afternoon, boxes of food and clothing arrived from the U.S. Sanitary Commission for general distribution to the inmates. He was delighted to see approximately thirty thousand letters addressed to individual prisoners, and he remembered one small package in particular. Instructed to open each letter and box to ensure that no contraband items were smuggled into the camp, Goss and several other clerks tore open the packages and rifled through the contents. "The first box opened had a little pocket Bible, and on the fly leaf was written the name of the prisoner, with the words, 'from your mother.'" Iverson was on hand to see the small token of maternal affection. "As if this incident had roused some tender recollections of his own home, the Colonel turned quickly away, saying, 'Put on the cover again, and let the poor boy have his box just as his mother packed it.'"[39]

Getting the right package to the right prisoner was an administrative nightmare because it was difficult to determine which soldiers were held in which prisons. After all, the men were shipped to different camps at different times, often without warning. The task of delivering letters addressed to Florence inmates fell to Goss. He checked the names on the letters against the names in the register. When he found that the addressee was deceased, he wrote a brief note to the correspondent at Colonel Iverson's direction. It was a time-consuming, often heartbreaking task, but Goss believed he was doing noble work in sorting through the mail. He was even rewarded by receiving two letters addressed to him from family and friends. They stirred feelings of hope and longing he had not felt for many months.[40]

In his capacity as a clerk, Goss observed soldiers of the Fifth Georgia Infantry at close quarters. He found most of them, notably Iverson and Cheatham, to be kindly men who were caught up in the exigencies of war. The most glaring exception aside from the "red-headed devil" Lieutenant Barrett was General Winder, the Confederate officer in charge of prisons east of the Mississippi. The general arrived at the camp one day that December and requested a meeting with Colonel Iverson. Goss found him to be about sixty years old and dressed in homespun "Secesh" clothes such as a butternut coat and gray pants. He was a tall, hefty man, "straight in figure, with an austere face: a firm, set mouth, a large Roman nose like a parrot's beak, and a cold, stony, stern eye."[41]

From his post stationed just outside Colonel Iverson's door, Goss overheard a heated conversation between the two men that confirmed his view of their respective characters. Judging by his tone of voice, Winder obviously was furious. At one point, he shouted at his subordinate. "Colonel Iverson, I can't have all these Yankees running around outside the prison. What are they doing?" When the colonel explained that he needed the prisoners to gather wood, repair damaged structures, care for the sick, and aid in the orderly administration of the camp, Winder interrupted him. "No necessity."

Colonel Iverson respectfully dissented. "General, the prisoners, in spite of all I have done, or can do, are starving."

Winder's rejoinder was chilling. In a voice devoid of emotion, he said, simply, "let them starve, then!"[42]

"I mention this incident, as I think it furnishes the key to the general inhumanity with which the prisoners were uniformly treated in all the rebel prisons," Goss explained. "First, public sentiment [in the] South forbade to prisoners civilized usage; second, the inflexible Winder was in general command of all the Confederate prisons, and received orders direct from the chief actors in the rebellion. Winder afterwards died of disease contracted at Florence military prison, and thus poetical justice was dealt out."[43]

However much he was tempted to embellish his adventures in later years—especially about almost universally vilified figures such as General Winder—no doubt Goss saw a great deal of prison life in his position as Iverson's clerk, and most of what he wrote was factually accurate. On the question of paroles, he kept meticulous records until the end of his days at Florence. Not long after he began compiling the register, he learned that General Hardee had sent orders to make out parole rolls for the sick and wounded prisoners to be exchanged. Approximately two thousand men were to be shipped to Charleston every other day until all the sick and wounded had been removed from the stockade. Goss found it a labor of joy to hand the parole slips to the men as they limped or dragged themselves before him.[44]

"You'll have to write my name," one prisoner said in a small voice. "I'm not the man I was when you and I were captured at Plymouth."

Goss had been hunched over the table, writing in his register when he heard the familiar voice. He jerked his head up from the pages. Squinting, he considered the shattered wreck of humanity who stood before him. He recognized a sergeant from his old unit, Company G of the Second Massachusetts Heavy Artillery Regiment. The change was astonishing. The man was a wasted, walking skeleton that seemed to be standing only through sheer force of will. Goss dropped his pen and ledger and helped the man to a nearby log hut. While the sergeant was lying down, Goss brought him food and drink.

"Do you think we're going home?" the man asked repeatedly through a cascade of tears. Goss was so touched he could not speak. He finally shook his head in response to the question. Yes, the men were going home. This time it was not a trick; he had it on good authority that the sick and wounded inmates would soon be on their way.

He had to return to his duties, so Goss left the man lying on his bunk. Later, when he returned, the fellow was gone. Many years after the war, Goss tried to learn what had become of his friend. The records were woefully incomplete—certainly missing, perhaps destroyed—and no one living could recall. In light of the sergeant's weakened condition that day, Goss thought he probably died during the trip to Charleston.[45]

Parole was a delicate subject in the camp because not everyone could leave. Goss asked several times that he be allowed to enter his own name on the list of parolees. In each instance the Rebels told him to be content with his position or they would send him back inside the stockade. He knew he risked incurring the wrath of his jailers, yet he could not help but entertain thoughts of release. After all he had been through during his two episodes of incarceration, to be so close to securing his parole and yet so far removed was torture of a most heinous and offensive kind.[46]

It was a long time coming, but Goss finally gained his freedom shortly before the new year began. After many delays, another order arrived from

General Hardee requiring fifteen hundred prisoners to be ready for transportation the following afternoon. To prepare their parole, Goss wrote the appropriate names, rank, and regiment numbers on the rolls. Each roll contained approximately three hundred names. In accordance with instructions, he entered the names in triplicate. On one roll, he wrote his own name.[47]

The procedure for paroling men was simple. A camp officer took the rolls and walked into the stockade where the men had congregated. As he called their names, the lucky prisoners shuffled forward and stood in line, if they could walk. Afterward, the line was marched outside the main gate to the railroad depot. There the men were loaded into boxcars for their journey.[48]

The crucial moment arrived the next afternoon when Goss heard his name called. He dropped his pen and stepped forward, desperately trying to blend into the line as unobtrusively as possible. Holding his breath, he waited to see if he could slip through the gates without complication.

"Here, here!" Colonel Iverson and Adjutant Cheatham exclaimed in unison. "What does this mean?"

Goss feigned surprise. "I thought you told me that I could go home with this squad, adjutant."

Cheatham laughed at Goss's audacity; even Colonel Iverson appeared amused by the attempted trickery. To Goss's enormous relief, the colonel seemed to consider the request. "Well, you can go, but you must confess that

Many prisoners, including Warren Lee Goss, were held temporarily in the Charleston jail yard while they waited to return home. Reprinted from *The Capture, the Prison Pen, and the Escape* by Willard W. Glazier.

it is a damned Yankee trick," he said at last. With that parting comment, the commandant turned and abruptly disappeared. Goss never saw him again.

As the men marched from the stockade, Cheatham fell beside Goss in the line.

"I'm glad for you. I intended you to go soon." He paused. "I expect next you will be telling the Yankees what a damned rascal Adjutant Cheatham was."[49]

Goss said nothing, but he thought about the adjutant's comment as the men were loaded into boxcars. It echoed through his mind as Charleston loomed before him. Temporarily herded into Roper Hospital, he saw men dying all about him, and there was nothing anyone could do to save them. "It seemed sad, when so near the Promised Land, that they should die."[50]

Thereafter, the men languished in the Charleston jail yard for two days before boarding a transport ship bound for Camp Parole in Annapolis, Maryland. Yes, he would tell the Yankees about Andersonville and Florence. He would not let his generation forget what had happened in the prison camps nestled amidst rural Georgia and South Carolina pine forests. If Warren Lee Goss had his way, the world would never forget.[51]

Prisoners released from the Florence Stockade were sent by ship to Camp Parole in Annapolis, Maryland. Courtesy of the Library of Congress.

TWELVE

Loathsome Bones of a Sad and Lamentable Past

Gen. Robert E. Lee finally surrendered the Army of Northern Virginia at Appomattox Courthouse, Virginia, on April 9, 1865. Although his was not the last Confederate fighting force in the field, Lee's stature was so large and his influence so profound that this act, more than any other, signaled the end of the Civil War. Gen. Joseph E. Johnston followed suit shortly thereafter by surrendering his troops at Durham Station, North Carolina, on April 26. Other forces laid down their arms in ensuing weeks. The Confederate leadership had evacuated Richmond in the first days of April, so the military portion of the conflict, in effect, ended in the fourth month of the year. It would take many more years of strife and contention before the nation was reconstructed.[1]

Prison administrators on both sides faced an especially difficult chore as the war ended. Simply opening the gates of the prisons and ushering sickly, embittered men into the surrounding countryside was not a viable option. Transporting newly liberated prisoners to the nearest line of Union troops was the most appropriate course of action for the defeated Confederates, and generally they did this when they could find locomotives and boxcars as well as railroad lines that were not damaged. Union prison administrators faced a more perplexing dilemma—what should they do with their prisoners once the Confederacy had been brought to its knees? Where should they ship displaced persons who no longer had a nation awaiting their arrival?

Anticipating the looming crisis, Colonel Johnson, commandant of the Rock Island Prison Barracks, telegraphed his superior, Colonel Hoffman, in February 1865 asking for permission to pay the costs of releasing and transporting men to a suitable location after they had sworn an oath of allegiance to the United States government. Hoffman replied in April that only men who had taken the oath before the fall of Richmond would be eligible for financial assistance. Although this decision alleviated some difficulties at the prison, it nonetheless begged the question of how the remaining inmates should be paroled. Moreover, because the prisoners were destitute, they required some semblance of food and clothing upon their release; otherwise, they would be forced to engage in all manner of mischief to ensure their survival.[2]

To make matters worse, Colonel Johnson entered into another bitter dispute, this time with a Chicago lawyer-turned-military-officer, Capt. Matthew Marx. Marx began his military service as part of the Eighty-second Illinois Regiment, but he claimed to have suffered a leg wound at Gettysburg that prevented him from carrying out his duties. In November 1863, he entered the Veteran Reserve Corps and came to the Rock Island Prison to serve in the Quartermaster Department. He and the commandant clashed after Marx claimed that Johnson's family had borrowed money from the Marx family and he, the captain, wanted it repaid immediately. Furious at this allegation, Johnson told the man, "I'll fix you, you damned Copperhead." And fix him Johnson did. He relieved Marx from duty in July 1864 on charges of financial irregularities in the quartermaster funds used to operate the prison. Marx was tried by a court-martial in October and cashiered the following March, just as the war ended. Far from defeated, the unrepentant Marx set up a law practice in Rock Island City where he kept an eye on Johnson and vexed his opponent at every opportunity.[3]

Marx immediately joined forces with Johnson's long-time adversary, J. B. Danforth of the Rock Island *Argus*. The two Johnson-bashers made quite a team. Captain Marx started the campaign by preferring charges against the colonel for various improprieties such as selling prison hay and pocketing the emolument himself, as well as using a soldier as his personal servant. To ensure that he would not be charged with prosecuting Johnson as part of a personal vendetta, Marx changed the complaint so it appeared to antedate his removal from the Quartermaster Department. For his part, Danforth happily published a pamphlet titled, "A Word to the Public: Col. A. J. Johnson's Record Examined," arguing that the commandant had created a deliberately horrible prison, every bit as hellish as Andersonville. Although these events were not the only source of the myth labeling the Rock Island Prison the "Andersonville of the North," they did much to exacerbate tensions between Johnson and his detractors. They also spread the reputation of the barracks as one of the most barbaric of Union prisons.[4]

As if the Marx-Danforth imbroglio was not enough controversy during the waning days of the prison's operation, Major Kingsbury, the arsenal commander, renewed his ongoing squabbling with Colonel Johnson. The major had been relatively quiescent during the winter of 1864–65, but with the coming spring his inactivity melted away. Incensed that one of his men had been arrested and "beaten like a dog" by Lieutenant Colonel Caraher and his troops, Kingsbury demanded that Johnson supply him with the facts of the case and an apology. Apparently unsatisfied merely to confront the prison commandant, Kingsbury also wrote to his superiors at the arsenal outlining the incident and preferring charges against Caraher.[5]

Kingsbury had been nursing a grudge against the prison administrators since the barracks were built. One of the aesthetically pleasing features of life on the island was the native beauty, especially the abundant trees. Ash, basswood, elm, hickory, oak, and walnut trees decorated the area, providing local residents with a pleasant place to enjoy picnics and other recreational outings during the antebellum years. With the arrival of the prison, Union troops had cut many of the trees to clear an area for the barracks and to provide wood to augment the lumber purchased for constructing the stockade walls. Kingsbury bitterly complained about excessive tree removal on several occasions. As in the past, his latest invectives did little more than damage his own military career; nonetheless, he remained a thorn in Colonel Johnson's side until the end of the war.[6]

In his reply to the mounting criticism—especially the accusations leveled by Marx and Danforth—Johnson wrote words that rivaled his unrestrained, angry prose printed by the *Argus* the preceding November. Arguing that Marx's charges were "both frivolous and malicious," he concluded that "only a disordered brain in a malicious heart" would believe such preposterous lies. Although he managed to stay in the service until July 1866, Johnson's reputation was forever sullied by this dispute, to say nothing of the critical newspaper coverage that appeared in the *Argus* throughout the life of the prison.[7]

Often the reality of the historical record is vastly different than the myths surrounding famous events. The story of Rock Island as a heinous place rivaling the worst Confederate prisons began to circulate by 1864, but the statistics told another tale. The barracks existed as a military prison for twenty months—from November 1863 to July 1865—and during that time between 12,192 and 12,409 men were held in captivity. Of that total, 730 were transferred to other prisons, 3,876 were exchanged, 41 successfully escaped, approximately 4,000 enlisted in the U.S. Army after swearing an oath of allegiance, and 1,960 men died. This translates into a mortality rate of about 16 percent, compared to the 35 percent rate for the Andersonville Stockade.[8]

While the myths were already beginning to coalesce, Johnson could do little but oversee the release of the prisoners. From March through July 1865, he authorized inmates to be released as soon as they took an oath of allegiance to the United States government. His plans were assisted by a communiqué from Washington, D.C. In May 1865, Secretary of War Edwin M. Stanton issued a decree allowing all officers below the rank of colonel and all enlisted men captured before the fall of Richmond to secure their liberty by swearing the oath. Men like John Minnich had been reluctant to betray the Confederacy in the past, but after the collapse of the Confederate government and its armies in April, their objections disappeared. Why continue to suffer on behalf of a lost cause?[9]

Grant's General Order No. 104, issued on June 2, 1865, required the U.S. Quartermaster Department to provide transportation for all released prisoners. This directive certainly helped ensure a measure of order in resolving the inherently chaotic problem of releasing thousands of men desperate to return home. Whenever possible, Colonel Johnson had the men loaded onto trains and shipped to large cities and key railroad depots. He developed a plan to release approximately fifty men a day until the camp was empty, in accordance with Commissary General Hoffman's orders. Despite Hoffman's instructions, however, Johnson usually exceeded this figure. On June 18, the day John Minnich was released, 163 Rock Island inmates tasted freedom. On July 7, the last two prisoners, J. W. Craddock and B. F. McCoy, walked across the bridge, and the Rock Island Prison was officially closed for business.[10]

By the time he was released, Minnich had been a prisoner of war for almost seventeen months, counting from the day he was captured January 27, 1864—until he finally took the oath of allegiance on June 18, 1865. He would not have taken the oath at that time, but he had no choice. When he filed his pension application in February 1915, he remarked that he "only took it on the day of release at Rock Island," and he "would not have taken it if there had been any other way of getting out." Union authorities placed him on a train bound for his mother's home in Pennsylvania, where he remained until January 1870, when he returned to Louisiana to marry, raise his four children, and live out his life.[11]

Reflecting on his experiences in later years, he marveled at the differences between how Confederate and Union prisons were remembered. Confederate prisons were held up to public derision while Union prisons were commonly considered not nearly as terrible as their Southern counterparts. "It is unseemly that, standing as we are, with one foot on the edge of the grave which is soon to be our last resting place, circumstances should force us in sheer self-defense to dig down through the putrid mold of forty years and bring forth in the sunlight the grinning skull and clanking, loathsome bones of a sad and lamentable past." Nonetheless, because of distorted historical memory, Minnich felt obliged to set the record straight for future generations. "It has been a painful task," he concluded, "one which I had hoped I would never be called upon to undertake; for should it come to light, there are those of my own blood and kindly friends who wore the blue, North and South, East and West, who must feel the stings conveyed by these pages."[12]

With his departure from the island, Minnich did not bear witness to subsequent events, but the story was not quite completed. As the long exodus from the prison came to an end, Johnson and his few remaining troops struggled to complete the voluminous paperwork associated with closing the camp. He also instructed his men to gather up all leftover rags and sell them, a measure that brought in an additional $118 for the prison fund. Later, the administrators auctioned off property that had been purchased with the prison fund. That last act of frugality netted $754. Apparently feeling sanguine in the wake of his recent travails, Johnson invited the public to visit the prison and partake of a "grand picnic." The irony of men, women, and children frolicking with their dogs and enjoying a picnic in a yard where only a few weeks earlier prisoners lay sick and starving seemed to have been lost on the myopic commandant.[13]

Finally, during the summer, the shoddy buildings of the prison compound stood empty of people and salvageable merchandise. Johnson and his men turned it over to the Ordnance Department on August 24, 1865, in exchange for $89,113—about two-thirds of the original cost of construction. Consisting of 214 wooden structures, 116,589 pounds of cast-iron piping, and approximately 1,400 feet of smaller wrought-iron pipe, the stockade was used as a storage site for surplus and captured war matériel, especially Confederate armaments. During the postwar period the island was home to the largest collection of Confederate cannon known to exist. In some cases, the more durable buildings served as temporary quarters for Union soldiers and occasionally as a makeshift hospital. The last original prison building stood until 1909.[14]

Although the prison passed out of existence in 1865, Rock Island remained an important site for the U.S. government. As early as July 11, 1862, when Congress authorized the construction of a series of arsenals, the U.S. Army had been planning to expand and upgrade the Rock Island Arsenal. The initial groundbreaking for the expansion occurred on September 1, 1863, before the first prisoners arrived elsewhere on the island. Additional construction was delayed for three years for a variety of reasons, not the least of which was the difficulty in procuring necessary equipment, land, and personnel during wartime.[15]

Major Kingsbury remained concerned that parts of the island were not under the exclusive ownership and control of the army. In a letter he wrote to the chief of ordnance in October 1863, he recommended that steps be taken to ensure that the land was procured. "Could not these lands be condemned for public uses and appraisers appointed to determine the compensation, if any, to which the parties may be entitled for their improvements?" he asked.[16]

Despite his preference for prohibiting private activity on the island, the major was a practical man. Until he received orders to that effect, he was forced to interact with private parties from surrounding communities. Accordingly, when the mayor of Rock Island asked for permission to build a road from a wagon bridge to the prison, Kingsbury assented, allowing a road to be constructed as long as it did not interfere with the business of the arsenal.[17]

He had many occasions to regret this bit of magnanimity. Not long after the road was completed, traffic increased to such an unexpected volume that it threatened to intrude on the arsenal building site. Moreover, nearby residents acted as though the island was their own personal possession. They sometimes allowed their livestock to run loose, invariably creating chaos and delays in construction whenever errant horses, cattle, or hogs wandered into restricted areas.[18]

Despite these annoyances, Kingsbury finally got his way when Congress passed a law in April 1864 placing the site under the command of the federal government. The statute instructed the secretary of war to "take and hold full, complete, and permanent possession, in behalf of the United States, of all lands and shores of the island of Rock Island, in the state of Illinois; the same, when so possessed, to be held and kept as a military reservation by the War Department, upon which shall be built and maintained an arsenal for the construction, deposit, and repair of arms and munitions of war, and such other military establishments as have been seen or may be authorized by law to be placed thereon." The new law authorized the army to purchase any private lands on the island and secure all necessary water rights. It took until 1867—at a cost of $237,392—before the transfer of all lands on Rock Island was completed.[19]

With the United States government firmly in charge, construction work began at the arsenal and continued throughout the remainder of the nineteenth century. In 1864, Major Kingsbury described the value of the site based on "the public works on the island." In his view, they were "of a more extensive and

The main gate of the Rock Island Arsenal, looking east, was a desolate scene in 1876. Courtesy of the Rock Island Arsenal Museum.

varied character than any other ordnance depot west of the Alleghenies; and if this idea is correct, it is evident that the buildings should be designed with reference to this fact, as well as the locality itself and the topographical surroundings." The chief of ordnance, General Ramsay, apparently agreed with Kingsbury's assessment. In 1864, he wrote to the secretary of war outlining an ambitious construction plan. New buildings, bridges, and waterpower generators were designed and eventually approved.[20]

Because it was used for other purposes, the site of the Rock Island Prison Barracks did not assume the symbolic importance that other prison sites—especially Confederate prisons like Andersonville—assumed. Although Rock Island was much discussed and debated by Confederate veterans after the war, the property itself, with the exception of the Confederate cemetery, was not considered hallowed ground. Memories of the prison would be preserved through memoirs of former inmates and in the pages of *Confederate Veteran.*

As for the two men who were instrumental in the Rock Island Prison story, Colonel Hoffman was brevetted to brigadier general and eventually to major general owing to his "faithful, meritorious, and distinguished services" in designing and operating the prison system. Despite his later portrayal as a monster that placed frugality ahead of human life, he enjoyed a reasonably good reputation when he retired from the army in 1870. For all of his faults—and the cramped, narrow vision of his duty towers above the rest—he wisely

The U.S. Government sponsored construction work on the Rock Island Arsenal in 1878. Courtesy of the Rock Island Arsenal Museum.

recognized the career-enhancing possibilities of providing competent service under budget. Accordingly, he proudly returned $1,845,125.99 to the federal treasury at the conclusion of the war.[21]

Hoffman lived the final dozen years of his life in Rock Island City. He had been a widower during the war, but after he moved to Rock Island he married a local woman and lived in a large, comfortable mansion near the banks of the Mississippi River until his death in 1883. He was interred in the Chippiannock Cemetery, not far from the original site of the Rock Island Prison Barracks.[22]

Adolphus Johnson did not enjoy a sterling reputation in his autumn years, and it was of little wonder. He never learned to hold his tongue when his critics took aim. Shortly before he left his post, he penned a pamphlet attacking a Democratic candidate in the fall elections in New Jersey, but he made the mistake of sending a few samples to Rock Island City. After procuring a copy, Danforth once more took the offensive, reveling in the chance to take a final swipe at his enemy before Johnson completely disappeared from view. Calling the pamphlet "a jargon of horrible English, bad grammar, vulgar slang, and brutal attacks upon the living and the dead," Danforth again delighted in disparaging the low character and sordid motives of the departing commandant. "It is really surprising that any man, having even a thimble full of brains, should . . . put himself in a position, in so many ways, for ridicule and contempt," Danforth concluded.[23]

On this unhappy note, Johnson moved on from Rock Island, never to return. When he left the army in July 1866, he spent a brief time in Chicago before returning to his native Newark, New Jersey. He knew that his name and service at Rock Island had been besmirched; he just did not know what to do about it. Each time he responded to charges leveled by Danforth in the *Argus*, he only magnified tensions and hurt his cause. Finally, after all the backbiting and heated exchanges, he surrendered in the war of words and fell silent.[24]

Never able to rehabilitate his reputation, Johnson lived out the remainder of his days hidden from public view. When he died in Newark in 1893, the cause of death was listed as "general paresis," a euphemistic description of syphilis. He did not live to see himself characterized as the "Devil's Archangel" and the final vilification of the Rock Island Prison during the twentieth century, but he would not have been surprised. Once the myth of the "Andersonville of the North" arose, it was difficult to destroy. In the decades to come, the myth would take on a life of its own, growing in potency as the era of Civil War prisons passed forever into the mists of time.[25]

While the Rock Island Prison Barracks continued to operate until July 1865, Confederate prisons wound to a close in tandem with the collapse of the Confederacy. Thus, the Florence Stockade operated for only two months after Warren Lee Goss departed in December 1864. Other Southern prisons shut down shortly thereafter. With General Sherman on the march—first to Savannah and then up through the Carolinas—and with the loss of Wilmington, North Carolina, the beleaguered commandant of prisons, General Winder, found himself in an untenable position. "I am at a loss to know where to send prisoners from Florence," he wrote at the end of January 1865. "In one direction the enemy are in the way. In the other the question of supplies presents an insuperable barrier." If the Confederacy were to maintain its prison system, something drastic must be done to alleviate the pressure from invading Union forces.[26]

Enter Gen. P. G. T. Beauregard. The patrician general who established himself as the Hero of Sumter and First Manassas during the early days of the conflict had faded as his ambitions exceeded his abilities. Relegated to a supporting role for three long years, he reemerged on the scene as commander of the newly created Military Division of the West in the waning days. He was eager to prove his mettle as a commander, but he possessed few resources with which to muster a defense. Shortly before Sherman captured Savannah, Beauregard arrived in the city and turned his attention to defending the Carolinas. He was concerned that Sherman might capture Gen. William Hardee's forces inside Savannah.[27]

A former West Point commandant who was not easily dissuaded from fulfilling his duty, "Old Reliable" Hardee—the same officer who had engaged in the jurisdictional dispute with General Gardner over the operation of the Florence Stockade—promised to defend the city, despite Sherman's threats to punish its citizens if they resisted. Hardee said he had followed "the rules of civilized warfare" in preparing his defenses, but he added, ominously, that he might be compelled to "deviate from them in the future" if his adversary proved to be ruthless. Despite his subordinate's defiant statements of valor, Beauregard rightly concluded that the ragged Confederate troops, barely numbering ten thousand, were no match for Sherman's men, which were at least six times that number. The Union army had built momentum, and Sherman was anxious to hook up with the U.S. Navy after his long march. Realizing that Savannah must be abandoned, Beauregard ordered Hardee to build a pontoon bridge to carry his troops to safety. If the enemy chose to travel inland through South Carolina instead of traveling by ship, Hardee's forces would be necessary to provide whatever meager resistance could be offered.[28]

Confederate Gen. P. G. T. Beauregard, second in command under Gen. Joseph E. Johnston in the Carolinas campaign, ordered General Winder to move the prisoners from the Florence Stockade back to Andersonville, if possible. Courtesy of the National Archives.

Hardee's troops could not stop Sherman's advance, but bad weather was another matter. The Union general had anticipated marching into South Carolina in mid-January 1865, but it rained incessantly. Most roads into the area were so poorly constructed and maintained that he was forced to delay his invasion until February 1. Although Sherman eventually veered west and headed into the state capital, Columbia, Beauregard ordered Hardee to evacuate Charleston to prevent the troops garrisoned there from becoming trapped.[29]

As Hardee essentially backed his forces through the South Carolina low country, Beauregard turned his attention to the Florence Stockade. General

Winder had urged Confederate authorities to close the prison for some time. With Sherman's troops firmly established on South Carolina soil, the commissary general finally found a supporter. Beauregard ordered the prisoners to be transported from Florence back to Andersonville, if possible. In a message sent from Kingsville, South Carolina, on February 6, Winder agreed with Beauregard that the inmates should be returned to southwest Georgia, and he asked if additional sentries could be made available. "I have not sufficient troops to guard them," he complained.[30]

After sending his message, Winder rode the train to Florence to examine the stockade himself and decide how best to transfer the prisoners. It was a bitterly cold day, and Winder was not in the best of health. Already sixty-five years old, he looked a full decade older than the calendar indicated. War-heavy burdens will do that to a man. His presence was needed in Columbia, but he wanted to inspect the Florence prison and discipline several camp administrators charged with unnecessary cruelty. Sherman's impending arrival in the state capital had made the Columbia prisons vulnerable to liberation, so the prisoners would have to be removed. It was likely that the Florence inmates would be moved as well. Winder had so much work to do and so little time in which to get the work done.[31]

He never knew how little time he had. On February 6, he arrived in Florence on the afternoon train and disembarked on Front Street across from the Gamble Hotel, the main edifice in the town. Accompanied by Col. Henry Forno, an aide who had been stationed in Florence since December, and Capt. Phillip Cashmeyer, an aide who served as the camp sutler, the old man rode south for two miles, turned onto Stockade Road adjacent to the burial ground, and entered the prison. He was greeted by the overpowering stench of decaying bodies and human waste. Despite apocryphal stories that later circulated about Winder preparing to enjoy a feast, the commissary general had just walked into the compound and asked to see the commandant when he clutched his chest. In a dramatic moment, the aged general fell to the ground, stricken with a massive heart attack. Stunned aides carried the old man's hefty body to Cashmeyer's tent and summoned the prison doctors, but to no avail. Winder was dead.[32]

In the ensuing confusion, Forno assumed responsibility for complying with General Beauregard's orders to move the Florence prisoners back to southwest Georgia. In a telegram to several Confederate leaders, Forno explained, "Genl. Winder died suddenly, on arriving here, last night. Have assumed command and shall endeavor to carry out the Dept. view, expressed to me, by Genl. Winder." This was a tall order, but Forno wasted no time in arranging to have trains sent to the depot and prisoners loaded into boxcars for the journey. Fate intervened yet again, for his plans were frustrated when Sherman cut the last railroad line leading back into Georgia. With his options to the south foreclosed, the colonel sent prisoners north in several shipments over the course of two weeks, with some men going to Greensboro and others to Wilmington for release.[33]

By the end of February, the Florence Stockade was deserted. Nonetheless, although Sherman had entered Columbia—some eighty miles from Florence—on February 17, he remained interested in the area because General Hardee's troops had retreated to the Great Pee Dee River. Moreover, a Confederate naval yard operated on the banks of the river just above the Wilmington and Manchester Railroad. Commanded by Lt. Oscar F. Johnson, the *C.S.S. Pee Dee*, a cruiser class wooden naval vessel, was docked at the site. Later, Confederate sailors scuttled the craft rather than allow it to fall into Union hands, but in mid-February Sherman could not be sure that the ship was harmless to his men. He also did not know whether the Florence camp had been abandoned. In light of these uncertainties, the Union general dispatched Capt. William K. Duncan and the Fifteenth Illinois Cavalry on a mission to reconnoiter the countryside, destroy railroad trestles over the nearby Lynches River and Sparrow Swamp, destroy railroad equipment, and liberate the Florence prison.[34]

Recognizing the possibility of invading troops pushing into the Pee Dee area, Hardee stationed a brigade from Gen. Alfred McLaw's division at Florence. As the Fifteenth Illinois Cavalry approached the town on February 27, Col. Hugh K. Aiken led the Fifth South Carolina Cavalry in a battle three miles below the Mt. Elon Baptist Church in Darlington County and repulsed Duncan's forces. Aiken was killed in the encounter, but his cavalry forced the enemy to retreat across Lynches River, thereby saving Florence from destruction.[35]

The area still was not safe. In March, as Sherman's troops passed through the nearby town of Cheraw, he sent another task force to assault Florence. Under the command of Col. Reuben Clark, the 546 men from the Seventh and Ninth Regiments of the Illinois Mounted Infantry, the Missouri Mounted Infantry, and thirty foragers left Cheraw on March 4. As was the custom of Union troops in that army, they tore up railroad tracks along their route, twisting steel beams into pretzel-shaped masses sarcastically referred to as "Sherman's neckties." They stopped in Darlington, ten miles from Florence, long enough to destroy a printing shop before heading for their primary target.[36]

Florence appeared to be doomed to suffer the wrath of Sherman's men until a train traveling to Darlington saw the advancing column. In an inspired bit of improvisation, the engineer halted on the tracks and retreated into Florence, sending up an alarm. Confederate troops stationed in the town put up a spirited defense, but they were overpowered. Forced to retreat, they left the depot in Union hands for the first and only time during the war.

The town was saved in a strange feat of deus ex machina. The cavalry literally rode to the rescue when Gen. Joseph Wheeler and Col. John Colcock arrived from Kingsville near the Wateree River. After receiving an urgent telegram to provide relief, "Fighting Joe" and his men rushed their horses off the boxcars that had transported them to the field of battle at a record pace. Galloping at full speed, the dashing cavalrymen arrived in the nick of time to skirmish with Clark's forces behind the Gamble Hotel. Four hundred Rebel artillerymen provided reinforcements. Realizing that the tide had turned against them, Union troops retreated without burning the town or destroying the railroad tracks or equipment. The zealous Confederates pursued them to Darlington, attacking repeatedly until the enemy was too close to its larger force to engage. Although this incident did little to slow Sherman's momentum, it ensured that his soldiers would abandon plans to renew an offensive into Florence.[37]

Despite the Confederates' valor, the war was all but concluded by the time the skirmish occurred at Florence. With the collapse of the Southern Confederacy a month later, prisoners went home to their families as starving, flesh-colored skeletons, or they did not go home at all. Many nameless souls lay buried in mass, unmarked graves. The Florence Stockade was abandoned, left standing as it had existed during its brief life, although some portions later appeared to have been burned. The ghostly landscape of the nearby cemetery was a final resting place for more than 2,300 of the 2,802 men who perished at Florence, but the stockade received little notice in light of the attention afforded other, more pressing national and regional issues.[38]

THIRTEEN

The Terribleness of the Sufferings

No sooner had the guns fallen silent than a new kind of war erupted—a propaganda war to influence public memory of the conflict. Although many commentators agree that the North won the second war as well as the first, the South established its own body of literature and cultural expression that propagated values important to the region. If the missions of the two sides were similar, however, their methods were different. Northerners were anxious to memorialize all aspects of the conflict, including the treatment of prisoners of war in Confederate prison camps. Many Northern politicians, especially Republicans, piously "waved the bloody shirt" and thereby tried to gain an advantage over their Democratic opponents, whose loyalty was suspect because of their affiliation with the party of the traitorous South. By contrast, Southerners generally did not memorialize prison experiences, with the exception of a concerted effort to rehabilitate Henry Wirz's name after his trial, conviction, and execution for "war crimes." Instead, they chose to remember the valor of Confederate soldiers who fought against overwhelming odds and those who died in battle; they venerated Dixie as a place where cherished values of family, home, self-reliance, and old times were not forgotten.[1]

Despite the considerable skills of Southerners in perpetuating a distinct Confederate identity, former Union soldiers set the tone for much of the early memorialization of the war. Hundreds of journals and firsthand accounts appeared from the end of the fighting until the turn of the century detailing the appalling treatment of prisoners. Many of the more famous and influential memoirs—notably works by Warren Lee Goss, John McElroy, Robert Kellogg, Samuel S. Boggs, and John Urban—have been referenced in these pages. McElroy's and Urban's works demanded particular attention, for both men were professional ex-prisoners and promoters of the image of Confederate prisons and

This drawing of the execution of Andersonville commandant Henry Wirz appeared in Frank Leslie's Illustrated Newspaper on November 25, 1865. Courtesy of the National Archives.

their administrators as deliberately cruel and infinitely worse than their Northern counterparts.[2]

In his later years, McElroy was a journalist with the *Toledo Blade*, printed by David Ross Locke, a sardonic humorist much beloved by Northern audiences during the war—especially President Abraham Lincoln—for his satirical writings under the nom de plume Petroleum V. Nasby. Despite statements to the contrary, McElroy was anything but a dispassionate reporter on life in Confederate prisons; his memoir was written partly in response to a pro-Confederate book, *The Southern Side* by R. Randolph Stevenson, which sought to rehabilitate Henry Wirz's reputation. McElroy's account was a bitter diatribe against the oppressive, evil forces of the Southern Confederacy. Such a reaction was hardly surprising in light of his terrible prison experiences as well as his association with Locke. Although he insisted that "nothing could be farther from the truth" that he hated the South and "no one has a deeper love for every part of our common country than I," he spoke of the region in vitriolic language that left little room for ambiguity. McElroy referred to his captors using biblical images of vengeance, expiation, sin, and redemption, as did many prisoners' accounts.[3]

Urban adopted a considerably more moderate tone than McElroy, but what he lacked in bitterness he compensated for in ubiquity. An accomplished self-promoter, Urban published his memoir three different times by repackaging it slightly—changing the title, a few words and phrases here and there, and dressing it up a bit. One can attribute any number of motives to this inspired bit of self-plagiarism, although most commentators have viewed money as the paramount consideration. One celebrated historian went so far as to characterize Urban as "ingenious if not prolific" and a practitioner of "charlatanry" of a high order.[4]

Prisoner of war literature of this type—lengthy invectives designed to demonize the conquered South by exposing the terrible conditions prevalent in Confederate prisons—especially increased in the 1870s. Union veterans were anxious to receive their pensions, and their published memoirs did much to support their claims. Moreover, as former soldiers died of recurring wounds and the normal complications of old age, survivors understandably sought to preserve their real or imagined experiences for future generations. Whatever the reason, the literature exploded after 1878: thirty-one books and articles adapted from the diaries of former Union prisoners were published in the decade following that pivotal year. From 1888 to 1892, thirty-nine such publications appeared, and from 1892 to 1901, thirty-two more accounts were printed. Fifty-one others joined the growing body of literature from 1901 to 1910.[5]

Some diaries and memoirs were matter-of-fact, day-to-day accounts of prison life containing notations about weather conditions, the quality and quantity of food, and treatment by Rebel authorities. Other accounts were written in the histrionic, hyperbolic language that characterized much of the romantic literature of the day, complete with a cast of heroes and villains. The protagonist—generally the author or his heroic comrades in arms—carried the mantle of righteous indignation and Christian piety when confronted by the dark powers of the evil camp administrators. Even when the Rebels were kindly, good-hearted souls struggling to care for the prisoners despite dwindling resources, they were surrounded by malignant persons. At the top of the Confederate hierarchy lurked the most dastardly villain of all—next to Satan himself the most despicable creature in human history—Gen. John H. Winder, the man who gleefully caused such misery and death through his callousness and his lack of human decency.[6]

Most Union accounts highlighted a common theme in postwar prison literature—a fervent acceptance of evangelical religion, especially the redemptive power of suffering, and a deep, spiritual appreciation of the noble sacrifices made by prisoners. With their emphasis on suffering in support of a noble cause—the defeat of the wicked South and the end of that pernicious institution, slavery—ex-prisoners' tales also represented a direct link to antebellum abolitionist writings. McElroy's book, for example, repeated these themes in almost every chapter. "I simply ask that the great sacrifices of my dead comrades shall not be suffered to pass unregarded to irrevocable oblivion," he explained in his conclusion. His purpose in writing was so "the example of their heroic self-abnegation shall not be lost, but the lesson it teaches be preserved and inculcated into the minds of their fellow countrymen, that future generations may profit by it, and others be as ready to die for right and honor and good government as they were."[7]

Even accounts authored by sources lacking firsthand experience in Confederate camps reflected this same self-righteousness. The Loyal League, a patriotic organization dedicated to disseminating propaganda favorable to the North, widely circulated the U.S. Sanitary Commission's 1864 account, *Narrative of Privations and Sufferings of United States Officers and Soldiers while Prisoners of War in the Hands of the Rebel Authorities, Being the Report of a Commission of Inquiry*. Like the prisoners' memoirs, the Sanitary Commission report was filled with apocrypha aimed at presenting a morality play in lieu of presenting a factual recitation of events. Because the commission relied almost exclusively on the memoirs and testimony of former Union prisoners, the report advanced a self-perpetuating myth: Confederate prisons were far more barbaric than Union prisons because the Confederates deliberately mistreated prisoners while the North did the best it could to ease the suffering of Southern inmates.[8]

The vilification of the South did not stop with the publication of Union prisoners' memoirs. Recognizing the political value in investigating Rebel prisons, the U.S. Congress entered the fray in 1869 as Republican leaders sought to condemn the barbarism of the South. After eliciting testimony from more than three thousand witnesses, the House of Representatives issued a report that in many ways reflected the Sanitary Commission's findings as well as an 1864 report issued by the 38th Congress examining the condition of Union prisoners returning to Camp Parole in Annapolis, Maryland. Once again, the South was the villain in this morality play, with characters such as John Winder, Henry Wirz, and Jefferson Davis reprising their popular roles as evil masterminds devoted to exterminating Yankee soldiers held in hellish Confederate prison camps.[9]

Warren Lee Goss assumed a prominent role in the 1869 congressional inquiry, serving as a key witness in the hearings. The investigating committee from the House of Representatives concluded that his testimony "is presented as an interesting and well-sustained account of prison life at Andersonville, sanctioned not only by the oath of the patriotic and accomplished author, but fully corroborated by all concurrent testimony." Indeed, Goss's words were afforded so much weight that whole chapters from his book, *The Soldier's Story*, were included in the congressional report. The credence given to the recollections of Goss and other former prisoners—generally at the exclusion of the "Southern view"—ensured that memory of Confederate prisons would forever be viewed through a distorted lens.[10]

For a variety of reasons, the Southern response to this propaganda war was delayed until the 1880s and 1890s, when former Confederates began to articulate and promote their own values. Former Confederate President Jefferson Davis probably was the most famous and vociferous respondent in this war of words. Winder and Wirz were dead, but the unapologetic former Confederate leader would take up the cause once again. Although he defended the Confederacy's policies in many writings, Davis's most vehement defense was set forth in his two-volume work, *The Rise and Fall of the Confederate Government.*[11]

He sounded a familiar refrain. The Union was responsible for the wretched privations that existed in Confederate prisons because Northern leaders suspended the exchange cartel and refused to negotiate. Davis's deceased friend, Winder, did all he could to care for the prisoners under his jurisdiction, but Union cruelties and a lack of sufficient resources hampered him at every turn. When he discovered that disease and misery were rampant at Andersonville, Winder took decisive and immediate action to alleviate the prisoners' suffering. As Davis remembered it, "as soon as arrangements could be made, he was instructed to disperse them to Millen and elsewhere, as in his judgment might be best for their health, comfort, and safety." When conditions continued to deteriorate, Winder "with the main body of the prisoners, removed first to Millen, Georgia, and then to Florence, South Carolina." General Sherman's rapid advance through Georgia was not a major factor in Winder's decision to remove the prisoners. Safety and comfort were the primary considerations; Sherman's advance was fortuitous—an ancillary issue, at best.[12]

Davis's bid to portray the South as a fledgling nation of chivalric people who never mistreated prisoners was fully consistent with a developing regional tradition. Southerners saw themselves as victims of Northern aggression while the North viewed the former Confederates as victimizers of Union prisoners, monsters in human form hell-bent on overseeing—and perhaps triggering—Yankee extirpation. Consistent with its self-image, the South embraced a romantic notion generally referred to as the "Lost Cause." This potent myth suggested that the Confederate States Army may have been defeated on the battlefield, but the region was superior to the North because traditional values such as home, family, and honor were alive and well. Southern icons arose—

especially Robert E. Lee, Thomas J. "Stonewall" Jackson, and Jefferson Davis—and became symbols of the noble character cherished by Southerners. Churches, schools, community and civic groups as well as political leaders in the region promoted this myth as a means of assuaging the fears and morose feelings of the people in a conquered territory.[13]

For the most part, memorializing Confederate prisons was not an integral part of the Southern tradition; consequently, many sites lapsed into disrepair unless Northern groups chose to commemorate them. Moreover, memory of their operation gradually faded away as the years passed. The exception was Andersonville, and primarily Northern veterans' groups memorialized that site.[14]

Aside from the sensationalism of the Wirz trial, Andersonville attracted attention because of several events. A series of drawings and photographs in *Harper's Weekly* in June 1865 publicized the deplorable physical condition of prisoners returning from Andersonville. The scenes would be familiar to anyone viewing pictures of emaciated concentration camp victims from World War II. The living skeletons presented a ghastly image to Northerners who had no conception of the abominable conditions in Southern prisons. This article did much to indict Henry Wirz and the Confederate prison system for a Union public that might otherwise have been more forgiving of the South.[15]

In July 1865, famed nurse Clara Barton, accompanied by Capt. James N. Moore, visited Andersonville to enclose the national cemetery and gather a list of names of the dead. Although she recognized that nothing good could come if she chose to "dwell upon the terribleness of the sufferings imposed upon our prisoners," Barton also understood that Northern families were anxious to know if their missing sons were interred there. Despite the War Department's plans to investigate matters in relative secrecy, she assisted reporters in publishing a partial list of the dead in the *New York Tribune*. Several newspapers republished the list as well as a letter that Barton wrote outlining her impressions and explaining the need for a national cemetery.[16]

After Barton's visit and the end of the Wirz trial, the land around the stockade was left to weather the forces of nature. Freedmen occupied the house where the Wirz family had lived and local citizens carried off pieces of wood to build fires or fences. Some curious souvenir hunters took artifacts as mementos of the camp's terrible history. From 1866 to 1874, two Rhode Island schoolteachers used the prison hospital as a schoolhouse for emancipated slaves. A black ten-ant farmer grew crops on the site in the 1870s and 1880s.[17]

As interest in memorializing the war reached a fever pitch starting late in the 1880s, the Grand Army of the Republic (GAR), an organization of Union veterans, purchased the property and established a prison park in 1890. Six years later, the members transferred title to the land to the Women's Relief Corps (WRC), an organization of Northern women dedicated to memorializing the heroism of Union troops. In 1897, the WRC purchased an additional fourteen acres and gradually improved the land. Thirteen years later, the group donated the five-hundred-acre parcel to the federal government to establish a national park and ensure its perpetual care.[18]

Shortly before World War I erupted, a group of New York women spearheaded an effort to memorialize New York prisoners who died at Andersonville. Reprinted from the Andersonville Monument Dedication Commission, Dedication of Monument Erected by the State of New York at Andersonville, Georgia, 1914.

Southerners were not content to sit by idly and allow Northern veterans' groups to direct all memorialization activities for Andersonville. In 1905, the Georgia chapter of the United Daughters of the Confederacy (UDC), the Southern analogue of the WRC, began discussing the possibility of erecting a monument to honor the much-maligned Captain Wirz. As part of the effort to rehabilitate the commandant, Confederate groups reiterated the arguments that Jefferson Davis had set forth in *The Rise and Fall of the Confederate Government*. This led to a bitter exchange of verbal fire between veterans' groups, North and South. Despite the brouhaha, the UDC eventually erected a monument honoring Wirz in 1909, not far from the prison site, where it stood well into the twenty-first century.[19]

On April 9, 1998—the 133rd anniversary of Lee's surrender at Appomattox Courthouse—a new chapter opened on the history of Andersonville. With the dedication of the National Prisoner of War Museum, the site assumed renewed importance in American history. The museum celebrated the ordeal endured by all prisoners in all wars, not simply the Union men held at Camp Sumter in

In the South after the war, a movement arose to construct monuments in honor of fallen Confederate soldiers. The Ladies Memorial Association of Florence, South Carolina, erected this obelisk in 1882. Courtesy of the author.

1864 and 1865. In light of this expanded symbolism, the land that once housed sick and starving Union soldiers could be honored and remembered by everyone, whatever their regional interests, as hallowed ground. By recasting the focus on prisoners of war in general instead of concentrating on Union inmates at Andersonville, the museum reached a broader constituency.[20]

Events at Andersonville were hardly typical of prison sites. By contrast, the land around the Florence Stockade did not receive the same attention and, in fact, the prison pen almost completely disappeared from public memory for many years after the war. Because it was not as well known as the Georgia prison, the swampy field that made up the Florence camp reverted to nature rapidly. Local residents carried off wood that was not left to rot and eventually plowed the field so they could plant crops. In 1882, the Florence Ladies' Memorial Association (LMA) erected a monument commemorating Florence soldiers who died in the war at the entrance to the Mount Hope Cemetery, a burial ground for many prominent Florentines located not far from the national cemetery. Although the LMA might have used the opportunity to memorialize the stockade, the record does not mention such an effort. The prison had operated only seventeen years earlier, yet it seemed to have receded from public memory by the 1880s.[21]

One of the few postwar references to the site in the nineteenth century occurred in the fall of 1865, when a thirty-one-year-old Northern journalist, Sidney Andrews, commenced an extraordinary journey through the former

Confederate states. He started his trek in Charleston, where he disembarked from a ship to travel overland via railroad. He spent the next six weeks in South Carolina, followed by three weeks in North Carolina and five weeks in Georgia. His timing was impeccable; each state he visited was holding a convention to determine how it would implement President Johnson's Reconstruction policies. By attending the conventions, Andrews gained an invaluable firsthand perspective on white Southerners' attitudes immediately following the cessation of hostilities.

He toured the Florence Stockade on the afternoon of October 19, 1865, and devoted a chapter in his book, *The South Since the War,* to the visit. "Everything remains as the Rebels left it when they evacuated Florence," he observed. Although time had dissipated the stench somewhat, the remnants of death and destruction lingered in the air. Sheltered huts that once had served as the prison hospital were charred; someone had tried to burn them, perhaps to conceal the evidence of what had occurred in the stockade. Finding a block of wood, Andrews knelt, balancing a notebook and his pen on his knee, and sat on it to outline the first draft of his ruminations on "The Great Military Prison of South Carolina." "Said I not that here was life arrested in the very pulsebeat?" he wrote as he prepared to leave the site. "The tale of Florence can be half read even now by the dullest eye."[22]

Bvt. Brig. Gen. James F. Rusling visited the Florence Stockade in May 1866 and issued a report on the conditions he found. Courtesy of the U.S. Army Military History Institute.

Seven months later, Bvt. Brig. Gen. James F. Rusling, an inspector in the Quartermaster Department, echoed Andrews's observations. Bvt. Maj. Gen. Montgomery C. Meigs, quartermaster general of the U.S. Army, dispatched Rusling to visit the national cemetery adjacent to the stockade and provide recommendations on how the national government should handle the bodies of Union soldiers buried there. Rusling issued his "Report of the Inspection of the National Cemetery at Florence,

S.C." from the Office of the Inspector, Quartermaster Department, in Charleston on May 27, 1866.[23]

He was so outraged by what he saw in the Florence Stockade and the nearby cemetery that he abandoned all pretense of objectivity. Adopting the florid prose so common in postwar memoirs, the general spewed forth a series of invectives. If anyone doubted that it boded well "for mankind that the Confederacy went down in darkness and blood" and its leaders "were 'moved and instigated by the Devil' and that its rank and file breathed only the 'sulfurous breath of Hell,'" he suggested they stand before the graves near the prison. "If any man doubts, let him visit Florence and Andersonville."[24]

When the Confederates thrust prisoners into the Florence Stockade, in Rusling's estimation, they did so "to dehumanize and bestialize themselves as far as men can! To roast! To freeze! To starve! To die! For from these came the 2,738 martyrs for freedom whose burial places I have essayed to describe. And this in the 19th Century! In 'chivalrous' South Carolina! The pride and pink of the Confederacy! History will not credit the tale, or if she does, will damn the Rebellion to a deeper infamy than we, its contemporaries, are capable of imagining. Her milk of human kindness will sour, and her bowels of compassion close forever against such unmitigated wretches."[25]

As devastating as Andrews's and Rusling's observations sounded, perhaps the most moving story to emerge from the Florence Stockade involved a mysterious woman named Florena Budwin. Not much is known about her. According to legend, she was a young woman, a native of Philadelphia who was no more than twenty years of age as the war stretched into its final year. She loved her soldier-husband, a captain in the Union army, so much it was beyond the power of words to convey its depth. When he was called into the service of his country and shipped to Plymouth, North Carolina, she followed him. She abandoned her crinoline skirts and hair bonnet to slide her petite frame into a blue uniform. Embracing a life of hardtack and musketry, she tracked the young captain to his camp and joined him in his tribulations. What must her groom have thought when he looked up from his soiled and sordid station to see his bride on her approach, disguised as a fellow soldier?

Falling in with the regiment, Florena shared in the sour misfortunes of war alongside the man for whom she had sacrificed so much. Disaster struck this young couple not long after she found the captain, for they were captured and sent to the Andersonville Stockade. According to one version of the legend, Captain Budwin was shot dead by a Confederate guard who fired into the crowd of anxious prisoners pushing and shoving to drink from the Providence

Spring that miraculously appeared in the earth near the deadline. Another version said the young man succumbed to disease.

Whatever happened to the gallant young officer, he did not survive his captivity in the Georgia prison pen. Florena, no doubt grief-stricken by his death and terrified by her predicament, kept her secret even as she was herded into a boxcar and shipped from Andersonville to Florence. A Confederate surgeon discovered her identity during a routine inspection. The timing and circumstances of the discovery vary according to who tells the tale. In some accounts, the Confederates paroled Florena immediately after she arrived in Florence and she spent months serving as a nurse in the stockade hospital, tirelessly and selflessly bathing the wounds of her husband's brethren. Many raconteurs insist that the woman hid her identity for some time. Later, when she was discovered because of her ailing condition, she left the prison and was tended to by the kind Southern ladies of the nearby community.

Florena Budwin died in the Florence Stockade in January 1865. She may be the first woman ever interred in a national cemetery in the United States. Courtesy of the author.

Whatever the particulars of her tale, Florena Budwin suffered much at the hands of fate. On January 25, 1865, only a month before the prisoners left the Florence Stockade, she died of a lung disease, probably pneumonia. No one was even certain of her real name—"Florena," with its alliterative possibilities for the town of Florence, seemed too perfect a coincidence for skeptical historians to accept—and her true motives remained a mystery as well. Even her appearance invited argument. Some romantics pictured her as a demure young woman of aristocratic background, with smooth, pale, almost translucent skin and fine, patrician features while others surmised that it was not difficult to disguise herself as a man because she was cursed with a coarse, plain appearance.

An article by Katherine Boling, an acclaimed writer from the Pee Dee region of South Carolina, summarized the meaning of this tale as well as anyone. "Despite her brief twenty years," Boling observed at the conclusion of her piece, "Florena Budwin must have understood in her heart as well as anyone can, the bitter cost of war." She was the first woman buried in a national cemetery in the United States. Her story—whichever version one accepts—is the stuff of books and movies. The mystery that surrounds her historical existence makes her more attractive because she becomes a template for anything or anyone people want her to be. She is a tabula rasa and readers may make of her story what they will. For people who know of her, she is *the* mystery woman of the Florence Stockade, a monument to the enduring power of love even in the midst of misery and death.[26]

Despite the reports filed by journalist Sidney Andrews and General Rusling of the Quartermaster Department and the dramatic tale of Florena Budwin, stories of the Florence Stockade faded with time. In 1895, a group of fifteen hundred blacks as well as a few whites held a memorial service for Union prisoners who died in the stockade, but it was a one-time event. Throughout the twentieth century, leading Florentines discussed restoring the site for its historic value and the possibility of tourism. Their efforts came to naught. In 1947, the UDC constructed a monument to the guards and prisoners in the stockade; by the dawn of the twenty-first century, however, the marker stood next to a busy thoroughfare, invisible to all but the most zealous Civil War enthusiasts.[27]

In 1947, the Florence Chapter of the United Daughters of the Confederacy erected a monument to memorialize the site of the Florence Stockade. Courtesy of the author.

The best hope of restoring the site of the prison occurred in May 1997, when a group of concerned citizens formed a nonprofit organization known as the "Friends of the Florence Stockade" (FFS). According to the group's literature, its "main purpose is the preservation of the stockade site and memory of those, both North & South, who served there during the prison's operation." Ideally, once the FFS raised the requisite funding and procured the property, its members intended to assist appropriate governmental entities—local, state, or federal—in constructing a memorial park and museum. In 2001, the group achieved its first goal when it purchased part of the site from private landowners.[28]

In some ways the Rock Island Prison experienced a postwar history similar to Andersonville and Florence. The prison buildings fell into disrepair in the decades that followed the end of the war but, after a period of inattention and decline, interest in memorializing the prison grew during the twentieth century. In 1951, the U.S. government erected a marker commemorating the prison on the northeast corner of the site. Sixteen years later, the Officers' Wives Club of the Illinois State Historical Society sponsored the construction of a second marker. A tradition grew up at the cemetery each Memorial Day honoring the 125 Union guards who died on duty as well as other United States veterans interred on the island. Confederate groups also honored the 1,960 dead prisoners by placing a small Confederate battle flag on each grave and playing "Taps." These events were relatively low-key affairs, little noticed by the general public.[29]

Major Kingsbury, the officer in charge of the arsenal who often quarreled with Colonel Johnson, left the post in June 1865. Bvt. Brig. Gen. Thomas Jefferson Rodman replaced him on August 4. After the change in command, Rodman oversaw the continuation of construction on the island while Kingsbury went on to an undistinguished career serving as the arsenal commander in Watertown, Massachusetts. Kingsbury finally retired from the army as a lieutenant colonel on December 31, 1870, and moved to Brooklyn, New York, where he lived for the remainder of the 1870s. He died on Christmas Day 1879 at the age of sixty-three.[30]

With the departure of Major Kingsbury as well administrators and former guards, institutional memory of the prison faded. Local citizens visited the island on special occasions, such as the centennial celebration of the establishment of a troop base in 1916, but these events were infrequent and not directly linked to the history of the prison. Even the diatribes penned by J. B. Danforth in the *Argus* and embittered former inmates in *Confederate Veteran* probably would not have sufficed to perpetuate the myth of the Rock Island Prison as the "Andersonville of the North" into the twentieth century and beyond. Had it not been for the publication of a popular novel, Rock Island might have faded into history as another Civil War prison site, forgotten by all but zealous Civil War enthusiasts and historians of the era.[31]

In 1936, the historical memory of the prison changed forever when a

Local citizens sometimes visited the Rock Island Arsenal. In this photograph, they were celebrating the establishment of a troop base in 1916, the year before the United States entered into World War I. Courtesy of the Rock Island Arsenal Museum.

Georgia writer, Margaret Mitchell, published a Pulitzer Prize–winning novel, *Gone with the Wind*. Three years later it appeared as one of the most popular motion pictures ever made. In telling the epic story of the Civil War from the Southern perspective, Mitchell did much to venerate the Confederate cause and portray the South as a mythical place of quintessential "American" values: chivalry, honor, and love of one's family. In an important subplot, Mitchell recounted the story of Ashley Wilkes, a debonair Confederate soldier captured and incarcerated in the Rock Island Barracks. One passage describing Wilkes's experiences in the prison did more than anything else ever written to propound the myth of Rock Island as equal to, or worse than, Andersonville. "Inflamed by reports from Andersonville, the North resorted to harsher treatment for Confederate prisoners and at no place were conditions worse than at Rock Island," she wrote. "Food was scanty, one blanket for three men, and the ravages of smallpox, pneumonia and typhoid gave the place the name of a pesthouse. Three-fourths of all the men sent there never came out alive."[32]

This last bit of hyperbole was especially damning. Never mind that the actual mortality rate—16 percent—was far below Mitchell's stated 75 percent rate or that Rock Island experienced about half as many deaths per capita as Andersonville; a popular work of fiction passed into public consciousness as gospel. Other prisons, North and South, may have posted higher death rates

Rock Island continued to function as a military installation long after the prison had disappeared. This photograph of an administration building on the island was taken in 1950. Courtesy of the Rock Island Arsenal Museum.

than Rock Island, but they could not compete with *Gone with the Wind* as a proponent of the Southern tradition.[33]

Even as the memory of the prison was manipulated, Rock Island remained an important site for ordnance and supply well into the twentieth century. Construction continued throughout the years to such an extent that John Minnich and his comrades would not have recognized the place. With the destruction of the last prison building in 1909, the site where the barracks once stood reverted back to what it had been before the war—part of a rocky out cropping standing majestically in the rapids of the mighty Mississippi River.[34]

FOURTEEN

The Last Bugle Call

John Wesley Minnich outlived the Southern Confederacy by sixty-seven years. He was twenty-one years old when he walked through the gates of the Rock Island Prison in June 1865 and eighty-eight when he died in Morgan City, Louisiana, in November 1932. He witnessed enormous changes during his long life: the Mexican War; the Civil War; the ratification of the Civil War amendments; the construction of the transcontinental railroad; the invention of the lightbulb, phonograph, telephone, automobile, and airplane; the Spanish-American War; World War I; the Gilded Age; the Jazz Age; the extension of the franchise to women; and the advent of the Great Depression, among other things.[1]

When he was born, John Tyler, the tenth president of the United States and a subsequent delegate to the provisional Confederate Congress, occupied the White House. Twenty-six states were in the Union. When he died, Herbert Hoover, the thirty-first president, presided over forty-eight states and a nation suffering from the ill effects of a worldwide economic depression. Although he probably did not realize it, John Minnich lived to see change on the horizon: Franklin Roosevelt won the presidential election on November 8, 1932, and Minnich died exactly one week later.[2]

He was forever touched by his Civil War experiences. Wherever he went and whatever he did in life, the war was never far from his mind. He was proud to have worn the gray uniform, and he never missed an opportunity to extol the virtues of his former comrades and commanders. Sifting through newspapers during the four and a half years he lived in Pennsylvania after his release from prison, he was incensed to read of the horrors of Andersonville with no mention of the privations and deliberate cruelties perpetrated in Union prisons. "Some things are not easily forgotten," he remarked. "I remember also that while Wirz was in prison, and the newspapers were manufacturing a character to saddle him with and hunting up witnesses to swear his life away at any and all costs, on the last Sunday in June, accompanied by my mother, I called upon some old-time neighbors whom I had not seen for a full dozen years (and with whose sons and daughters I had attended the same school during two sessions), and there met their oldest son, who had been a lieutenant in a Pennsylvania regiment, and who had passed seven months in Andersonville and was supposed to know something about the occurrences there." The gentleman was James Hastings, the older brother of a man who later became governor of Pennsylvania, Daniel Hastings. Minnich quizzed his acquaintance on events that occurred in the infamous Confederate stockade.

"How long were you in Andersonville, Jim?" he asked.

"Seven months."

"Well, now, I wish you would tell me the truth about that place. Was it really as bad as the papers say it was?"

"No, it wasn't. It was bad, of course. We did not have the shelter we needed because we were too many, and we did not have food enough nor machines for our sick; but I guess they didn't have enough themselves."

When Minnich asked the fellow if the stories of the atrocities supposedly committed by Wirz were true, Hastings muttered, "not that I know of."[3]

This little morality tale sounds awfully convenient, but Minnich swore that the exchange occurred. As the vignette suggests, the quest to set the record straight consumed most of his postwar years. After he moved back to Louisiana early in 1870, he became an indefatigable crusader for the Southern view of history. When *Confederate Veteran* magazine appeared in the 1890s, Minnich became a faithful and tireless correspondent.[4]

On returning to his adopted state, he settled in Grand Isle, a secluded hamlet in Jefferson Parish south of New Orleans. This quaint little fishing village would earn the sobriquet "a sportsman's paradise" in later years, but in 1870 it was still a sparsely populated township. In contrast to surrounding towns, which were depicted as "little more than sand-bars covered with wiry grasses, prairie-cane, and scrub timber," Grand Isle was described as an idyllic place. "Existence here is so facile, happy, primitively simple, that trifles give joy unspeakable," wrote one contemporary observer. It was an area where "neither misery nor malady may live. To such contented minds surely the Past must ever appear in a sunset glow of gold, the Future in an eternal dawn of rose."[5]

An eclectic group of men and women trickled into Grand Isle in the years following the war. They were not the officers and leaders entitled to the encomiums of history; rather, they were veterans who had served as enlisted men on the grimy, bloody battlefields of the war. They gravitated to small towns like Grand Isle searching for exactly the kind of peace and isolation found in a small fishing village tucked in the middle of nowhere at the bottom of America. The inhabitants who drifted to Grand Isle during the two decades after Appomattox were so diverse in their heritage that one commentator found the town a breeding ground for "a hybrid population from all ends of heaven, white, yellow, brown, cinnamon-color, and tints of bronze and gold—Basques, Andalusians, Portugese, Malays, Chinamen, etc."[6]

Sometime after March 28, 1870—the date when he settled in Grand Isle—Minnich married a young woman almost exactly his age, Eloise Anwise Keith. He also bought a small tract of land measuring 180 by 230 feet, and built a modest house—he called it a "shack"—for himself and his soon-to-be-growing family. The land originally came from Francois Rigaud, Sr., a prominent resident, who sold a large tract to Myrtil Plessala, described as a fisherman and a "free man of color," in 1852. Plessala divided the property into smaller lots and sold them after the war. It was no small irony that Minnich, the spirited Confederate who had been so outraged to see black men guarding prisoners at Rock Island, purchased his land from a man of color, but the history of Reconstruction America was filled with many such ironies as impoverished Confederates were forced to coexist with diverse peoples. Moreover, the diverse ethnicity of the Louisiana culture, with it mixture of Cajuns, Creoles, and other persons of color, ensured that strict distinctions between black and white were not possible or, for that matter, desirable. Even more ironic than the land purchase was the fact that Myrtil Plessala became John Minnich's brother-in-law after he married Eloise Minnich's sister, Marie.[7]

During the 1870s, once he had found a new home, Minnich began to raise his family. The 1880 census listed 249 permanent residents in Grand Isle. At the time, John W. Minnich, aged thirty-six, identified himself as a carpenter with seven people in his household. Of course, his wife, Eloise (recorded as "Heloise") lived there; as did his mother-in-law, Marguerite Lefort; his son, Adam, six years old; another son, George, five years old; and his daughter Edna, two years old. His last child, a daughter named Anna Marguerite, was born after 1880, so she wasn't included in the census. Although his brother, George Minnich, was not listed as a member of the household, the seventh member was not identified. Because John and George lived in the same house from time to time throughout the years, it is reasonable to conclude that George probably lived under his brother's roof in 1880.[8]

Minnich spent the rest of his life in or near Grand Isle. He was very close to his brother, but he also stayed in contact with Lt. John R. Lay, one of his commanding officers in the Sixth Georgia Cavalry Regiment, and several barracks mates from his sixteen-month stay in the Rock Island Prison. He may have seen these men upon occasion, but it is more likely that they kept in touch through correspondence.[9]

Minnich was active in the life of the community, taking part in, and sometimes organizing, athletic contests involving young people. He also served as a commissioner of election polls, most notably during the 1880 elections. In addition to his carpentry business, he served as the local postmaster for twenty years, a vocation that allowed him to peruse *Confederate Veteran* regularly. Always interested in veterans' affairs, he traveled to meetings of the United Confederate Veterans, especially when events were held in or near New Orleans.[10]

His life for the most part was quiet and uneventful, but he was no stranger to heartache. In 1893, he and other residents of his adopted township endured one of the worst hurricanes to strike Louisiana during the nineteenth century. In 1905, his wife died after more than thirty years of marriage. Although he did not advertise his grief to the world, it was probably no coincidence that his frequent letters to *Confederate Veteran* and the publication of his memoir about life in the Rock Island Prison followed on the heels of her death.[11]

He was well into his sixties before he put pen to paper and recalled his sixteen months as a "guest of the Yankees." Although Minnich had been a frequent contributor to *Confederate Veteran*, his correspondence usually reflected on life in the ranks. In his short letters and articles, he preferred to accentuate the glories and camaraderie of his wartime adventures with the Louisiana Zouaves, Rowan's Kentucky Rangers, and the Sixth Georgia Cavalry Regiment. He occasionally corrected the record on the treatment or number of prisoners at Rock Island, but for four decades he did not provide an in-depth chronology of his experiences. By 1908, the year he published his memoir *Inside of Rock Island Prison from December, 1863, to June, 1865*, Minnich believed that he could no longer remain silent. Former Union soldiers continually wrote shrill stories of their mistreatment in Confederate prisons. As a result, in his words, "the South is still being held up to the gaze of this and future generations as a people devoid of humanity as Kurd or Cossack." He was determined to set the record straight.[12]

In light of the deprivations he suffered as a prisoner of war, Minnich's longevity was improbable, but he somehow managed to persevere even as others of his generation slipped into their graves. In 1915, with his health declining and his financial fortunes on the wane, he applied for a pension from the state of Louisiana, swearing an oath "that I remained true to the Confederate cause until the surrender, and *that I am now in indigent circumstances, and unable to earn a livelihood by my own labor or skill.*" He won his pension and eventually moved to several nearby towns before settling in with brother George at 1027 Fourth Street in Morgan City. He spent a dozen or so years living there before his death.[13]

John Minnich was a frequent contributor to Confederate Veteran. *This photograph of the 80-year-old former prisoner appeared in the magazine in 1924.* Courtesy of the Museum of the Confederacy. Copy photography by Katherine Wetzel.

Reflecting on his advanced age in one of his last articles for *Confederate Veteran*, the eighty-five-year-old Minnich wrote that "I am proud of the fact that I am privileged to trail along with the fast-thinning line of the gray." Professing his continued allegiance to the Confederacy until the end of his days, he grew pensive. "I am now waiting patiently, if not cheerfully, for the last bugle call, confident that when at last my name is called, I can answer clearly: 'Here!'"[14]

The call came three and a half years after he wrote those words, in the wee morning hours of Tuesday, November 15, 1932, at the home he shared with his brother in Morgan City. His surviving kin held his funeral the following day, after which he was buried in the Army of Tennessee Tomb in historic Metairie Cemetery in New Orleans. It was fitting that John Wesley Minnich's final resting place was among the men of his generation who spent their energies in proud service, rightly or wrongly, of the Confederate cause.[15]

—∾—

Like Minnich, Warren Lee Goss carried vestiges of the war with him for the rest of his life. No sooner had he left the Charleston jail and arrived at Camp

Parole in Annapolis, Maryland, on December 16, 1864, than he was stricken with typhus. He spent many days in a delirium, anxiously awaiting either death or recovery. The only sight he clearly remembered was an American flag hanging on the wall of his sickroom. It brought him great comfort to know that whatever else happened, at least he would die a free man on free soil.[16]

But he did not die in December 1864. He survived the ravages of disease to live another sixty-one years. During that time, Goss carved out a writing career notable, if not for the majesty of his words or the originality of his plots, for the singularity of his mission. He would tell a tale of hardship and woe, casting Union men as heroes and Confederates as villains, and he would retell the tale endlessly in a slightly different form each time. His inaugural book, *The Soldier's Story of His Captivity at Andersonville, Belle Isle, and Other Rebel Prisons*—first published in 1866, and then reprinted in 1867, 1869, and 1872—was among the first of many works excoriating the South and her officers. It was a bitter denunciation of the Southern camps, perhaps not as vitriolic as many diatribes that followed, but certainly not as balanced and dispassionate as accounts penned by historians. *The Soldier's Story* originally was published a few years before a congressional investigation into the conditions prevalent in Confederate prisons, and so it served as a precedent for the members of Congress who wished to condemn the barbarity of the Confederate leadership. Goss was a prominent witness at the 1869 congressional hearings, and many parts of *The Soldier's Story* were introduced verbatim into the record.[17]

The book was important because, along with Robert H. Kellogg's *Life and Death in Rebel Prisons*, it set the standard for many works to follow. In fact, each subsequent work directly or obliquely referenced episodes recounted in Kellogg's and Goss's books as well as anecdotes included in the congressional report—which also cited Kellogg's and Goss's works. Thus, each new diary or memoir that appeared beginning in the 1870s repeated and often embellished the same horror stories that had come to light earlier. As the years passed, it became virtually impossible to separate reality from myth. Perhaps this development was Goss's intent all along—history as polemic.[18]

At the conclusion of *The Soldier's Story*, Goss explained his purpose in writing, and it could have served as a thesis statement for all memoirs written by former Union prisoners of war. "Today, though broken in health, and perhaps crippled for life, I record these sufferings as a remembrance to coming generations, and dedicate these pages to the memory of the living and the dead, who in the 'great struggle' have suffered or died in prisons, and upon well-fought battlefields, for our country's preservation and honor."[19]

As he went through his life after the 1860s, Goss remained active in several Union veterans' organizations, including the Grand Army of the Republic, the Connecticut Union Prisoners' Association, and the National Union of Andersonville Survivors. Because of his leadership role in these groups, he was always on the lookout for opportunities to promote the Union perspective on the war in general, and Confederate prisons in particular. One notable chance arose early in 1876. After reading an article written by former Confederate President Jefferson Davis, Goss felt compelled to express his outrage in a letter to the editor of the *New York Times*. "Though I was a prisoner at Andersonville, and the sworn testimony of thousands was published in 1869 by the committee appointed by Congress to show the treatment of prisoners of war by rebel authorities, yet it will not be necessary for me to appeal to this overwhelming testimony to show that Union soldiers were brutally murdered under the pretense of treating them as prisoners of war," he wrote. "As Jefferson Davis has appealed to the records, let him be judged by them." In Goss's view, the leaders, not the Southern people, were to blame for the atrocities committed in Confederate prisons. The crimes should be "fastened upon its proper authors," not upon "a great, brave though mistaken people." He returned to this theme in many books and articles he wrote throughout the years, including a signature piece he published in the *North American Review* in 1890.[20]

Unlike Minnich, who settled down in one state after 1870, Goss changed residences several times during the postwar years. He returned to his home state of Massachusetts for a brief period after he left the army in September 1865, but afterward he chose to live in Norwich, Connecticut, and, later, in Rutherford, New Jersey, on the outskirts of New York City. He was featured in a lengthy *New York Times* article in 1894 when the Connecticut chapter of the Grand Army of the Republic met to discuss important business, including the management and operation of the soldiers' homes provided for ailing and aging Union veterans in several northeastern states. Having achieved a measure of status as an author of adventure stories—most of which involved brave children taking part on the periphery of Union war activities—Goss's mustachioed face merited a sketch in the *Times*.[21]

He followed up *The Soldier's Story* with many books, mostly action stories and morality tales of the Civil War suitable for young readers. His prodigious output included: *Jed* (1889); *Recollections of a Private: A Story of the Army of the Potomac* (1890); *Tom Clifton* (1892); *Jack Alden* (1895); *In the Navy* (1898); *Boys' and Girls' Life of Grant* (1911); *The Boys' Life of General Sheridan* (1913); and *Jed's Boy* (1919). Although hardly literary masterworks, the yarns exhibited a certain charm in the Horatio Alger tradition: an impoverished but plucky lad came through in the clutch, learning the value of hard work and honor along the way. The biographies of Grant and Sheridan were hortatory tales on the virtues of exemplary Union leaders, men who had preserved the nation in its darkest hour.[22]

This sketch of Warren Lee Goss at age fifty-eight appeared in the New York Times *in 1894*. Courtesy of the General Research Division, the New York Public Library, Astor, Lenox and Tilden Foundations.

Aside from *The Soldier's Story*, his most popular work probably was *Recollections of a Private*. In that book, Goss painstakingly detailed the experiences of an "Everyman" soldier as he struggled to become attenuated to life in the Army of the Potomac. He began the book as a series of adventure stories published in *The Century: A Popular Quarterly* during the 1880s. The stories, thinly disguised autobiographical vignettes and "as told to" hearsay coupled with historical research, earned Goss a measure of fame, to say nothing of the accompanying mammon. He may have suffered grievously during the war, but afterward he was determined to reap the benefits of his tribulations. Just as he had demonstrated during his periods of confinement, Goss's business sense served him well. When the articles proved to be popular, he no doubt decided that a full-length book was in the offing.[23]

Goss's private life was far less accessible than his burgeoning public career. In an era when few writers were celebrities, he wrote little of his family. In 1871, he married Emily Antoinette Torbush of Rutherford, New Jersey, a woman eleven years his junior. The couple produced one son, Harry T. Goss. Like John Minnich, he enjoyed a long marriage, although Goss, too, outlived his wife. Warren and Emily lived as man and wife for more than forty years, until her death in 1912, thirteen years before he died.[24]

He probably should not have lived to a ripe old age. His prison experiences left him sickly and emaciated, little more than one of the flesh-colored skeletons that so enraged the Northern public. Yet, like John Minnich, he defied the odds, outliving virtually all of his contemporaries. Goss was ninety years old when he died in his home in Rutherford, New Jersey, on November 20, 1925.[25]

As the years passed and he awoke each day alive and well, perhaps he recalled a moment in his youth when he wandered through the Andersonville Stockade, despondent at his plight, seeking solace from any source he could find. Fearing that he would soon die if his circumstances or outlook did not change, Goss stumbled upon a shred of paper lying face down on the ground. He said to himself, "if there is one word of hope on that piece of paper I will take courage and live." Leaning forward, he grasped the page in his bony hand and turned it over. The words leapt off the page as if they had been written especially for him:

> Ye fearful saints, fresh courage take,
> The clouds ye so much dread
> Are big with mercy and will break
> With blessings on your head.

It was hardly inspired poetry, but the message of hope was not lost on Goss, especially when the August rains brought forth the waters of the Providence Spring. He straightened up, gazed around at the scenes of horror littered about the prison pen, and told himself that he must not succumb to despair. John Minnich would have understood this newfound attitude completely. A man can endure any experience—no matter how terrible, no matter how dehumanizing, no matter how long it lasts—if he can hold on to the hope that the promise of the future is preferable to the reality of the present or the mistakes of the past. More than anything else, this was the lesson he carried with him from the shattered landscape of Civil War prisons: a man who hopes is a man who lives. Perhaps this insight is as fitting an epitaph as any for men like John Wesley Minnich and Warren Lee Goss—indeed, for all survivors of Civil War prisons.[26]

Notes

Citations may be fully identified by referring to the bibliography. One frequently cited source, the United States War Department, *War of the Rebellion: A Compilation of the Official Records of the Union and Confederate Armies* (Washington, D.C.: Government Printing Office, 1880–1901), is identified as "OR." A useful secondary source for delving into the OR is Aimone and Aimone.

INTRODUCTION: The Fires of Sectional Hatred

1. Minnich, *Inside of Rock Island Prison*, 4; State of Louisiana, Secretary of State, Division of Archives, Records Management and History, "Soldier's Application for Pension: John Wesley Minnich"; "Story of Rock Island Prison," 378.
2. Asbury, esp. 197–231 and 315–27; Chaitin, 54, 77; "D'Gournay's Battalion of Artillery," 30; Lonn, 102; Wallace, "Coppens' Louisiana Zouaves," 269.
3. Bergeron, *Guide to Confederate Military Units*, 152–54; Clarkson, 235–36; Current, 357–69, especially 359; Davis, *Brother Against Brother*, 127; Detzer, 152–59; "First Meeting Since the War," 333.
4. Bergeron, *Guide to Confederate Military Units*, 152–54; Booth, 581; Chaitin, 54, 77; "D'Gournay's Battalion of Artillery," 30; Joslyn, "Well-Born Paul Francois de Gournay," 85–88; Lonn, 102; Minnich, "About Re-Enlistments for the War," 552; Minnich, "Picturesque Soldiery," 295; Minnich, "With the Louisiana Zouaves," 425; Wallace, "Coppens' Louisiana Zouaves," 269–70, 272–73.
5. See Minnich, *Inside of Rock Island Prison*, published in 1908.
6. Adams, 152; Burke and Howe, 287; *Commemorative Biographical Record of Tolland and Windham Counties*, 939; Lawrence, 347; Marquis, 818; *Who Was Who Among North American Writers, 1921–1939*, Vol. 1, 605. The Harvard Law School Alumni Directory indicates that Warren Lee Goss entered the school on September 30, 1859, when he was twenty-four years old, and left in 1860. Like many of his peers, he did not earn the LL.B. degree; however, in an era before graduation from an accredited law school was a mandatory requirement, he could have chosen to practice law had he been inclined to sit for the bar examination. *Quinquennial Catalogue of the Law School of Harvard University, 1817–1904*.
7. The Adjutant General of Massachusetts, Vol. V, 730; Goss, *Recollections of a Private*, 2; Goss, *The Soldier's Story*, 2; Miller, "I Only Wait for the River," 43–65,

especially 47; Schreckenhost, 54–61; "Virtual American Biographies: James Chatham Duane."

8. Burke and Howe, 287; Kirk, Vol. I, 692; Minnich, *Inside of Rock Island Prison*, 4; Wallace, *A Dictionary of North American Authors Deceased Before 1950*, 176; *Who Was Who Among North American Writers, 1921–1939*, Vol. I, A-J, 605.
9. Adams, 152; Crandell, 7; "Deaths: Minnich," 2; Gandolfo, esp. Chapter 3; "John W. Minnich," 439; Lawrence, 347; Marquis, 818; *Who Was Who Among North American Writers, 1921–1939*, Vol. I, A-J, 605; State of Louisiana, Secretary of State, Division of Archives, Records Management and History, "Soldier's Application for Pension: John Wesley Minnich"; Wallace, *A Dictionary of North American Authors Deceased Before 1950*, 25.

CHAPTER 1: Surrendering Just Then Was Not on My Program

1. Minnich, "The Affair at May's Ferry, Tenn.," 55–56.
2. Ibid., 56.
3. Ibid.
4. Ibid.
5. Ibid.
6. Ibid.
7. Booth, 581; "D'Gournay's Battalion of Artillery," 30; Joslyn, "Well-Born Francois de Gournay," 8; Wallace, "Coppens' Louisiana Zouaves," 272–73; Weigley, 26.
8. Minnich, "Picturesque Soldiery," 295; Minnich, "With the Louisiana Zouaves," 425; Wallace, "Coppens' Louisiana Zouaves," 272–73. For a good source on the reasons why men on both sides of the conflict presented themselves for military service, see, for example, McPherson, *What They Fought For, 1861–1865*.
9. Bergeron, *Guide to Confederate Military Units*, 153; Joslyn, "Well-Born Francois de Gournay," 85–86; Wallace, "Coppens' Louisiana Zouaves," 271.
10. Carmichael, 96–129; Davis, *First Blood*, 78–84; Freeman, 57–59; Minnich, "Picturesque Soldiery," 296; Wallace, "Coppens' Louisiana Zouaves," 271–72.
11. Minnich, "Picturesque Soldiery," 297; Wallace, "Coppens' Louisiana Zouaves," 276–79.
12. Bailey, *Forward to Richmond*, 93; Minnich, "Incidents of the Peninsular Campaign," 53; Minnich, "Lightning Bugs in Virginia," 393.
13. Bailey, *Forward to Richmond*, 92–109; McPherson, *Battle Cry of Freedom*, 425–27; Weigley, 123–25.
14. Minnich, "Incidents of the Peninsular Campaign," 56. Many commentators have agreed with Minnich's low opinion of General McClellan's generalship. The issue is discussed especially well in Harsh, 55–72; McPherson, *Battle Cry of Freedom*, 359–65; Weigley, 119–20. For a contrary view, see Campbell, especially 166–77, and Rowland, *George B. McClellan and Civil War History*.
15. Bergeron, *Guide to Confederate Military Units*, 11, 153; Booth, 581; "Service Record: John W. Minich [*sic*]," 993; Wallace, "Coppens' Louisiana Zouaves," 279–80.
16. The Editors of Time-Life Books, *Spies, Scouts and Raiders*, 106–09; Korn, *The Fight for Chattanooga*, 112–14; Minnich, "At Bean's Station, Tenn.," 18–19; Minnich, "The Cavalry at Knoxville," 11–12; Minnich, "Famous Rifles," 247; Minnich, "Freezing and Fighting, December 10, 1863," 60; Minnich, "Hiding Out," 287; Minnich, "How Some History Is Written," 111; Minnich, "The 6th Georgia

Cavalry," 156. Confederate records list George W. Minnich (alternately spelled "Minich," "Minnick," or "Mimic") as a member of two cavalry units, first Jesse's Battalion, Kentucky Mounted Riflemen, and later, Company G of the Georgia Sixth Cavalry Regiment. Georgia State Archives, "Compiled Service Records," M226, Roll #CSR-34. For more on this and other unit histories, see, for example, Crute. For information on the Battle of Chickamauga and Minnich's role, see, for example: Bell, 71; Bowers, 320–21; The Editors of Time-Life Books, *Voices of the Civil War: Chickamauga*, 9–15; Franks; Korn, *The Fight for Chattanooga*, 44–73; McPherson, *Battle Cry of Freedom*, 670–76; Minnich, "Liddell's Division at Chickamauga," 22; Minnich, "Query Concerning Chickamauga"; Minnich, "Unique Experiences in the Chickamauga Campaign" (June 1927), 222; Minnich, "Unique Experiences in the Chickamauga Campaign" (Oct. 1927), 381; Morris, 66–73; Rone; Tucker, *Chickamauga: Bloody Battle in the West*, 388–89; Weigley; Woodworth, beginning at 79; Wyeth, 221–48.

17. The Adjutant General of Massachusetts, Vol. V, 730; Goss, *The Soldier's Story*, 2.
18. Miller, "I Only Wait for the River," 43–65, especially 47; Schreckenhost, 54–61; "Virtual American Biographies: James Chatham Duane."
19. Goss, *The Soldier's Story*, 2.
20. Ibid., 18–19.
21. Ibid.
22. Ibid., 19.
23. Connelly, 50–64; The Editors of Time-Life Books, *Lee Takes Command*, 22–27; Gallagher, 3–27; Hubbell, 28–43; Rowland, "Heaven Save a Country Governed by Such Counsels!" 5–17; Schreckenhost, 54–61; Thomas, *Robert E. Lee*, 224–29.
24. Goss, *The Soldier's Story*, 20.
25. Ibid., 21.
26. Ibid., 22.
27. Ibid., 22–23.
28. Ibid., 23.
29. Ibid., 23, 25.
30. Ibid., 25.
31. Ibid., 25–26.
32. Ibid., 26.
33. Ibid., 26–27.
34. Ibid.

CHAPTER 2: The Black and Reeking Pits

1. Minnich, "Freezing and Fighting: December 10, 1863," 60.
2. Minnich, "Hiding Out," 287.
3. Ibid.
4. Ibid.
5. Ibid., 287–88.
6. Ibid., 288.
7. Ibid.
8. Minnich, "Hiding Out," 288; Minnich, "That Affair at Dandridge, Tenn.," 294.
9. Minnich, "That Affair at Dandridge, Tenn.," 296.
10. Ibid., 296–97.

11. Ibid., 297.
12. Ibid.
13. Ibid.; Minnich, "The Cavalry at Knoxville," 13; Minnich, "The 6th Georgia Cavalry," 157.
14. Burr, 1; McAdams, 3; Walker, 48–49.
15. Putnam, 19. Another good physical description of the Libby Prison and life inside its walls can be found in Boaz.
16. Byrne, "Libby Prison: A Study in Emotions," 430–32; Jones, "Libby Prison Break," 93–94; Morgan, 36–37; Speer, 89–90; Thompson, "The Prisons of the War," 60.
17. Cavada, 25–27.
18. Abbott, 24–25.
19. United States Sanitary Commission, 31.
20. Isham, et al., 415–16.
21. Domschcke, 38; Glazier, 47; Cavada, 26. For a more detailed discussion of prisoners' beliefs that the Confederates deliberately engaged in acts of cruelty at the Libby Prison, see especially Byrne" Libby Prison: A Study in Emotions," 430–46.
22. Goss, *The Soldier's Story*, 27.
23. Ibid., 27–28.
24. Ibid., 28.
25. Ibid., 26–28.
26. Putnam, 39.
27. Jeffrey, 51–52.
28. Goss, *The Soldier's Story*, 29.
29. Bill, 138–45; Dabney, 184; Parker, *Richmond's Civil War Prisons*, 14–15; Speer, 92–93.

CHAPTER 3: He Is Lost, Indeed, Who Loses Hope

1. McAdams, 3; Walker, 48–49.
2. Burr, 1; Kost, 7–11; McAdams, 19; Speer, 154; Walker, 48.
3. McAdams, 3; Speer, 154; Walker, 48.
4. OR, Series II, VI, 115, 281, 634, 663, 938, 948; England, 1; Walker, 48.
5. McAdams, 12–13.
6. McAdams, 19, 24, 29; Speer, 175; United States Army, Rock Island Arsenal, Vol. I, 101.
7. England, 2–3; McAdams, 21–22.
8. McAdams, 22–23.
9. McAdams, 26–27.
10. England, 3; Thompson, "The Prisons of the War," 66–68; Walker, 48–49.
11. England, 3; Speer, 154–55; Tillinghast, 31–34; Walker, 48–49.
12. McAdams, 30; United States Army, Rock Island Arsenal, Vol. I, 103; Walker, 49.
13. England, 3; McAdams, 34–35; Walker, 49.
14. England, 5; Perry-Mosher, 29.
15. McAdams, 35–36; Walker, 49.
16. McAdams, 30–33; Speer, 174–77.
17. McAdams, 32.
18. Wright, 283.
19. McAdams, 45–46; Perry-Mosher, 30; Wright, 283–84.
20. England, 7, 9–11; McAdams, 48–53; Minnich, *Inside of Rock Island Prison*, 10.

21. Bill, 72, 138–45, 198; Dabney, 184; Isham, et al., 416–17; Thompson, "The Prisons of the War," 70–72.
22. Hesseltine, *Civil War Prisons*, 122; Parker, *Richmond's Civil War Prisons*, 14; Speer, 92–93; Thompson, "The Prisons of the War," 70–72.
23. Isham, et al., 417–18.
24. Boggs, 9–10.
25. McElroy, 114.
26. Goss, *The Soldier's Story*, 29–30.
27. Ibid., 30.
28. Ibid., 30–31.
29. Ibid., 34–35; United States Sanitary Commission, frontispiece.
30. Goss, *The Soldier's Story*, 35.
31. Ibid., 37.
32. Ibid., 43.
33. Ibid., 38.
34. Ibid., 38–39.
35. Ibid., 39.
36. Ibid., 39–40.
37. Ibid., 41–42.
38. Ibid., 43–45.
39. Ibid., 45–47.
40. Ibid., 48.
41. Ibid., 48–49; Speer, 92–93.
42. Goss, *The Soldier's Story*, 50.
43. Ibid., 51–52.
44. Ibid., 52–53.
45. Ibid., 54.

CHAPTER 4: The Exigencies of the Moment

1. Hesseltine, *Civil War Prisons*, 34–39.
2. Speer, xiv.
3. Speer, 9–10. See also Thompson, "The Prisons of the War," 54–64.
4. Gardner; Gordon-Burr, 125–41; Hesseltine, "The Propaganda Literature of Confederate Prisons," 56–66; Marvel, "Johnny Ransom's Imagination," 181–89; Roberts, "The Afterlife of Civil War Prisons"; United States Sanitary Commission.
5. Hesseltine, "The Propaganda Literature of Confederate Prisons," 63–66; United States House of Representatives, *Treatment of Prisoners of War by the Rebel Authorities*.
6. Burnham, 367–81; Gillispie, 41; Gragg, 137; Hesseltine, "The Propaganda Literature of Confederate Prisons," 56–66; Speer, xiv. The official U.S. Army estimate of the number of Americans killed in Vietnam as a result of hostile action (46,498); other causes (10,388), such as disease; and those presumed dead (719) was 56,146. Lewy, 451.
7. Hesseltine, *Civil War Prisons*, 34–39; McAdams, 3–12.
8. Gillispie, 41–42; Hesseltine, *Civil War Prisons*, 34–39; McAdams, 3–12; Speer, 11; Thompson, "The Prisons of the War," 64.
9. See, for example, Doig and Hargrove.

10. OR, Series II, III, 122–23; OR, Series II, VI, 115, 196; Gillispie, 42; Hesseltine, *Civil War Prisons*, 35, 181–85; McAdams, 6–12.
11. McAdams, 203.
12. Brown, 18–25; Byrne, "Prisons," 458–59; Hesseltine, *Civil War Prisons*, 34–39; McAdams, 3–12; Speer, 19–25.
13. Blakey, 46–48; Speer, 13.
14. Blakey, 175–201; Marvel, *Andersonville: The Last Depot*, 225–32.
15. Blakey, 2–5; Byrne, "Prisons," 460–61; Hesseltine, *Civil War Prisons*, 254–58; Speer, 15; Davis, *The Rise and Fall of the Confederate Government*, 505.
16. McElroy, 563; Boggs, 72; Hamlin, 24; United States House of Representatives, *Treatment of Prisoners of War by Rebel Authorities*, 31.
17. Blakey, 1–5; Jones, *A Rebel War Clerk's Diary*, 495; King, "Death Camp at Florence," 41.
18. OR, Series II, I, 166–67; Byrne, "Prisoners of War," 451–53; Hesseltine, *Civil War Prisons*, 68; Speer, 102; Weigley, 189–90. For an excellent overview of the myriad issues associated with the operation of the cartel, see also Thomas, "Prisoner of War Exchange During the American Civil War."
19. OR, Series II, I, 167; Weigley, 189–90. A good discussion of Lincoln's problems in the conduct of the war, including the issues associated with the question of prisoners, can be found in Tap.
20. Hesseltine, *Civil War Prisons*, 69–94; Speer, 97–105.
21. OR, Series II, IV, 283–84; Hesseltine, *Civil War Prisons*, 69–71; Jones, *A Rebel War Clerk's Diary*, 342; Speer, 103–105.
22. Byrne, "Prisoners of War," 451–53; Robertson, *Tenting Tonight*, 110–11; McPherson, *Battle Cry of Freedom*, 791–802.
23. McPherson, *Battle Cry of Freedom*, 791–802; Speer, 103–105.
24. Byrne, "Prisoners of War," 453; McPherson, *Battle Cry of Freedom*, 788–96; Toppin, 1–5; Weigley, 189–91.
25. Catton, *This Hallowed Ground*, 122; Jordan, 218–22; Toppin, 1–5; Weigley, 190–91; Williams, *A History of the Negro Troops in the War of the Rebellion*, 86, 110.
26. Gladstone, 104; Speer, 97–105; Toppin, 3–5; Weigley, 191.
27. Speer, 107–115; Toppin, 4–5.
28. McPherson, *Abraham Lincoln and the Second American Revolution*, 86–87; Speer, 107–115; Toppin, 3–5.
29. OR, Series II, VII, 64–65, 155–56; Dyer, 273, 282; Speer, 110–11; Toppin, 3–5; Trudeau, 382–94; Urwin, 193–210; Williams, *A History of the Negro Troops in the War of the Rebellion*, 257–72; Wilson, *The Black Phalanx*, 239, 349–53.
30. Cornish, 177–78; Dyer, 273, 282; Speer, 111–15; Sprague, 54–55; Toppin, 1–5; Westwood, "Captive Black Union Soldiers in Charleston," 30–31, 38; Williams, "Again in Chains," 40–43; Williams, *A History of the Negro Troops in the War of the Rebellion*, 110–15.
31. Bergeron, "Free Men of Color in Grey," 247–55; Rhea, 364–65; Silverman and Silverman, 35–43; Speer, 107–115; Toppin, 1–5. For more information on the experiences of black soldiers in the war, see, for example, Cornish; Gladstone; Glatthaar; Jordan; Quarles; Westwood, *Black Troops, White Commanders*; Williams, *A History of the Negro Troops in the War of the Rebellion*; Wilson, *The Black Phalanx*.
32. Hesseltine, *Civil War Prisons*, 111–113; Speer, 14.
33. McPherson, *Battle Cry of Freedom*, 796–802; Speer, 14.

CHAPTER 5: We Were Ushered into What Seemed to Us Hades Itself

1. England, 27; McAdams, 29; Tillinghast, 34.
2. McAdams, 29.
3. England, 27; McAdams, 29.
4. England, 27; McAdams, 29; Speer, 175.
5. England, 27–28; McAdams, xi–xiii, 29, 211.
6. Minnich, *Inside of Rock Island Prison*, 20–21.
7. England, 25; McAdams, 162.
8. England, 25; McAdams, 163–64.
9. England, 27–28; McAdams, xi, 208.
10. England, 26–27; McAdams, 164–65.
11. McAdams, 165.
12. McAdams, 165–66.
13. Minnich, *Inside of Rock Island Prison*, 23.
14. Ibid., 37.
15. Ibid., 38.
16. England, 27–32; McAdams, 207–08; Minnich, 37–39.
17. McAdams, 208–11.
18. Goss, *The Soldier's Story*, 54.
19. Ibid., 54–55; The Adjutant General of Massachusetts, Vol. VII, 51.
20. Chaitin, 91–96; Foote, 113–14; Goss, *The Soldier's Story*, 54–55.
21. Chaitin, 91–93.
22. Chaitin, 93–95.
23. Chaitin, 94–95; Goss, *The Soldier's Story*, 54–55.
24. Goss, *The Soldier's Story*, 55–57.
25. Ibid., 57–58.
26. Ibid., 58–59.
27. Ibid., 59–60. Margaret Leonard was the wife of Private Isaac Newton Leonard of Company H. She was captured at Plymouth along with her husband and most of his regiment. From there, she was sent to the Confederate prison at Camp Sumter, Andersonville, Georgia, where she served as a hospital matron. Later, she was transferred to Macon, Georgia, and Castle Thunder in Richmond, Virginia. She eventually applied for a widow's pension in California in 1890. The Civil War Plymouth Pilgrims Descendants Society, "Roster of the 2nd Massachusetts Heavy Artillery, Companies G & H."
28. Goss, *The Soldier's Story*, 60. Union Gen. Henry W. Wessells later explained that the intense Confederate artillery barrage gave him few options but to surrender Fort Williams. "The condition of affairs could not be long endured without reckless sacrifice of life," he said. Chaitin, 95–96.
29. The name "Plymouth Pilgrims" refers to the Union soldiers captured at Plymouth, North Carolina, in April 1864. Aside from the name of the town where the troops were captured and the appealing alliteration, the origin and exact meaning of the term are obscure. It may have referred to the resemblance of the soldiers' original hats—which Goss described as a "tall dress hat" with "an ostrich plume which embellished it"—to the hats worn by the Mayflower Pilgrims, or it may have been a sardonic reference to the slow, somber walk of the prisoners, "like Pilgrims on their way to church." Goss, *The Soldier's Story*, 60–61. See also: Chaitin, 94–97; Kellogg, 33–46, 51, 61.

30. Goss, *The Soldier's Story*, 61.
31. Ibid.
32. Ibid.
33. Ibid, 61–62.
34. Kellogg, 45.
35. Goss, *The Soldier's Story*, 63–64.
36. Ibid.
37. Ibid., 65; Kellogg, 47.
38. Goss, *The Soldier's Story*, 65–67.
40. Ibid., 65–66.
41. Ibid., 66–67.
42. Futch, *History of Andersonville Prison*, 2–4; Hesseltine, *Civil War Prisons*, 133–36.
43. Joyner, 120–21; Smith, 29–30; Kelley, 31.
44. Goss, *The Soldier's Story*, 68; Kellogg, 49.
45. Goss, *The Soldier's Story*, 68.
46. Ibid., 68–70.
47. Ibid., 70–71.
48. Ibid., 71.
49. Futch, *History of Andersonville Prison*, 16–17; Genoways and Genoways, 251–53; Jervey, 31–32; Marvel, *Andersonville: The Last Depot*, 35–36; Rutman, 118–19; Spencer, 56; Thompson, *A Captive of War*, 92–93.
50. Byrne, "Andersonville Prison," 13; Futch, *History of Andersonville Prison*, 16–17; Marvel, *Andersonville: The Last Depot*, 36; Rutman, 118–19.
51. Futch, *History of Andersonville Prison*, 17; Marvel, *Andersonville: The Last Depot*, 37; Rutman, 118–19.
52. Futch, *History of Andersonville Prison*, 17; Marvel, *Andersonville: The Last Depot*, 37–38; Rutman, 118–19.
53. Futch, *History of Andersonville Prison*, 14–17; Marvel, *Andersonville: The Last Depot*, 21, 38; Rutman, 118–19; Speer, 260.
54. Byrne, "Andersonville Prison," 13; Hesseltine, *Civil War Prisons*, 140; Phillips, 19; Hamlin, 26; Brownell, 7; McElroy, 143.
55. Davis, *The Rise and Fall of the Confederate Government*, 505; Stevenson, "Andersonville Prison," 28. For more on the Southern position, see, for example, Andrews, "The Treatment of Prisoners of the Confederacy," 147–50; Ashe, "The Treatment of Prisoners in 1864–65"; Ashe, *The Trial and Death of Henry Wirz*; Jones, *Confederate View of the Treatment of Prisoners*, esp. 160–77; Joslyn, "Who Caused Andersonville?" 181–91; Murray, 210–15; "Union Officer Who Was in Prison," 167; Young, 470–73.
56. Hesseltine, *Civil War Prisons*, 134; Marvel, *Andersonville: The Last Depot*, 14–17; Speer, 259.
57. Byrne, "Andersonville Prison," 12; Futch, *History of Andersonville Prison*, 1–6; Hesseltine, *Civil War Prisons*, 134–37; Lutz, 54–55; Marvel, *Andersonville: The Last Depot*, 17–20; Speer, 259–60.
58. Hesseltine, *Civil War Prisons*, 135–36; Styple and Fitzpatricks, 73–74; Thompson, *A Captive of War*, 93–95; Watson, 227–32.
59. Futch, *History of Andersonville Prison*, 19–20; Hesseltine, *Civil War Prisons*, 135–36; Speer, 259–61; Styple and Fitzpatricks, 73–74; Thompson, *A Captive of War*, 94.

60. McElroy, 128; Forbes, 11; Miller, *The Story of Andersonville and Florence*, 16.
61. Kellogg, 56; Watson, 232; Ripple, 18.
62. Goss, *The Soldier's Story*, 72–73. See also, for example: Bastile, 63–84; Boggs, 18–19; Broomfield, 28; Brownell, 9–13; Creelman, 6–12; Dufur, 69–84; Harrold, 42–55; Jervey, 32–34; Miller, *The Story of Andersonville and Florence*, 15–17; Phillips, 18–19; Urban, 454–68.

CHAPTER 6: Too Much Fuss over a Very Small Matter

1. Minnich, *Inside of Rock Island Prison*, 22–23; Wright, 284–85.
2. England, 32–33; McAdams, 88, 102; Walker, 54–55.
3. McAdams, 88.
4. Minnich, *Inside of Rock Island Prison*, 16.
5. Ibid.
6. Ibid.
7. Ibid., 17.
8. Ibid., 19.
9. Ibid., 19–20.
10. Ibid., 20.
11. Ibid.
12. Ibid., 21.
13. Walker, 54–55.
14. England, 33.
15. England, 33; McAdams, 107–08.
16. England, 33.
17. McAdams, 108.
18. Minnich, *Inside of Rock Island Prison*, 34.
19. Wright, 285.
20. OR, Series II, VII, 1037; McAdams, 106–07; Walker, 54–55; Wright, 285.
21. McAdams, 107.
22. Minnich, *Inside of Rock Island Prison*, 28.
23. Ibid.
24. Ibid., 29–30.
25. Ibid., 34; Wright, 285.
26. England, 24; McAdams, 210; National Archives & Records Administration, *Record of Prisoners of War Who Have Died at Rock Island Barracks, Illinois.*
27. Goss, *The Soldier's Story*, 85.
28. Ibid., 85–86.
29. Kellogg, 61; United States Sanitary Commission, 260; Brownell, 10. See also, for example, Boggs, 32–33; Broomfield, 29; Creelman, 10; Helmreich, 15–16; McElroy, 141; Miller, *The Story of Andersonville and Florence*, 17.
30. McElroy, 141; Ripple, 19; Smith, 36; Futch, *History of Andersonville Prison*, 42–43.
31. OR, Series II, VII, 393; Boggs, 31; Hesseltine, *Civil War Prisons*, 143–44; Speer, 263–64.
32. Goss, *The Soldier's Story*, 86–87.
33. Boggs, 21–22; Futch, *History of Andersonville Prison*, 50–51; Marvel, *Andersonville: The Last Depot*, 64.
34. Futch, *History of Andersonville Prison*, 40–41, 63–64; Hesseltine, *Civil War Prisons*, 144–46; Marvel, *Andersonville: The Last Depot*, 110–11.

35. Futch, *History of Andersonville Prison*, 40–41; Marvel, *Andersonville: The Last Depot*, 110–12.
36. Ransom, 53; Goss, *The Soldier's Story*, 150; McElroy, 226.
37. Kelley, 50–51; Boggs, 35; Miller, *The Story of Andersonville and Florence*, 22.
38. Goss, *The Soldier's Story*, 152–53; Smith, 41; The Civil War Plymouth Pilgrims Descendants Society. "Big Peter" Aubrey should not be confused with "Big Pete" McCullough, a soldier from Company G, Eighth Missouri Infantry, who also served briefly as chief of the inmate police force and later acted as judge advocate for the trial of the Raiders at Andersonville. Sallee, 22–25.
39. Futch, *History of Andersonville Prison*, 71; McElroy, 225–29; Marvel, *Andersonville: The Last Depot*, 144.
40. Futch, "Andersonville Raiders," 49; Futch, *History of Andersonville Prison*, 63–64; Marvel, *Andersonville: The Last Depot*, 69–71.
41. Futch, "Andersonville Raiders," 51; Futch, *History of Andersonville Prison*, 64–66; Hesseltine, *Civil War Prisons*, 144–45; McElroy, 225–27; Ripple, 26–27.
42. Futch, *History of Andersonville Prison*, 64–66; Hesseltine, *Civil War Prisons*, 144–46; Marvel, *Andersonville: The Last Depot*, 97–100; Speer, 264.
43. Goss, *The Soldier's Story*, 153–54.
44. Futch, "Andersonville Raiders," 53–54; Marvel, *Andersonville: The Last Depot*, 96–97; McElroy, 227–29.
45. Futch, "Andersonville Raiders," 54; Marvel, *Andersonville: The Last Depot*, 96–97; McElroy, 228–29.
46. Forbes, 25–26; Futch, *History of Andersonville Prison*, 68–69; Marvel, *Andersonville: The Last Depot*, 97–98.
47. Forbes, 25–26; Futch, "Andersonville Raiders," 57–60; Futch, *History of Andersonville Prison*, 69–71; Marvel, *Andersonville: The Last Depot*, 97–98.
48. Forbes, 25; Kellogg, 156; Ripple, 27. The notorious character "Limber Jim" Laughlin is discussed in detail in Futch, "Andersonville Raiders," beginning at 53.
49. OR, Series II, VII, 426; Futch, *History of Andersonville Prison*, 71; Kellogg, 155–56; Marvel, *Andersonville: The Last Depot*, 99–100; Sallee, 22–25.
50. Futch, *History of Andersonville Prison*, 71; Hesseltine, *Civil War Prisons*, 144–45; Kellogg, 156; Marvel, *Andersonville: The Last Depot*, 99–100; Sallee, 23.
51. Goss, *The Soldier's Story*, 156.
52. Futch, *History of Andersonville Prison*, 71; Hesseltine, *Civil War Prisons*, 145; Marvel, *Andersonville: The Last Depot*, 100; Sallee, 22.
53. Forbes, 29; Futch, "Andersonville Raiders," 58–60; Futch, *History of Andersonville Prison*, 72–73; Marvel, *Andersonville: The Last Depot*, 142–43.
54. Ibid.; Hammer, 86–88.
55. Futch, "Andersonville Raiders," 58–60; Futch, *History of Andersonville Prison*, 73; Lutz, 54–55; Marvel, *Andersonville: The Last Depot*, 143.
56. Futch, *History of Andersonville Prison*, 73; Marvel, *Andersonville: The Last Depot*, 143–44; Thompson, *A Captive of War*, 111–12.
57. Forbes, 29; Futch, *History of Andersonville Prison*, 73–74; Hammer, 86–88; Marvel, *Andersonville: The Last Depot*, 143–44; Thompson, *A Captive of War*, 111–12.
58. Forbes, 29; Futch, "Andersonville Raiders," 58–60; Futch, *History of Andersonville Prison*, 73–74; Hammer, 86–88; Helmreich, 21; Marvel, *Andersonville: The Last Depot*, 143–44; Spencer, 132–35; Thompson, "The Prisons of the War," 111–12.

CHAPTER 7: The Grave Question of Escape

1. McAdams, 140; "One of the C7K," 527; "Treatment of Prisoners at Rock Island," 60.
2. England, 22. Inmate Charles Wright remembered the initial call for volunteers for U.S. service coming in March, not January. He concluded that 1,077 recruits stepped forward. A second call in September 1864 netted virtually no new recruits. Wright, 286.
3. England, 25; McAdams, 141.
4. McAdams, 140–41; "One of the C7K," 527; "Treatment of Prisoners at Rock Island," 60; "C7K," 455.
5. "One of the C7K," 527; "Treatment of Prisoners at Rock Island," 60.
6. England, 21; McAdams, 82; Pullen, 287.
7. Perry-Mosher, 33–34.
8. McAdams, 82; Pullen, 287.
9. England, 17–18; Speer, 230.
10. Berry, 65–69; England, 16; National Archives & Records Administration, *General Register of Prisoners: 1864–1865*.
11. Hord, 385–89; England, 16–17.
12. OR, Series II, VIII, 523–25, 896; England, 21; McAdams, 154. An excellent source on the lives of Civil War prisoners as well as a compendium on escape attempts is Denney.
13. Minnich, "Tunnels to Release Prisoners," 554; Walker, 54–55.
14. Minnich, "Tunnels to Release Prisoners," 554.
15. Ibid.
16. England, 17; Walker, 54.
17. England, 18.
18. Minnich, "Tunnels to Release Prisoners," 554.
19. Ibid.
20. Walker, 54.
21. Goss, *The Soldier's Story*, 116–17; Futch, *History of Andersonville Prison*, 52–54.
22. Futch, *History of Andersonville Prison*, 50–51; Futch, "Prison Life at Andersonville," 125–28.
23. Goss, *The Soldier's Story*, 117.
24. Some of the most dramatic tales recounting the use of dogs to apprehend escaped prisoners include Dufur; Ransom; Ripple; Smith; Stafford; Williams, *From Spotsylvania to Wilmington, N.C.*
25. Goss, *The Soldier's Story*, 117–18.
26. Ibid., 118.
27. Ibid., 119.
28. Ibid., 119–20.
29. Ibid., 120–21.
30. Ibid., 122.
31. Ibid., 122–23.
32. Ibid., 123–24.
33. Ibid.
34. Ibid., 124–25.
35. Ibid.
36. Ibid., 125–26.
37. Ibid.

38. Ibid., 126.
39. Ibid., 126–27.
40. Ibid., 127.
41. Ibid., 127–28.
42. Ibid., 128.
43. Ibid.
44. Ibid., 128–29.
45. Ibid., 129.
46. Ibid.
47. Ibid., 130.
48. Ibid., 130–31.
49. Ibid., 131.
50. Ibid., 131–32.
51. Ibid., 132–33.
52. Ibid., 134.
53. Ibid., 134–35.
54. Ibid., 137.
55. Ibid., 135; Futch, *History of Andersonville Prison*, 49–50; Futch, "Prison Life at Andersonville," 124.

CHAPTER 8: That Most Terrible of Afflictions—Hunger

1. Minnich, *Inside of Rock Island Prison*, 7–8; Speer, 216.
2. McAdams, 80–83; Minnich, *Inside of Rock Island Prison*, 8–9; Perry-Mosher, 30–31; Tillinghast, 31, 33.
3. McAdams, 82; Minnich, *Inside of Rock Island Prison*, 8–9; Perry-Mosher, 30.
4. Minnich, *Inside of Rock Island Prison*, 8.
5. Johnson, "Some Prison Experiences," 82; Wright, 287; Minnich, *Inside of Rock Island Prison*, 9; United States Army, Rock Island Arsenal, Vol. I, 103–04.
6. Minnich, *Inside of Rock Island Prison*, 9.
7. McAdams, 96–97.
8. Ibid., 96–98; Tillinghast, 33–34.
9. McAdams, 98–99; Minnich, *Inside of Rock Island Prison*, 10–11.
10. McAdams, 147–50; Speer, 14–15.
11. McAdams, 169; Minnich, *Inside of Rock Island Prison*, 10–11.
12. Minnich, *Inside of Rock Island Prison*, 11.
13. McAdams, 149; Minnich, *Inside of Rock Island Prison*, 11.
14. McAdams, 82; Minnich, *Inside of Rock Island Prison*, 8–9; Perry-Mosher, 30.
15. Miller, *The Story of Andersonville and Florence*, 26; McElroy, 205; Goss, *The Soldier's Story*, 88. See also Brooks, 111.
16. Goss, *The Soldier's Story*, 89.
17. Ibid., 75; Lutz, 54–55; Speer, 261.
18. Goss, *The Soldier's Story*, 75–76.
19. Ibid., 78.
20. Ibid., 78–83.
21. Ibid., 94–95.
22. Ibid., 97–98.
23. Ibid., 98–99.
24. Ibid., 99.

25. Ibid., 99–100.
26. Marvel, *Andersonville: The Last Depot*, 179–80.

CHAPTER 9: Sickness and Death Were Inevitable Accompaniments

1. Blustein, 22–41; Freemon, 19–26; Gillispie, 46; Hesseltine, *Civil War Prisons*, 151; McPherson, *Battle Cry of Freedom*, 485–89.
2. Brooks, 120; Gillispie, 46–47; McPherson, *Battle Cry of Freedom*, 487.
3. Brooks, 111–120; Gillispie, 46–48; McPherson, *Battle Cry of Freedom*, 487–88; Smart, 45–46; Speer, 14. The Woodward volume, *The Medical and Surgical History of the War of the Rebellion, Volume 1, Part II: Medical History*, is devoted almost exclusively to diseases associated with "inflammation of the bowels," especially diarrhea and dysentery. Dr. David F. Cross has argued that hookworm disease was responsible for many deaths, especially in the Andersonville Stockade. Cross, 26–32.
4. Gillispie, 47–48; Speer, 155.
5. Brooks, 120; Creehan, 6–7; McAdams, 49–51.
6. Brooks, 120; Creehan, 6–7.
7. Creehan, 6; McAdams, 49.
8. Lewis-Jones and Baxby, 77–78.
9. Walker, 49; Wright, 283–84.
10. OR, Series II, VI, 1004; Speer, 154–55; Stephens, *Rock Island Confederate Prison Deaths*, 41, 51–52; Walker, 49–50.
11. OR, Series II, VII, 13–15; England, 9; United States Army, Rock Island Arsenal, Vol. I, 103–04; Walker, 52.
12. Minnich, *Inside of Rock Island Prison*, 7–8; Speer, 216.
13. Goss, *The Soldier's Story*, 87–88; Futch, *History of Andersonville Prison*, 98–88; Marvel, *Andersonville: The Last Depot*, 39.
14. Futch, *History of Andersonville Prison*, 98–99; Marvel, *Andersonville: The Last Depot*, 40.
15. OR, Series II, VII, 89; Futch, *History of Andersonville Prison*, 98–99; Hesseltine, *Civil War Prisons*, 138–39; Marvel, *Andersonville: The Last Depot*, 40–41.
16. Marvel, *Andersonville: The Last Depot*, 179–80.
17. Goss, *The Soldier's Story*, 175–76.
18. Futch, *History of Andersonville Prison*, 95; Hammer, 91–92; Hesseltine, *Civil War Prisons*, 153; Kelley, 61–62; Kellogg, 209–14.
19. Futch, *History of Andersonville Prison*, 94–95; Hesseltine, *Civil War Prisons*, 153; Marvel, *Andersonville: The Last Depot*, 179–80.
20. OR, Series II, VII, 583–84, 586, 588–89; Forbes, 37; Futch, *History of Andersonville Prison*, 95; Hammer, 91–92; Kellogg, 209–13; Marvel, *Andersonville: The Last Depot*, 179–80.
21. Watson, 248; Boggs, 54.
22. Ripple, 38–39; Creelman, 13–14; McElroy, 353; Miller, *The Story of Andersonville and Florence*, 17. See also Futch, "Prison Life at Andersonville," 135.
23. Goss, *The Soldier's Story*, 176–77.
24. Ibid., 174.

CHAPTER 10: Crazy with the Idea of Freedom and Home

1. England, 35; McAdams, 142–43.
2. England, 35; McAdams, 142–43; McPherson, *Battle Cry of Freedom*, 500.

3. England, 35; McAdams, 143–44; Minnich, *Inside of Rock Island Prison*, 32.
4. McAdams, 143–45.
5. See, for example, Cornish; Glatthaar; Quarles; Toppin; Westwood, *Black Troops, White Commanders*; Williams, *A History of the Negro Troops in the War of the Rebellion*.
6. England, 35; McAdams, 142–43; McPherson, 564–66.
7. Quoted in England, 36.
8. Ibid.
9. McAdams, 144.
10. McAdams, 146; Minnich, "Comment on Rock Island Prison," 394.
11. McAdams, 146; Walker, 54–55.
12. Minnich, *Inside of Rock Island Prison*, 31–32.
13. Ibid., 32.
14. Hord, 387; McAdams, 144–45.
15. McAdams, 145.
16. England, 35; McAdams, 142–44; Minnich, *Inside of Rock Island Prison*, 31–32.
17. Byrne, "Prisons," 458–59; Hesseltine, *Civil War Prisons*, 34–39; Speer, 19–25.
18. Davis, *An Honorable Defeat*, 4–35; Davis, *Look Away!*, 397–400, 402–05; McPherson, *Battle Cry of Freedom*, 819–30; Weigley, 386–402; Winik, esp. 73–75, 102–11.
19. Catton, *The American Heritage New History of the Civil War*, 512–28, 533–39; Nevin, 8–43; Simpson, 382–84; Ward, 321–49; Weigley, 389–96.
20. Donald, 530–32; The Editors of Time-Life Books, *Voices of the Civil War: Atlanta*, 89–142; Foote, 374, 596, 600, 654; McMurry, 141–42, 174–76; McPherson, *Abraham Lincoln and the Second American Revolution*, 87–91; Oates, *With Malice Toward None*, 419–23, 437–39, 451; Rhea, 260–61; Waugh, 296–98; Winik, 303–11.
21. Sherman did not abandon his role as a liberator lightly or without attempting a rescue. During the summer, he allowed General George Stoneman to lead five thousand men to a point near Lovejoy's Station, Georgia, to destroy the railroad line between Macon and Atlanta. As part of that mission, Stoneman was authorized to "proceed to Macon & Andersonville and release our prisoners of war confined at those points." After Stoneman was repulsed by a ragtag force of Georgia reserves, local citizens, and the state militia as well as captured—he was sent to the Camp Oglethorpe Confederate Prison to await exchange—Sherman abandoned his plans to free the Andersonville captives. In the larger scope of his strategy, he could not alter his March to the Sea to undertake a side mission, no matter how symbolically welcome such a campaign might have been. Evans, *Sherman's Horsemen*, 205–06, 294, 356–57, 362–63, 376; Futch, *History of Andersonville Prison*, 84–85; Lewis, *Sherman: Fighting Prophet*, 431; Marvel, *Andersonville: The Last Depot*, 158–61; McMurry, 157–58; Montgomery, 122–23.
22. OR, Series II, VII, 817; Byrne, "Prisons," 462; Helmreich, 21; King, "Death Camp at Florence," 35; Martinez, 10.
23. Goss, *The Soldier's Story*, 181.
24. Ibid., 185.
25. Ibid., 186–87.
26. Ibid., 188; Speer, 28, 29, 213–15.
27. OR, Series II, VII, 817.

28. Andrews, *The South Since the War*, 191.
29. Gregg, 2; Northrop, 135; Fosdick, 72.
30. Baker, 5–7; Davis, *A History of Florence*, 587–614; King, "The Emergence of Florence, South Carolina," 197–200; King, *Rise Up So Early*, 45–58; Roberts, "The Afterlife of Civil War Prisons," 177–80.
31. Baker, 5–7; Davis, *A History of Florence*, 587–614; King, "The Emergence of Florence, South Carolina," 197–98; King, *Rise Up So Early*, 45–58.
32. Baker, 6; Byrne, "Prisons," 462; King, "The Emergence of Florence, South Carolina," 199–200. For more on the hardships endured by towns and crossroads, even those relatively insulated from the fighting, see especially Curry, 169–75.
33. King, "The Emergence of Florence, South Carolina," 197–98; King, *Rise Up So Early*, 36–39; Martinez, 10–17.
34. Clarkson, 234–36; Davis, *A History of Florence*, 583; Detzer, 155–65; King, *Rise Up So Early*, 45–46; Muldrow, 233; Ramsdell, 259–88.
35. Davis, *A History of Florence*, 589–90; Gragg, 163–66; Martinez, 10, 12; Tucker, "Fifty Exposed as the 'Six Hundred,'" 364.
36. Davis, *A History of Florence*, 591–93; Isham, et al., 423–24; Kellogg, 315–19; King, "Death Camp at Florence," 37; Smith, 78–79; Watson, 274–77.
37. Davis, *A History of Florence*, 593–95; King, "Death Camp at Florence," 35–37.
38. OR, Series II, VII, 449; King, "Death Camp at Florence," 36; King, *Rise Up So Early*, 49–50; Rogers, "Pee Dee Pen: Mass Prison Escape Narrowly Averted at Florence Stockade," n.p. Slave impressments by the Confederate military, especially late in the war, were not uncommon. See, for example, Channing, 23; Davis, *Look Away!*, 154–56.
39. In addition to contacting General Jones, on September 18, Warley also telegraphed Brig. Gen. Roswell S. Ripley, the Confederate commander in charge of Charleston, asking that Ripley "send every available man that can be spared" as soon as possible to prevent a mass escape. General Ripley no doubt was sympathetic to Major Warley's precarious position. A large, rotund career military officer and West Point graduate who had commanded the South Carolina artillery forces that fired on Fort Sumter and later served in the Seven Days' Battles before suffering a wound at South Mountain, Ripley understood the dangers of guarding prisoners with an inadequate force. Unfortunately, he, too, faced an untenable situation as he struggled to maintain law and order in Charleston while the Confederacy collapsed all around him. He simply could spare no men. Freeman, 148, 363, 376, 379, 382, 386; King, "Death Camp at Florence," 36–37; Martinez, 10, 12.
40. King, "Death Camp at Florence," 36–37; King, *Rise Up So Early*, 49–50; Martinez, 10, 12; Rogers, "Pee Dee Pen: Mass Prison Escape Narrowly Averted at Florence Stockade," n.p.
41. OR, Series II, VIII, 765–66; Davis, *A History of Florence*, 591–93; Isham, et al., 423–24; Kellogg, 315–19; Smith, 78–79; Styple and Fitzpatricks, 144–67; Woods, "Notes on the Confederate Stockade"; "The Yankee Prisoners at Florence," 1.
42. OR, Series II, VII, 974, 986; Byrne, "Prisons," 460; Catton, "A Civil, and Sometimes Uncivil, War," 51; Davis, *A History of Florence*, 595–601; Freeman, 652; King, "Death Camp at Florence," 37; King, *Rise Up So Early*, 50–51.
43. OR, Series II, VII, 962–64, 975.
44. OR, Series II, VII, 972; Davis, *A History of Florence*, 597–98; King, "Death Camp at Florence," 35–37; Woods, "Notes on the Confederate Stockade," 11. Of all the

men who served at the Florence Stockade, Colonel Harrison was the most celebrated, especially in the years after the war. By all accounts, he was an ambitious young man on the rise who stopped only briefly at Florence during his ascendancy. Born on the Montieth Plantation near Savannah, Georgia, on March 19, 1841, he hailed from an illustrious family, for he was the son of George P. Harrison, Sr., a distinguished Georgia state legislator and general officer in the Confederate States Army. Both men eventually served as generals for the Confederacy during the Civil War, making them one of five father-son combinations of generals who held that distinction.

The younger Harrison began his academic career by enrolling in the Effingham Academy. He was a student at the Georgia Military Institute when the first states seceded from the Union. In January 1861, he left school to assist in seizing Fort Pulaski on the Georgia coast. Later, he enlisted in the Confederate Army as a lieutenant in the First Georgia Regulars. After briefly returning to school to take his degree, he rejoined the army and advanced through the ranks. On May 15, 1862, he was elected colonel of the Thirty-second Georgia Infantry. He still held this position when he was assigned to the Florence Stockade two years later.

For much of his military career, Harrison was stationed in or near Charleston. At various times, he commanded Fort Johnson, Morris Island, and John's Island. He was twice wounded in battle. Following the Battle of Olustee in 1864, Harrison received a citation for his "brave and daring" actions under fire. In September of that year, he came to Florence and served for about a month. Later, he commanded a mixed brigade of Georgia infantry and reserves in the Carolinas campaign and at the Battle of Bentonville, the last major engagement in the eastern theater. He was promoted to brigadier general two months before he surrendered at Greensboro, North Carolina, on April 26, 1865.

Harrison's postwar career proved that his early promise was no fluke. After the conflict ended, he moved to Alabama. In 1872–73, he served as commandant of cadets at Alabama A & M University (later renamed Auburn University). He also became a lawyer and planter, and attended the 1875 Alabama constitutional convention. The retired general eventually moved to nearby Opelika and won election to the state senate in 1878. During the last two years of his six years in office, he served as president of the senate. After attending the 1892 Democratic National Convention as a delegate, Harrison was elected to the U.S. House of Representatives as a Democrat to represent Alabama in the Fifty-third Congress. He served out the unexpired term of William C. Oates, who resigned late in 1894. That November, Harrison won election to his own term in the Fifty-fourth Congress.

When his term ended on March 3, 1897, Harrison returned to Opelika and practiced law. He won reelection to the state senate in 1900 and 1902. As a prominent lawyer and political figure, he served as a delegate to the state constitutional convention in 1901 and represented the Western Railway of Alabama as general counsel for many years. Always interested in the activities of Confederate veterans, Harrison rose to the rank of major general in the Alabama Division of the United Confederate Veterans, a position he held at the time of his death on July 17, 1922, at the age of eighty-one. He was buried in the Rosemere Cemetery in Opelika. Allardice, 123–24; "Commander of the Army of Tennessee Department, U.C.V.," 57; Cox, 16; "Gen. George P. Harrison," 283; "Harrison,

George Paul, 1841–1922"; King, "Death Camp at Florence," 37–38; Martinez, 13–14; Wise, 175; "Youngest General in the Confederate Army," 55–58.

45. OR, Series II, VII, 972–74; Davis, *A History of Florence*, 598–99; Thompson, "The Prisons of the War," 86–87.
46. OR, Series II, VII, 972–74; King, "Death Camp at Florence," 37; King, *Rise Up So Early*, 50–51.
47. OR, Series II, VII, 973–74; King, "Death Camp at Florence," 37; King, *Rise Up So Early*, 50–51.
48. OR, Series II, VII, 974; King, "Death Camp at Florence," 37–38.
49. OR, Series II, VII, 1097–1110; Davis, *A History of Florence*, 600–01; United States House of Representatives, *Treatment of Prisoners of War by the Rebel Authorities*, 185–86.
50. King, "Death Camp at Florence," 37; Martinez, 13.
51. Goss, *The Soldier's Story*, 216.
52. Ibid., 217–18; Dowling, 326; Harrold, 61–62; Leonard, 62.

CHAPTER 11: It's Twelve O'clock and All Is Well, and Old Jeff Davis Is Gone to Hell!

1. Minnich, *Inside of Rock Island Prison*, 33.
2. Ibid., 33–34.
3. Ibid., 34.
4. Ibid., 34–35.
5. Ibid., 23, 36.
6. Ibid., 36; McAdams, 83–84.
7. Minnich, *Inside of Rock Island Prison*, 36. Emphases in the original. It is difficult to corroborate this episode in Minnich's account. He may have been describing the "deranged" guard, William Boyd, as the black soldier who wantonly shot prisoners; unfortunately, Minnich provided no dates or other details, so it is impossible to resolve the matter.
8. Minnich, *Inside of Rock Island Prison*, 33–34.
9. Goss, *The Soldier's Story*, 216–17.
10. Ibid.
11. Ibid., 217–18.
12. Ibid., 218.
13. Ibid., 218–19.
14. Ibid., 219–20.
15. Ibid., 220–21.
16. Ibid., 221.
17. Ibid., 235–36.
18. Ibid., 221–22.
19. Ibid., 222; Phillips, 62.
20. Goss, *The Soldier's Story*, 222–23.
21. Kellogg, 341; Urban, 613; Boggs, 60; McElroy, 578; Fosdick, 77–78; Miller, *The Story of Andersonville and Florence*, 37; Northrop, 161–62.
22. Goss, *The Soldier's Story*, 225–26. The dastardly Lieutenant Barrett either was Thomas Glascock Barrett or James Barrett Jr. Both men served as lieutenants in Company C, Fifth Georgia Volunteer Infantry Regiment, at the time that the unit served at the Florence Stockade. Barrett was a relatively common name in Richmond County, which includes the area around Augusta, Georgia, so it is dif-

ficult to resolve the issue definitively. Some sources indicate that Thomas Glascock was the offending officer while others suggest that James was the likely culprit. According to his service record, James Barrett Jr. originally enlisted in Company A ("The Clinch Rifles") of the Fifth Georgia before eventually transferring to Company C. He was detailed to Florence as inspector of military prisons in November 1864. Thomas Glascock Barrett's service record does not indicate that he ever reported to Florence, but Civil War service records are not always known to be accurate or complete. Moreover, the Officials Records indicate that Thomas Glascock Barrett was the Florence Stockade guard that General Winder intended to discipline in February 1865. The two men's service records are reprinted in Rigdon, 106, 134–35. The sources that identify "Lieutenant Barrett" as Thomas Glascock Barrett include OR, Series II, VIII, 172, 184, 191, 451–53, 754, 765–66; Blakey, 4; Speer, 274–75, 278, 288, 293. Editor Mark Snell makes a more persuasive case that James Barrett Jr. was the infamous lieutenant on duty. Ripple, 160–61. The Reverend Albert H. Ledoux, a member of the Friends of the Florence Stockade, made a similar case for identifying James Barrett Jr. in private correspondence with the author.

23. Goss, *The Soldier's Story*, 228–29.
24. Ibid; Styple and Fitzpatricks, 152; Waugh; Winther, 440–58.
25. Massey; Rogers, "Pee Dee Pen: McClellan Won in Florence"; Rogers, "Vote at Stockade Opposed Lincoln," n.p.; Woods, "Notes on the Confederate Stockade," 10–11. For more on Walter D. Woods and his memoirs about the Florence Stockade as well as local postwar history, see, for example, Massey; "Walter D. Woods (Obituary)"; Woods, "Confederate Memorial Day."
26. Dufur, 228; Bastile, 93; Keys, entry dated November 9, 1864; Forbes, 60; Hoster, 116; Goss, *The Soldier's Story*, 229.
27. Goss, *The Soldier's Story*, 248.
28. Ibid., 248–49.
29. Ibid., 249.
30. Ibid., 250.
31. Ibid., 251.
32. Ibid.
33. Ibid.
34. Ibid., 248; Williams, *From Spotsylvania to Wilmington*, N.C., 41; Ripple, 91–92.
35. McElroy, 576–77.
36. Ibid., 577–78.
36. The episode is recounted in Ibid., 536–37.
38. Quoted in Speer, 276. See also Boggs, 64; Fosdick, 89; McElroy, 544–45.
39. Goss, *The Soldier's Story*, 252.
40. Ibid., 252–53.
41. Ibid., 253–56. A good, readily accessible account of the Fifth Georgia Volunteer Infantry Regiment's unit history can be found in Mosser, 12, 52.
42. Goss, *The Soldier's Story*, 256–57.
43. Although this story of Winder's naked malice toward the prisoners smacks of apocryphal moralizing, it was typical of the Union perspective on the much-maligned Confederate general. Inmates swapped similar tall tales during their time in the Andersonville and Florence stockades. One often-repeated story recounted the general's disposition when he greeted a group of captives while he

served as provost marshal of the Richmond prisons. A Union brigadier general stood among the prisoners and asked, in a sycophantic voice, "Ah, general, what are you going to do with me?" According to the story, Winder regarded the man with a contemptuous sneer. Turning abruptly on his heel, he said, in a sharp tone, "Hang you, sir." That was the end of the matter, and of the brigadier general as well. Ibid., 257. The U.S. House of Representatives made much of these incidents in its 1869 investigation of Confederate prisons. United States House of Representatives, *Treatment of Prisoners of War by the Rebel Authorities*, 195.

44. Goss, *The Soldier's Story*, 261–62.
45. Ibid., 262.
46. Ibid., 262–63.
47. Ibid., 263.
48. Ibid.
49. Ibid., 263–64.
50. Ibid., 264.
51. Ibid., 264–67. For more on Camp Parole and the U.S. Sanitary Commission's work, see, for example, Blustein, 23–24, and Thompson, "The U.S. Sanitary Commission," 41–63.

CHAPTER 12: Loathsome Bones of a Sad and Lamentable Past

1. Connelly, 50–64; Davis, *An Honorable Defeat*, 109–13, 193–99; McPherson, *Battle Cry of Freedom*, 848–51, 853; Weigley, 440–42, 446–50, 453–57.
2. McAdams, 186.
3. Ibid., 187–88.
4. Ibid., 188.
5. Ibid., 191–93.
6. Ibid., 192–93; Tillinghast, 37–38.
7. England, 41; McAdams, 188–89.
8. OR, Series II, VIII, 1002; Marvel, *Andersonville: The Last Depot*, 238–39; McAdams, xi, 206; Speer, 329, 332; Walker, 58.
9. McAdams, 190–93.
10. Ibid., 193–94, 196, 200–201.
11. State of Louisiana, Secretary of State, Division of Archives, Records Management and History, "Soldier's Application for Pension: John Wesley Minnich"; "Statistics from Rock Island Prison," 100.
12. Minnich, *Inside of Rock Island Prison*, 38–39.
13. McAdams, 197.
14. Ibid., 201; Burr, 4–5; England, 41; Walker, 59.
15. Burr, 1; United States Army, Rock Island Arsenal, Vol. I, 117–18.
16. Ibid., 119–20.
17. Ibid.
18. Ibid., 120–21.
19. Ibid., 121–22; McAdams, 201.
20. United States Army, Rock Island Arsenal, Vol. I, 122, 125–27.
21. England, 41; McAdams, 205.
22. McAdams, 205.
23. England, 41; McAdams, 199–200.
24. England, 41; McAdams, 199–200, 207–09.

25. England, 41; McAdams, 207–11.
26. Blakey, 1–5; Davis, *A History of Florence*, 605–07; King, "Death Camp at Florence," 42; King, *Rise Up So Early*, 54–55. The quote is from the latter source, 54–55.
27. Freeman, 770–71; King, "Death Camp at Florence," 41–42; Nevin, 28–29, 147–50; Rhea, 18–19; Weigley, 418–22.
28. Blakey, 3, 201; King, "Death Camp at Florence," 41; King, *Rise Up So Early*, 54–55.
29. Korn, *Pursuit to Appomattox*, 52–54.
30. OR, Series II, VIII, 111, 159, 172, 184, 191; Blakey, 3, 201; King, "Death Camp at Florence," 41; King, *Rise Up So Early*, 54–55.
31. Blakey, 4–5; Jones, *A Rebel War Clerk's Diary*, 495; King, "Death Camp at Florence," 41; King, "The Emergence of Florence, South Carolina," 202.
32. Denney, 346–47; King, "Death Camp at Florence," 41–42; King, *Rise Up So Early*, 55; Martinez, 16; United States House of Representatives, *Treatment of Prisoners of War by the Rebel Authorities*, 31.
33. OR, Series II, VIII, 198; Blakey, 201; Martinez, 16.
34. OR, Series II, VII, 33, 538; Cromie, 247; King, "Death Camp at Florence," 42; King, "The Emergence of Florence, South Carolina," 202; King, *Rise Up So Early*, 55–58; Martinez, 16–17; Nelson, 328–54, esp. 330–31.
35. King, *Rise Up So Early*, 55–58.
36. Ibid., 56–58; Nelson, 330–33.
37. King, *Rise Up So Early*, 57–58.
38. King, "Death Camp at Florence," 42; Martinez, 16–17; Parker, Letter to H. F. Rudisill.

CHAPTER 13: The Terribleness of the Sufferings

1. Foster, 67; Gardner, 1–23, 228–55; Gordon-Burr, 587–600; Hesseltine, "Civil War Prisons: Introduction," 117–20; Hesseltine, "The Propaganda Literature of Confederate Prisons," 64–66; Rutman, 117–23; United States House of Representatives, *The Trial of Henry Wirz*.
2. Goss, *The Soldier's Story*; McElroy; Kellogg; Boggs; Urban.
3. Andrews, "The Treatment of Prisoners of the Confederacy," 147–50; Ashe, "The Treatment of Prisoners in 1864–65"; Ashe, *The Trial and Death of Henry Wirz*; Gardner, 1–23; Genoways and Genoways, 6–9; Jones, *Confederate View of the Treatment of Prisoners*, esp. 160–77; McElroy, xiv; Roberts, "The Afterlife of Civil War Prisons," 150–65; Stevenson, *The Southern Side*. For more on Petroleum V. Nasby, see Locke. McElroy greatly influenced later accounts, such as the influential, albeit fanciful, memoir penned by John Ransom. See Marvel, "Johnny Ransom's Imagination," 181–89; Ransom.
4. Hesseltine, "The Propaganda Literature of Civil War Prisons," 64–66.
5. Ibid.; Catton, "A Civil, and Sometimes Uncivil, War," 51; Hesseltine, "The Propaganda Literature of Civil War Prisons," 64–66; Marvel, "Johnny Ransom's Imagination," 181–89; Roberts, "The Afterlife of Civil War Prisons," 150–65. Literature on public memory of the war continues to appear in voluminous numbers even today, although the participants are long dead. One of the most exciting publications of recent times occurred after the Virginia Historical Society acquired four tattered scrapbook albums in 1994 containing five hundred vivid

watercolor drawings and maps made by Union soldier and cartographer Robert Knox Sneden. Born in Nova Scotia in 1832, Sneden was a Canadian citizen who immigrated to the United States in 1850. During the Civil War, he served with the Fortieth New York Infantry Regiment as a topographical engineer to Maj. Gen. Samuel P. Heintzelman in the III Corps, Army of the Potomac. He was present at many of the famous battles in the Virginia theater and constantly sketched scenes of carnage and destruction. Captured in 1863, Sneden was incarcerated in the Andersonville Stockade before he was paroled in November 1864. Afterward, he joined the staff of Confederate surgeon Isaiah H. White. As a member of White's "staff," Sneden traveled to numerous Confederate prisons, including Camp Lawton (Millen), Savannah, Charleston, and Florence. His sketches of the Florence Stockade, one of which is reproduced in this book on page 167 are among the few surviving artifacts that depict the prison site from that period. Sneden, 2000, 2001.

6. Gillispie, 41–42; Hesseltine, "Civil War Prisons: Introduction," 117–20; Hesseltine, "The Propaganda Literature of Civil War Prisons," 64–66; Gardner, 1–23; Marvel, "Johnny Ransom's Imagination," 181–89.
7. Gillispie, 41–42, 46–48; Hesseltine, "The Propaganda Literature of Civil War Prisons," 58–59; McElroy, 654.
8. United States Sanitary Commission. The dubious nature of this conclusion is discussed at length in Gardner, 1–23; Gillispie, 41–43, 46–48; Hesseltine, "The Propaganda Literature of Confederate Prisons," 64–66. See also Blustein, 23–24, and Thompson, "The U.S. Sanitary Commission," 41–63.
9. United States House of Representatives, *Treatment of Prisoners of War by the Rebel Authorities*. The earlier 1864 congressional report was United States House of Representatives, *Report on the Condition of Returned Prisoners of War at Annapolis*. The 1864 report was unquestionably inflammatory, concluding that evidence demonstrated "beyond all manner of doubt" the existence of "a system of treatment which has resulted in reducing many of those who have survived and been permitted to return to us to a condition, both physically and mentally, which no language we can use can adequately describe . . . literally the appearance of living skeletons," 1 2.
10. United States House of Representatives, *Treatment of Prisoners of War by the Rebel Authorities*, 54. This modern analog to this distorted view was carried over in MacKinlay Kantor's 1955 Pultizer Prize–winning novel, *Andersonville*, which especially casts Winder in a negative light. It is a marvelous read, even if it is historically inaccurate. Byrne, "Prisoners of War," 458.
11. Byrne, "Prisoners of War," 458; Davis, *The Rise and Fall of the Confederate Government*.
12. Davis, *The Rise and Fall of the Confederate Government*, 501–13. Alexander Stephens, vice president of the Confederacy, expressed a similar perspective in his two-volume apologia, *A Constitutional View of the Late War Between the States*, 507–09. This point of view is discussed in Byrne, "Prisoners of War," 458; McPherson, *Battle Cry of Freedom*, 800–02; Tucker, "Andersonville Prison: What Happened?," 1–34; and eloquently expressed by an "average" Confederate in Andrews, *The War-Time Journal of a Georgia Girl*, 63–79. Davis follows a similar line of argument in essays reprinted long after his death in Davis, "Andersonville and Other War Prisons" in the March and April 1907 issues of *Confederate Veteran*.

13. Anderson, "Memorial Day," 164; Ashe, *A Southern View of the Invasion*; Cave; "The Confederate Memorial Day," 20; Coulter; Eaton; Foster, 47–55, 103–14; 113; *History of the Confederated Memorial Associations of the South*, esp. 32–39; Jimerson, 245–51; Kennedy and Kennedy; Pollard; "The Sentiment of Our Memorial Day," 163; Wilson, "The Religion of the Lost Cause," 229–34. See, also, Bishir, Catton, *The American Heritage New History of the Civil War*, 600–11; Davies, "The Problem of Race Segregation in the GAR," 354–72; Davis, "Empty Eyes, Marble Hand," 2–21; Dearing; Gulley, 125–41; Jastremski, 425; Martinez and Harris, 130–92; McConnell; Mendenhall, 334–53; Murphy, 160–62; Poppenheim; Starnes, 177–94; White; Winberry, 107–21. For more on the role of women in the war effort, especially in the South, see, for example, Faust and Fox-Genovese.
14. Anderson, "Andersonville Remembers America's POWs," 18; Bearss; Marvel, *Andersonville: The Last Depot*, 241–43; Potter, 16; Roberts, "The Aftermath of Civil War Prisons," 150–65; Roberts, *Andersonville Journey*.
15. Gardner, 135–52; Marvel, *Andersonville: The Last Depot*, 242–43; Roberts, "The Aftermath of Civil War Prisons," 151; United States Sanitary Commission, 259–74. The judge advocate who prosecuted the case, Norton P. Chipman, also fanned the flames of sectional hatred over Andersonville in several postwar works. Chipman, *The Andersonville Prison Trial*; Chipman, *The Horrors of the Andersonville Rebel Prison*. For a summary and critique of Chipman's argument, see, for example, Rutman, 123–26, and Spencer.
16. Bearss, 143–50; Marvel, *Andersonville: The Last Depot*, 242–43; Oates, *A Woman of Valor*, 295–97, 310–19; Roberts, "The Aftermath of Civil War Prisons," 151–53.
17. Andrews, *The South Since the War*, 301–17; Bearss, 163, 165–71; Marvel, *Andersonville: The Last Depot*, 247–48; Roberts, "The Aftermath of Civil War Prisons," 154–55.
18. Andersonville Monument Dedication Commission; Averill, 9–15; Bearss, 171; Byrne, "Andersonville Prison," 14; Davies, *Patriotism on Parade*, 228; Roberts, "The Aftermath of Civil War Prisons," 155–56.
19. See, for example, Ashe, *The Trial and Death of Henry Wirz*; Davis, "Andersonville and Other War Prisons" (March 1907), 107–13, and (April 1907), 161–66; "Georgia Daughters to Captain Wirz," (Jan. 1906), 10–11, and (April 1906), 181–82; Joslyn, "Who Caused Andersonville?," 181–91; Joyner, 119–31; Marvel, *Andersonville: The Last Depot*, 247; Rutherford; "Wirz Monument Dedicated in Kind Spirit," 263.
20. Bates, S20–S21; Fordney, 30–33; Hendrick, Telling the Story," G1, G3; Hendrick, "Together, in Andersonville," D1, D6; "New Museum Honors American POWs," 3; "New Museum Honors POWs," 4.
21. King, *Rise Up So Early*, 239; Roberts, "The Aftermath of Civil War Prisons," 178–80; Townsend, n.p.
22. Andrews, *The South Since the War*, i–vi, 191–200; King, "History Lesson," 2A; Reid; Trowbridge. Andrews was not the only Northern correspondent to journey through the South. The classic exposition of the character of the antebellum South remains Olmstead's *The Cotton Kingdom*, a one-volume summary of several earlier works, which usually is contrasted with Pike's postbellum classic, *The Prostrate State*.
23. Rusling.

24. Ibid., 7–8.
25. Ibid., 5–6. The records showing the identities of the dead bodies buried in the cemetery also were missing, and Rusling despaired of ever matching the names with the corpses. The records never turned up; consequently, most of the dead Union prisoners remained interred in unmarked graves well into the next century. During the 1990s, the Reverend Albert H. Ledoux laboriously worked to identify the bodies of the Union prisoners interred in the Florence National cemetery. See Ledoux, *The Union Dead of the Florence Stockade*.
26. The Florena Budwin story is recounted in many sources. Blakey, 4; Boling, 53, 55; Brunson; Creelman, 40–41; Dorrell, 1A, 3A; Fincher; Floyd, 1C; Ford, 1D; Hicklin, "Grave in Florence Holds Woman-Soldier's Secret," n.p.; Hicklin, "Woman in Grave of Union Soldier," n.p.; James, "Behind Marker There's a Story," n.p.; Johnson, *Civil War Blunders*, 83; King, "Death Camp at Florence," 38; King, *Rise Up So Early*, 52–53; Lewis, "Florence Grave Recalls Story of Great Love," n.p.; Martinez, 16; "The Mystery of Florena Budwin," 6–7; Singleton and Lewis, n.p.
27. Baker, 6–10; Bigger, n.p.; "Florence Listed as Prison Site," n.p.; James, "Museum Planned at Stockade Here," n.p.; King, *Rise Up So Early*, 239; Rogers, "Good Morning: A Reminder of the Past," n.p.; "Stockade Here Held Over 12,000 Prisoners at War's End," 4B.
28. The FFS formed an active board of directors composed of prominent citizens and longtime proponents of preserving the site. In his position as chairman, local attorney Mark Buyck III entered into negotiations with the Keels family, owners of a major part of the prison land, to purchase their parcel for preservation purposes. Other influential board members included Dr. Al Harley; Horace F. Rudisill (who passed away in 2003), a well-known historian from the Darlington County Historical Commission; J. R. Fisher, a local historian and Civil War enthusiast; John Andrews of nearby Hartsville, a member of the Old Darlington Chapter of the South Carolina Genealogical Society who served as FFS treasurer; Chas. Brand Livingstone, a Maine resident and longtime expert on Civil War history who served as vice chairman of the group; and the Reverend Albert Ledoux, a professor of theology at Mount St. Mary's Seminary in Emmitsburg, Maryland. By all accounts, Livingstone was the leading force behind the creation of the group. According to fellow board member John Andrews, "I will give all the credit for the formation of our group to Mr. Brand Livingstone. He has been, and still is, the driving force behind our organization and preservation efforts." Andrews expressed no doubt that the FFS would achieve its goals. "When we eventually succeed in our efforts to permanently preserve this historic site," he stated, "it will be because of Brand's foresight in suggesting that we form this organization."

    Even as the board struggled to raise funds and purchase the land, group members made impressive progress on reconstructing parts of the prison's history. Under board member Ledoux's leadership, the FFS began the arduous task of identifying the twenty-three hundred Union soldiers buried in the Florence National Cemetery by examining records compiled by the National Archives & Records Administration in Washington, D.C., as well as regimental histories, soldiers' letters and diaries, and other difficult-to-find sources. As of this writing, the Reverend Ledoux's painstaking research had helped to identify 1,531 Union bodies. The results were published in a book printed by the Old Darlington Chapter of the South Carolina Genealogical Society in 2000.

As part of its effort, the Friends formed a website at www.homeatt.net/~florencestockade/friends.htm to provide interested parties with a brief history of the stockade, sources for research, and the latest news on the group's preservation activities. One early success stemmed from the group's decision in 1998 to erect a sign in the Florence National Cemetery informing the public about the history of the stockade.The group erected a second sign five years later. The FFS board also began writing and distributing a newsletter to anyone who joined the group as a member and provided a financial contribution toward the purchase of the land. From the time the group was formed until 2001, Brand Livingstone served as the newsletter editor.

The FFS was instrumental in raising awareness about the prison at the close of the twentieth century. This led to new investigations aimed at identifying the parameters of the site and preserving as much of the remaining land as possible. In 1997 and 1998, the South Carolina Institute of Archaeology and Anthropology (SCIAA) began excavating the site at the request of the Florence Historical Society and the city of Florence. In a July 1999 report titled *Walking the Deadline: Recent Archaeological Investigations at the Florence Stockade*, Dr. Jonathan M. Leader, deputy state archaeologist and principal project investigator, issued a report recommending that the site be preserved and restored. In 2000, the FFS announced that it had acquired an option to purchase 15.6 acres of the Florence Stockade land. According to the FFS newsletter, the group said it would develop the land and eventually (with assistance from appropriate units of government and private support from foundations) build a museum and/or kiosks to disseminate historical information about the stockade. Bailey; Burton, 5A; e-mail interview with John Andrews, Hartsville, South Carolina, Monday, Sept. 25, 2000; *Florence Mornings News*, April 23, 1995, n.p.; Friends of the Florence Stockade, "Florence Prison Stockade History"; Friends of the Florence Stockade, "Join Efforts to Preserve an Important Civil War Site"; Friends of the Florence Stockade newsletters, especially Supplemental Newsletter (Jan. 2001); Hite, 1D; Kauffman; Leader; Ledoux, "Remarks"; MacDonald, n.p.; Martin, 3A; Martinez, 17; Rummel; Swindler, 1D; Tucker, *Florence Prison Pen*.

29. Burr, 4–5; *Dedication of State of Illinois Historical Marker Commemorating Rock Island Arsenal and Rock Island as Historic Landmarks*, 3; England, 41; United States Army, Rock Island Arsenal, Vol. I, 116–23.
30. Kett, 138; McAdams, 201–02; United States Army, Rock Island Arsenal, Appendix.
31. Daffan, 422; England, 28; Kett, 138; Kost, 94; McAdams, xi.
32. Quoted in England, 28.
33. England, 28, 42; Gragg, 137; McAdams, xi, 208; Speer, 329, 332. If any Union prison qualified as the "Andersonville of the North," most historians agree that the prison at Elmira, New York—nicknamed "Helmira"—probably deserved the designation. Burnham, 368; Denney; Gragg, 144–46; Gray; Horigan; Robertson, "The Scourge of Elmira," 184–201; Stephens, *Rock Island Confederate Prison Deaths*, 41, 51–52.
34. Daffan, 422; *Dedication of State of Illinois Historical Marker Commemorating Rock Island Arsenal and Rock Island as Historic Landmarks*, 3; England, 41; Lassen, 82; McAdams, 201; Sitz, 58–62; Stephens, *Rock Island Confederate Prison Deaths*, 51–52; Walker, 59.

CHAPTER 14: The Last Bugle Call

1. "Deaths: Minnich," 2; "First Meeting Since the War," 333; "John W. Minnich," 439; Kane, 127, 204, 217, 267, 324, 333.
2. "Deaths: Minnich," 2; "John W. Minnich," 439; Kane, 116–23, 328–37.
3. Minnich, *Inside of Rock Island Prison*, 12–13.
4. Foster, 140–44; State of Louisiana, Secretary of State, Division of Archives, Records Management and History, "Soldier's Application for Pension: John Wesley Minnich."
5. Evans, et al., *Grand Isle on the Gulf*, 51.
6. Ibid., 51–52.
7. Ibid., 53; Rousse, 44; State of Louisiana, Secretary of State, Division of Archives, Records Management and History, "Soldier's Application for Pension: John Wesley Minnich."
8. Evans, et al., *Grand Isle on the Gulf*, 55–56; "John W. Minnich," 439; Rousse, 44–45; State of Louisiana, Secretary of State, Division of Archives, Records Management and History, "Soldier's Application for Pension: John Wesley Minnich."
9. "John W. Minnich," 439; State of Louisiana, Secretary of State, Division of Archives, Records Management and History, "Soldier's Application for Pension: John Wesley Minnich."
10. Germann, et al., 99–100; Historical Records Survey, *Transcriptions of Parish Records of Louisiana: Vol. V: 1879–1888*, 21; Historical Records Survey, *Transcriptions of Parish Records of Louisiana: Vol. VII: 1859–1904*, 214–15; "John W. Minnich," 439; State of Louisiana, Secretary of State, Division of Archives, Records Management and History, "Soldier's Application for Pension: John Wesley Minnich."
11. "First Meeting Since the War," 333; Evans, et al., *Grand Isle on the Gulf*, 69; "John W. Minnich," 439; Minnich, "Comment and Correction," 223; Minnich, *Inside of Rock Island Prison*; Minnich, "Proposed Design for Woman's Monument," 69; "A Serious Error," 339; "What Our Patrons Think," 43.
12. Minnich, *Inside of Rock Island Prison*, 4; "Story of Rock Island Prison," 378. The phrase "guest of the Yankees" is borrowed from Gillispie, 40–49.
13. "John W. Minnich," 439; State of Louisiana, Secretary of State, Division of Archives, Records Management and History, "Soldier's Application for Pension: John Wesley Minnich." Emphasis in the original.
14. Minnich, "Comment and Correction," 223; "Story of Rock Island Prison," 378.
15. "Deaths: Minnich," 2; Gandolfo, esp. Chapter 3; "John W. Minnich," 439; State of Louisiana, Secretary of State, Division of Archives, Records Management and History, "Soldier's Application for Pension: John Wesley Minnich."
16. Goss, *The Soldier's Story*, 266–67.
17. Gardner, 232–45; Genoways and Genoways, 4–9; Hesseltine, *Civil War Prisons*, 252–53; Hesseltine, "The Propaganda Literature of Confederate Prisons," 65; United States House of Representatives, *Treatment of Prisoners of War by the Rebel Authorities*, esp. 53–76, 190–98.
18. Hesseltine, "The Propaganda Literature of Confederate Prisons," 64–66; Kellogg.
19. Goss, *The Soldier's Story*, 267.
20. "Jeff. Davis Letter Answered," 2. Goss's 1890 article was titled "The Responsibility of Andersonville." The National Union of Andersonville Survivors was founded

on April 9, 1874—the ninth anniversary of General Lee's surrender at Appomattox Courthouse—with Goss elected as the group's first president. "The object of this association," the inaugural charter stated, "shall be to strengthen the ties of fraternal fellowship and sympathy, formed by companionship in arms during the war for the Union, among the survivors of Rebel Military Prisons." On April 19, 1877, the name was changed to the "National Union of Survivors of Andersonville and Other Southern Military Prisons" and Ezra Hoyt Ripple was elected president. In 1878, Robert H. Kellogg served as president, as did John McElroy in 1886. In September 1887, the group changed its name one final time. It ended its existence as the "Union Ex-Prisoners of War Association." Beath, 680–81.

21. "Connecticut's Grand Army," 21.
22. Burke and Howe, 287; Kirk, Vol. I, 692; Wallace, *A Dictionary of North American Authors Deceased Before 1950*, 176; *Who Was Who Among North American Writers, 1921–1939*, Vol. I, A–J, 605.
23. The book was published as: Warren Lee Goss, *Recollections of a Private: A Story of the Army of the Potomac* (New York: Thomas Y. Crowell & Company, 1890). Before the work appeared, Goss's "Everyman" episodes were recounted in several issues of *The Century: A Popular Quarterly*: Volume 29, Number 1, November 1884; Volume 29, Number 2, December 1884; Volume 29, Number 5, March 1885; Volume 30, Number 1, May 1885; Volume 30, Number 4, August 1885; Volume 31, Number 3, January 1886; Volume 32, Number 1, May 1886.
24. Adams, 152; Lawrence, 347; Marquis, 818; *Who Was Who Among North American Writers, 1921–1939*, Vol. I, A–J, 605.
25. Ibid.; Wallace, *A Dictionary of North American Authors Deceased Before 1950*, 176. Goss was one of the lucky prison survivors, apparently suffering less of the post-traumatic stress syndrome that afflicted many of his contemporaries. See, for example, Marten, 57–70.
26. Crandell, 7.

Selected Bibliography

I. Archives, Historical Societies, and Research Libraries

The Alabama Department of Archives & History, Montgomery, Alabama.
The Alexandria Library, Special Collections Department, Alexandria, Virginia.
The Augusta Richmond County Museum, Augusta, Georgia.
The Bailey Howe Library, University of Vermont, Burlington, Vermont.
The Darlington County Historical Commission, Darlington, South Carolina.
The Eastbank Regional Library, Metairie, Louisiana.
The Eleanor S. Brockenbrough Library, Museum of the Confederacy, Richmond, Virginia.
The Florence Public Library, Florence, South Carolina.
The Friends of the Florence Stockade, Florence, South Carolina.
The Georgia Department of Archives & History, Atlanta, Georgia.
The Harvard University Archives, Cambridge, Massachusetts.
The Historic New Orleans Collection, Williams Research Center, New Orleans, Louisiana.
The Horace W. Sturgis Library, Kennesaw State University, Kennesaw, Georgia.
The Illinois State Historical Library, Springfield, Illinois.
The Kansas State Historical Society, Topeka, Kansas.
The Lackawanna Historical Society, Scranton, Pennsylvania.
The Library of Congress, Washington, D.C.
The Massachusetts Historical Society, Boston, Massachusetts.
The National Archives & Records Administration, Washington, D.C., and College Park, Maryland.
The New Orleans Public Library, Louisiana Division, New Orleans, Louisiana.
The New York Public Library, New York, New York.
The Nicholls State University Library, Special Collections Division, Thibodaux, Louisiana.
The Ralph Brown Draughon Library, Auburn University, Auburn, Alabama.
The Reese Library, Augusta State University, Augusta, Georgia.
The Robert W. Woodruff Library, Special Collections Department, Emory University, Atlanta, Georgia.
The Rock Island Arsenal Museum, Rock Island, Illinois.
The Rutgers University Libraries, New Brunswick, New Jersey.
The South Carolina Department of Archives & History, Columbia, South Carolina.
The State Library of Massachusetts, Boston, Massachusetts.

The State of Louisiana, Secretary of State, Division of Archives, Records Management, and History, Baton Rouge, Louisiana.
The University of Georgia Library, Athens, Georgia.
The University of Iowa Libraries, Iowa City, Iowa.
The U.S. Army Military History Institute, Carlisle Barracks, Pennsylvania.
The Virginia Historical Society, Richmond, Virginia.
The War Between the States Museum, Florence, South Carolina.
The Wilson Library, Southern Historical Society Papers, the University of North Carolina, Chapel Hill, North Carolina.

II. Sources

Abbott, A. O., *Prison Life in the South: At Richmond, Macon, Savannah, Charleston, Columbia, Charlotte, Raleigh, Goldsborough, and Andersonville During the Years 1864 and 1865* (New York: Harper & Brothers, 1865).

Adams, Oscar Fay, *A Dictionary of American Authors* (4th ed.) (Boston and New York: Houghton-Mifflin, and Cambridge, Mass.: The Riverside Press, 1901).

The Adjutant General of Massachusetts, *Massachusetts Soldiers, Sailors, and Marines in the Civil War* (Norwood, Mass.: The Norwood Press, 1933).

Aimone, Alan C., and Barbara A. Aimone, *A User's Guide to the Official Records of the American Civil War* (Shippensburg, Pa.: White Mane Publishing Company, 1993).

Allardice, Bruce S., *More Generals in Gray* (Baton Rouge: Louisiana State University Press, 1995).

Anderson, Mrs. John H., "Memorial Day" in *Confederate Veteran* 40 (May 1932).

Anderson, Kristine F., "Andersonville Remembers America's POWs" in *Civil War Times Illustrated* 35 (April 1996).

Andersonville Monument Dedication Commission, *Dedication of Monument Erected by the State of New York at Andersonville, Georgia, 1914* (Albany, N.Y.: J. B. Lyon Company, 1916).

Andrews, Eliza Frances, *The War-Time Journal of a Georgia Girl, 1864–1865* (New York: D. Appleton & Company, 1908).

Andrews, John, e-mail interview with the author, Monday, September 25, 2000.

Andrews, Matthew Page, "The Treatment of Prisoners of the Confederacy" in *Confederate Veteran* 26 (April 1918).

Andrews, Sidney, *The South Since the War* (New York: Arno Press and the *New York Times*, 1969; Originally published in Boston: Ticknor and Fields, 1866).

Asbury, Herbert, *The French Quarter: An Informal History of the New Orleans Underworld* (New York: Alfred A. Knopf, 1936).

Ashe, Samuel A., *A Southern View of the Invasion of the Southern States and War of 1861–65* (Crawfordville, Ga.: Ruffin Flag Company, n.d. Originally published in 1938).

———, "The Treatment of Prisoners in 1864–65" in *Confederate Veteran* 35 (April 1927).

Ashe, Sarah Williams, *The Trial and Death of Henry Wirz and Other Matters Pertaining Thereto* (Raleigh, N.C.: E. M. Uzzell & Company, 1908).

Averill, James P., *Andersonville Prison Park; Report of Its Purchase and Improvement* (Atlanta: Byrd Printing Company for the Grand Army of the Republic, 1898).

Bailey, Justin, "Florence Stockade No Longer in Danger" in *Florence Morning News*, Florence, S.C. (July 7, 2001).

Bailey, Ronald H., *Forward to Richmond: McClellan's Peninsula Campaign* (Alexandria, Va.: Time-Life Books, 1983).

Baker, Steve, A *Brief History of Florence* (Florence, S.C.: Home Federal Savings and Loan, n.d.)

Bastile, Leon (ed.), *The Civil War Diary of Amos E. Stearns, a Prisoner at Andersonville* (East Brunswick, N.J.: Associated University Presses, Inc., 1981).

Bates, Lincoln S., "Go to Jail! A Hell on Earth: Andersonville was Once a Notorious Confederate Prison Camp in Georgia; Today There's More than Just Civil War History Here" in *American History* 37 (Oct. 2002).

Bearss, Edwin C., *Andersonville National Historic Site: Historic Resource Study and Historical Base Map* (Washington, D.C.: Office of History and Historic Architecture, U.S. Department of the Interior, National Park Service, 1970).

Beath, Robert B., *History of the Grand Army of the Republic* (New York: Bryan, Taylor, & Company, 1889).

Bell, G. W. R., "Reminiscences of Chickamauga" in *Confederate Veteran* 12 (Feb. 1904).

Bergeron, Arthur W. Jr., "Free Men of Color in Grey" in *Civil War History* 32 (Sept. 1986).

———, *Guide to Confederate Military Units, 1861–1865* (Baton Rouge and London: Louisiana State University Press, 1989).

Berry, Thomas F., "Prison Experiences on Rock Island" in *Confederate Veteran* 20 (Feb. 1912).

Bigger, Frank, "Veterans Honor Dead; Men of Five Wars Interred in Cemetery" in *Florence Morning News*, Florence, S.C. (Nov. 11, 1955).

Bill, Alfred Hoyt, *The Beleaguered City: Richmond, 1861–1865* (New York: Alfred A. Knopf, 1946).

Bishir, Catherine W., "Landmarks of Power: Building a Southern Past, 1885–1915" in *Southern Cultures* (Inaugural Issue, 1994).

Blakey, Arch Fredric, *General John H. Winder, C.S.A.* (Gainesville: University of Florida Press, 1990).

Blustein, Bonnie Ellen, "'To Increase the Efficiency of the Medical Department': A New Approach to U.S. Civil War Medicine" in *Civil War History* 33 (March 1987).

Boaz, Thomas M., *Libby Prison and Beyond: A Union Staff Officer in the East, 1862–1865* (Shippensburg, Pa.: White Mane Publishing Company, 1999).

Boggs, S. S., *Eighteen Months a Prisoner under the Rebel Flag: A Condensed Pen-Picture of Belle Isle, Danville, Andersonville, Charleston, Florence and Libby Prisons from Actual Experience* (Lovington, Ill.: Author, 1887).

Boling, Katharine, "A Tragic First: Florena Budwin" in *Pee Dee Magazine* (Darlington, S.C.: Darlington County Historical Commission Files, n.d.).

Booth, Andrew, *Records of Louisiana Confederate Soldiers and Louisiana Confederate Commands: Vols I & II:* A–G (Spartanburg, S.C.: The Reprint Company, 1984).

Bowers, John, "The Rock of Chickamauga: George H. Thomas" in *With My Face to the Enemy: Perspectives on the Civil War*, Robert Cowley (ed.) (New York: G. P. Putnam's Sons, 2001).

Brooks, Stewart, *Civil War Medicine* (Springfield, Ill.: Charles C. Thomas, Publisher, 1966).

Broomfield, William, "My Imprisonment Down in Dixie," Richard E. Shue (ed.) in *Civil War Times Illustrated* 27 (Jan. 1989).

Brown, Louis A., *The Salisbury Prison: A Case Study of Confederate Military Prisons, 1861–1865, Revised and Enlarged* (Wilmington, N.C.: Broadfoot Publishing Company, 1992).

Brownell, Josiah C., At *Andersonville: A Narrative of Personal Adventure at Andersonville,*

Florence and Charleston Rebel Prisons (Glen Cove, N.Y.: Glen Cove Public Library and the Friends of the Glen Cove Public Library, 1981).

Brunson, Mason Jr., "Only Woman in Soldiers Graveyard in Nation" (newspaper clipping) (Darlington, S.C.: Darlington County Historical Commission Files, n.d.).

Burke, W. J., and Will D. Howe, *American Authors and Books, 1640–1940* (New York: Gramercy Publishing Company, 1943).

Burnham, Philip, "The Andersonvilles of the North" in *With My Face to the Enemy: Perspectives on the Civil War*, Robert Cowley (ed.) (New York: G. P. Putnam's Sons, 2001).

Burr, George W., *History of Rock Island Arsenal, 1862–1913* (Rock Island, Ill.: The Rock Island Arsenal, 1913).

Burton, Michele, "Historical Society Looks at Market for 'Florence'" in *Florence Morning News*, Florence, S.C. (Dec. 4, 2000).

Byrne, Frank L., "Andersonville Prison" in *Macmillan Information Now Encyclopedia: The Confederacy*, Richard N. Current (ed.) (New York: Simon & Schuster Macmillan Reference USA, 1993).

———, "Libby Prison: A Study in Emotions" in *Journal of Southern History* 24 (Oct. 1958).

———, "Prisoners of War" in *Macmillan Information Now Encyclopedia: The Confederacy*, Richard N. Current (ed.) (New York: Simon & Schuster Macmillan Reference USA, 1993).

———, "Prisons" in *Macmillan Information Now Encyclopedia: The Confederacy*, Richard N. Current (ed.) (New York: Simon & Schuster Macmillan Reference USA, 1993).

"C7K" in *Confederate Veteran* 12 (Sept. 1904).

Campbell, James Havelock, *McClellan: A Vindication of the Military Career of General George B. McClellan—A Lawyer's Brief* (New York: The Neale Publishing Company, 1916).

Carmichael, Peter S., "The Great Paragon of Virtue and Sobriety: John Bankhead Magruder and the Seven Days" in *The Richmond Campaign of 1862: The Peninsula and the Seven Days*, Gary W. Gallagher (ed.) (Chapel Hill, N.C.: University of North Carolina Press, 2000).

Catton, Bruce, *The American Heritage New History of the Civil War*, James M. McPherson (ed.) (New York: Viking, 1996).

———, "A Civil, and Sometimes Uncivil, War" in *American Heritage* 10 (Oct. 1964).

———, *This Hallowed Ground* (Garden City, N.Y.: Doubleday, 1956).

Cavada, F. F., *Libby Life: Experiences of a Prisoner of War in Richmond, VA., 1863–64* (Philadelphia: J. B. Lippincott & Company, 1865).

Cave, Robert Catlett, *The Men in Gray* (Crawfordville, Ga.: Ruffin Flag Company, 1997. Originally published by *Confederate Veteran*, Nashville, 1911).

Chaitin, Peter M., *The Coastal War: Cheseapeake Bay to Rio Grande* (Alexandria, Va.: Time-Life Books, 1984).

Channing, Steven A., *Confederate Ordeal: The Southern Home Front* (Alexandria, Va.: Time-Life Books, 1989).

Chipman, N. P., *The Andersonville Prison Trial: The Trial of Captain Henry Wirz* (Birmingham: The Notable Trials Library, 1990. Originally published by the Blair Murdock Company, San Francisco, 1911).

———, *The Horrors of the Andersonville Rebel Prison; Trial of Henry Wirz, the Andersonville Jailer; Jefferson Davis' Defense of Andersonville Fully Refuted* (San Francisco: The Blair Murdock Company, 1891).

The Civil War Plymouth Pilgrims Descendants Society, "Roster of the 2nd Massachusetts Heavy Artillery, Companies G & H" at http://home.att.net.net/~cwppds/2ma.htm (Sept. 4, 2002).

Clarkson, H. M., "Story of the Star of the West" in *Confederate Veteran* 21 (May 1913).

"Commander Army of Tennessee Department, U.C.V" in *Confederate Veteran* 24 (Feb. 1916).

Commemorative Biographical Record of Tolland and Windham Counties; Biographical Sketches of Prominent and Representative Citizens and of Many of the Early Settled Families (Chicago: J. H. Beers & Company, 1903).

"The Confederate Memorial Day" in *Confederate Veteran* 1 (January 1893).

"Connecticut's Grand Army; Its Annual Encampment to Be Held This Month" in *New York Times*, New York, N.Y. (Feb. 4, 1894).

Connelly, Thomas L., "The Image and the General: Robert E. Lee in American Historiography" in *Civil War History* 19 (March 1973).

Cornish, Dudley Taylor, *The Sable Arm: Negro Troops in the Union Army, 1861–1865* (New York: Longmans, Green and Company, 1956).

Coulter, E. Merton, *The South During Reconstruction, 1865–1877* (Baton Rouge: Louisiana State University Press, 1947).

Cox, Francis M., *Official Congressional Directory for the Use of the United States Congress* (2d ed.) (Washington, D.C.: Government Printing Office, 1895).

Crandell, Fern, "War Ancestors Learned the Necessity of Hope" in *The Genealogical Helper* 7 (March 1953).

Creehan, Sean, "A Forgotten Enemy" in *Harvard International Review* 23 (Spring 2001).

Creelman, Samuel, *Collections of a Coffee Cooler, Consisting of Daily Prison Scenes in Andersonville, Ga., and Florence, S.C.* (Pittsburgh: Pittsburgh Photo-Engraving Company, 1889).

Cromie, Alice, A *Tour Guide to the Civil War* (4th ed.) (Nashville: Rutledge Hill Press, 1992).

Cross, David F., "Why Did the Yankees Die at Andersonville?" in *North & South* 6 (Sept. 2003).

Crute, Joseph H. Jr., *Units of the Confederate States Army* (Midlothian, Va.: Derwent Books, 1987).

Current, Richard N., "The Confederates and the First Shot" in *Civil War History* 7 (Dec. 1961).

Curry, J. L. M., *Civil History of the Government of the Confederate States with Some Personal Reminiscences* (Richmond: B. F. Johnson Publishing Company, 1901).

Dabney, Virginius, *Richmond: The Story of a City* (2d. ed.) (Charlottesville: University Press of Virginia, 1990).

Daffan, Katie, "Rock Island in Peace" in *Confederate Veteran* 20 (Sept. 1912).

Davies, Wallace E., *Patriotism on Parade: The Story of Veterans' and Hereditary Organizations in America, 1783–1900* (Cambridge: Harvard University Press, 1955).

———, "The Problem of Race Segregation in the GAR" in *Journal of Southern History* 13 (Aug. 1947).

Davis, Henry E., *A History of Florence, City and County, and Portions of the Pee Dee Valley, South Carolina* (Florence, S.C.: Florence County Library, n.d.).

Davis, Jefferson, "Andersonville and Other War Prisons" in *Confederate Veteran* 15 (March 1907).

———, "Andersonville and Other War Prisons" in *Confederate Veteran* 15 (April 1907).

———, *The Rise and Fall of the Confederate Government*, Vol. II (New York: Da Capo Press, 1990. Originally published in 1881).

Davis, Stephen, "Empty Eyes, Marble Hand: The Confederate Monument and the South" in *Journal of Popular Culture* 16 (1982).

Davis, William C., *Brother Against Brother: The War Begins* (Alexandria, Va.: Time-Life Books, 1983).

———, *First Blood: Fort Sumter to Bull Run* (Alexandria, Va.: Time-Life Books, 1983).

———, *An Honorable Defeat: The Last Days of the Confederate Government* (New York: Harcourt, 2001).

———, *Look Away! A History of the Confederate States of America* (New York: The Free Press, 2002).

Dearing, Mary R., *Veterans in Politics: The Story of the GAR* (Baton Rouge: Louisiana State University Press, 1952).

"Deaths: Minnich" in *The Times Picayune*, New Orleans, La. (Nov. 17, 1932).

Dedication of State of Illinois Historical Marker Commemorating Rock Island Arsenal and Rock Island as Historic Landmarks (Rock Island: Author, 1968).

Denney, Robert E., *Civil War Prisons & Escapes: A Day-by-Day Chronicle* (New York: Sterling Publishing Company, 1995).

Detzer, David, *Allegiance: Fort Sumter, Charleston, and the Beginning of the Civil War* (New York: Harcourt, 2001).

"D'Gournay's Battalion of Artillery" in *Confederate Veteran* 13 (Jan. 1905).

Doig, Jameson W., and Erwin C. Hargrove, *Leadership and Innovation: Entrepreneurs in Government, Abridged Edition* (Baltimore and London: The Johns Hopkins University Press, 1990).

Domschcke, Bernhard, *Twenty Months in Captivity: Memoirs of a Union Officer in Confederate Prisons* (Frederic Trautmann, trans. and ed.) (London and Toronto: Associated University Presses, 1987).

Donald, David Herbert, *Lincoln* (New York: Simon & Schuster, 1995).

Dorrell, Linda, "National Cemeteries Mark Years of Honoring Veterans" in *The News and Shopper*, Florence, S.C. (July 15, 1987).

Dowling, Morgan E., *Southern Prisons; Or Josie, The Heroine of Florence; Four Years of Battle and Imprisonment; Richmond, Atlanta, Belle Isle, Andersonville and Florence; A Complete History of All Southern Prisons, Embracing a Thrilling Episode of Romance and Love, With Illustrations* (Detroit: William Graham, 1870).

Dufur, S. M., *Over the Dead Line or Tracked by Blood-Hounds* (Burlington, Vt.: Free Press Association, 1902).

Dyer, Brainerd, "The Treatment of Colored Union Troops by the Confederates, 1861–1865" in *Journal of Negro History* 20 (July 1935).

Eaton, Clement, *The Waning of the Old South Civilization: 1860–1880's* (Athens, Ga.: University of Georgia Press, 1968).

The Editors of Time-Life Books, *Lee Takes Command: From Seven Days to Second Bull Run* (Alexandria, Va.: Time-Life Books, 1984).

———, *Spies, Scouts and Raiders: Irregular Operations* (Alexandria, Va.: Time-Life Books, 1985).

———, *Voices of the Civil War: Atlanta* (Alexandria, Va.: Time-Life Books, 1996).

———, *Voices of the Civil War: Chickamauga* (Alexandria, Va.: Time-Life Books, 1997).

England, Otis Bryan, *A Short History of the Rock Island Prison Barracks* (Rock Island, Ill.: Historical Office, U.S. Army Armament, Munitions, and Chemical Compound, 1985).

Evans, David, *Sherman's Horsemen: Union Cavalry Operations in the Atlanta Campaign* (Bloomington and Indianapolis: Indiana University Press, 1996).

Evans, Sally Kittredge, Frederick Stielow, and Betsy Swanson, *Grand Isle on the Gulf—An Early History* (Metairie, La.: Jefferson Parish Historical Commission, 1979).

Faust, Drew Gilpin, *Mothers of Invention* (Chapel Hill, N.C.: University of North Carolina Press, 1996).

Fincher, Judy, "Civil War Prison Location Led to National Cemetery" in *Florence Morning News*, Florence, S.C. (Darlington, S.C.: Darlington County Historical Commission Files, n.d.).

"First Meeting Since the War" in *Confederate Veteran* 32 (Sept. 1924).

"Florence Listed as Prison Site" in *Florence Morning News*, Florence, S.C. (July 17, 1958).

Florence Morning News, Florence, S.C. (April 23, 1995).

Floyd, Blanche W., "Woman Civil War Veteran Buried Here," *Florence Morning News*, Florence, S.C. (Dec. 29, 1985).

Foote, Shelby, *The Civil War: A Narrative. Vol. III: Red River to Appomattox* (New York: Random House, 1974).

Forbes, Eugene, *Diary of a Soldier, and Prisoner of War in the Rebel Prisons* (Trenton, N.J.: Murphy & Bechtel, 1865).

Ford, Wayne, "General or Private: Monumental Markings Tell Appreciation Story" in *Florence Morning News*, Florence, S.C. (Jan. 18, 1976).

Fordney, Chris, "The Long Road to Andersonville" in *National Parks* 72 (Sept./Oct. 1998).

Fosdick, Charles, *Five Hundred Days in Rebel Prisons* (Chicago: Chicago Electrotype & Stereotype Company, 1887).

Foster, Gaines M., *Ghosts of the Confederacy: Defeat, the Lost Cause, and the Emergence of the New South* (New York: Oxford University Press, 1987).

Fox-Genovese, Elizabeth, *Within the Plantation Household: Black and White Women of the Old South* (Chapel Hill, N.C.: University of North Carolina Press, 1988).

Franks, Edward Carr, "In Defense of Braxton Bragg: The Detachment of Longstreet Reconsidered" in *North & South* 5 (July 2002).

Freeman, Douglas Southall, *Lee's Lieutenants: A Study in Command*, Abridged in One Volume by Stephen W. Sears (New York: Scribner, 1998).

Freemon, Frank R., *Gangrene and Glory: Medical Care During the American Civil War* (Cranbury, N.J.: Associated University Presses, Inc., 1998).

Friends of the Florence Stockade, "Florence Prison Stockade History" (Pamphlet) (Florence, S.C.: Author, n.d.).

Friends of the Florence Stockade, "Join Efforts to Preserve an Important Civil War Site in Florence, South Carolina" (Pamphlet) (Florence, S.C.: Author, 2000).

Friends of the Florence Stockade, 12th Newsletter (March 2000); 13th Newsletter (June 2000); 14th Newsletter (Oct. 2000); Supplemental Newsletter Update (Dec. 2000); 15th Newsletter (Jan. 2001); 16th Newsletter (March 2001); 17th Newsletter (June/July 2001); 18th Newsletter (Sept./Oct. 2001).

Friends of the Florence Stockade Web site at http.//home.att.net/~florencestockade/friends.htm (2000).

Futch, Ovid L., "Andersonville Raiders" in *Civil War History* 2 (Dec. 1956).

———, *History of Andersonville Prison* (Gainesville: University of Florida Press, 1968).

———, "Prison Life at Andersonville" in *Civil War History* 8 (June 1962).

Gallagher, Gary W., "A Civil War Watershed: The 1862 Richmond Campaign in Perspective" in *The Richmond Campaign of 1862: The Peninsula and the Seven Days*,

Gary W. Gallagher (ed.) (Chapel Hill, N.C.: University of North Carolina Press, 2000).

Gandolfo, Henri A., *Metairie Cemetery: An Historical Memoir: Tales of Its Statesmen, Soldiers and Great Families* (New Orleans: Stewart Enterprises, 1981).

Gardner, Douglas Gibson, "Andersonville and American Memory: Civil War Prisoners and Narratives of Suffering and Redemption" (Ph.D. dissertation, Miami University of Ohio, 1998).

"Gen. George P. Harrison" in *Confederate Veteran* 30 (Aug. 1922).

Genoways, Ted, and Hugh H. Genoways (eds.), *A Perfect Picture of Hell: Eyewitness Accounts by Civil War Prisoners from the 12th Iowa* (Iowa City: University of Iowa Press, 2001).

"Georgia Daughters to Captain Wirz" in *Confederate Veteran* 14 (Jan. 1906). Continued in *Confederate Veteran* 14 (April 1906).

Georgia State Archives, "Compiled Service Records," M226, Roll #CSR-34 (n.d.).

Germann, John J., Alan H. Patera, and John S. Gallagher, *Louisiana Post Offices* (Lake Grove, Or.: The Depot, 1990).

Gillispie, James M., "Guests of the Yankees: A Reevaluation of Union Treatment of Confederate Prisoners" in *North & South* 5 (July 2002).

Gladstone, William A., *United States Colored Troops* (Gettysburg, Pa.: Thomas Publications, 1990).

Glatthaar, Joseph T., *Forged in Battle: The Civil War Alliance of Black Soldiers and White Officers* (New York: The Free Press, 1990).

Glazier, Willard W., *The Capture, the Prison Pen, and the Escape; Giving a Complete History of Prison Life in the South* (New York: R. H. Ferguson & Company, Publishers, 1870).

Gordon-Burr, Lesley Jill, "Storms of Indignation: The Art of Andersonville as Postwar Propaganda" in *Georgia Historical Quarterly* 75 (1991).

Goss, Warren Lee, *Recollections of a Private: A Story of the Army of the Potomac* (New York: Thomas Y. Crowell, 1890).

———, "The Responsibility of Andersonville" in *North American Review* 150 (May 1890).

———, *The Soldier's Story of His Captivity at Andersonville, Belle Isle, and Other Rebel Prisons* (Boston: Lee and Shepard, 1867).

Gragg, Rod, *The Illustrated Confederate Reader* (New York: Harper & Row, 1989).

Gray, Michael P., *The Business of Captivity: Elmira and Its Civil War Prison* (Kent, Ohio: Kent State University Press, 2001).

Gregg, Bessie A., "The War in Our Country: An Address Before the Maxcy Gregg Chapter of the United Daughters of the Confederacy" (Darlington, S.C.: Darlington County Historical Commission Files, n.d.).

Gulley, H. E., "Women and the Lost Cause: Conserving a Confederate Identity in the Deep South" in *Journal of Historical Geography* 19 (1993).

Hamlin, Augustus C., *Martyria; Or, Andersonville Prison* (Boston: Lee and Shepard, 1866).

Hammer, Jefferson J. (ed.), *Frederic Augustus Jones's Civil War Diary: Sumter to Andersonville* (Cranbury, N.J.: Associated University Presses, Inc., 1973).

"Harrison, George Paul, 1841–1922" in *Biographical History of the United States Congress* (http://bioguide.congress.gov/scripts/biodisplay.pl?index=H000270) (June 13, 2001).

Harrold, John, *Libby, Andersonville, Florence: The Capture, Imprisonment, Escape and Rescue of John Harrold, a Union Soldier in the War of the Rebellion* (Philadelphia: W. B. Selheimer, 1870).

Harsh, John L., "On the McClellan-Go-Round" in *Battles Lost and Won: Essays from Civil War History*, John T. Hubbell (ed.) (Westport, Conn.: Greenwood Press, 1975).

Helmreich, Paul C., "The Diary of Charles G. Lee in the Andersonville and Florence Prison Camps, 1864" in *The Connecticut Historical Society Bulletin* 41 (Jan. 1976).

Hendrick, Bill, "Telling the Story: Former Prisoners Celebrate the Opening of Remembrance in Andersonville" in *Atlanta Journal & Constitution*, Atlanta, Ga. (April 10, 1998).

———, "Together, in Andersonville: Ex-Prisoners from Different Wars Converge in Georgia for Memorial's Opening" in *Atlanta Journal & Constitution*, Atlanta, Ga. (April 9, 1998).

Hesseltine, William Best, "Civil War Prisons: Introduction" in *Civil War History* 8 (June 1962).

———, *Civil War Prisons: A Study in War Psychology* (Columbus: Ohio State University Press, 1930).

———,"The Propaganda Literature of Confederate Prisons" in *Journal of Southern History* 1 (1935).

Hicklin, J. B., "Grave in Florence Holds Woman-Soldier's Secret" in *The State*, Columbia, S.C. (Feb. 13, 1938).

———, "Woman in Grave of Soldier" in *The State*, Columbia, S.C. (Feb. 13, 1938).

Historical Records Survey, Division of Professional and Service Projects, Works Projects Administration, *Transcriptions of Parish Records of Louisiana: Vol. V: 1879–1888* (New Orleans, La.: The Police Jury, Parish of Jefferson, April 1940).

———, *Transcriptions of Parish Records of Louisiana: Vol. VII: 1959–1904* (New Orleans, La.: The Police Jury, Parish of Jefferson, June 1940).

History of the Confederate Memorial Associations of the South (New Orleans: Graham Press, 1904).

Hite, Alice, "Memorial Proposed: Stockade Evidence Remains" in *Florence Morning News*, Florence, S.C. (Jan. 16, 1975).

Hord, B. M., "Forty Hours in a Dungeon at Rock Island" in *Confederate Veteran* 12 (Aug. 1904).

Horigan, Michael, *Elmira: Death Camp of the North* (Mechanicsburg, Pa.: Stackpole Books, 2002).

Hoster, John L., *Adventures of a Soldier* (Darlington, S.C.: Darlington County Historical Commission Files, Typeset Manuscript, n.d.)

Hubbell, John T., "The Seven Days of George Brinton McClellan" in *The Richmond Campaign of 1862: The Peninsula and the Seven Days*, Gary W. Gallagher (ed.) (Chapel Hill, N.C.: University of North Carolina Press, 2000).

Isham, Asa B., Henry M. Davidson, and Henry B. Furness, *Prisoners of War and Military Prisons* (Cincinnati: Lyman & Cushing, 1890).

James, Dew, "Behind Marker There's a Story" in *Florence Morning News*, Florence, S.C. (June 2, 1968).

———, "Museum Planned at Stockade Here" in *Florence Morning News*, Florence, S.C. (Dec. 23, 1959).

Jastremski, Leon, "The Organization of U.C.V." in *Confederate Veteran* 12 (Sept. 1904).

"Jeff. Davis' Letter Answered" in *New York Times*, New York, N.Y. (Feb. 9, 1876).

Jeffrey, William H., *Richmond Prisons, 1861–1862: Compiled from the Original Records Kept by the Confederate Government; Journals Kept by Union Prisoners of War, Together with the Name, Rank, Company, Regiment and State of the Four Thousand Who Were Confined There* (St. Johnsbury, Vt.: The Republican Press, 1893).

Jervey, Edward D., "Prison Life Among the Rebels: Recollections of a Union Chaplain" in *Civil War History* 34 (March 1988).

Jimerson, Randall C., *The Private Civil War: Popular Thought During the Sectional Conflict* (Baton Rouge: Louisiana State University Press, 1988).

"John W. Minnich" in *Confederate Veteran* 40 (Dec. 1932).

Johnson, Clint, *Civil War Blunders* (Winston-Salem, N.C.: John F. Blair, Publishers, 1997).

Johnson, E. Polk, "Some Prison Experiences" in *Confederate Veteran* 27 (Jan. 1919).

Jones, John B., *A Rebel War Clerk's Diary*, Earl Schenck Miers (ed.) (New York: A.S. Barnes & Company, 1961).

Jones, J. William, *Confederate View of the Treatment of Prisoners; Compiled from Official Records and Other Documents* (Richmond: Southern Historical Society, 1876).

Jones, Virgil Carrington, "Libby Prison Break" in *Civil War History* 4 (June 1958).

Jordan, Ervin L. Jr., *Black Confederates and Afro-Yankees in Civil War Virginia* (Charlottesville: University Press of Virginia, 1995).

Joslyn, Mauriel, "Well-Born Col. Paul Francois de Gournay was the South's Adopted 'Marquis in Gray'" in *America's Civil War* 8 (Sept. 1995).

———,"Who Caused Andersonville?" in *Andersonville: The Southern Perspective*, J. H. Segars (ed.) (Atlanta: Southern Heritage Press, 1995).

Joyner, Lee, "Life in the Stockade" in *Andersonville: The Southern Perspective*, J. H. Segars (ed.) (Atlanta: Southern Heritage Press, 1995).

Kane, Joseph Nathan, *Facts about the Presidents* (New York: Ace Books, 1976).

Kantor, MacKinlay, *Andersonville* (New York: Plume Books, 1993. Originally published in 1955).

Kauffman, Tim, "Archaeologists Mark Prison Boundaries; Local Group Fights to Preserve Remnants of Florence Stockade" in *Florence Morning News*, Florence, S.C. (Darlington, S.C.: Darlington County Historical Commission Files, n.d.).

Kelley, Daniel G., *What I Saw and Suffered in Rebel Prisons* (Buffalo, N.Y.: Thomas, Howard & Johnson, 1868).

Kellogg, Robert H., *Life and Death in Rebel Prisons: Giving a Complete History of the Inhuman and Barbarous Treatment of Our Brave Soldiers by Rebel Authorities, Inflicting Terrible Suffering and Frightful Mortality, Principally at Andersonville, Ga., and Florence, S.C.* (Hartford, Conn.: L. Stebbins, 1865).

Kennedy, James Ronald and Walter Donald Kennedy, *The South Was Right!* (Gretna, La.: Pelican Publishing Company, 1994).

Kett, H. F., *The Past and Present of Rock Island County, Ill.* (Chicago: H. F. Kett & Company, 1877).

Keys, William C., *William C. Keys War Journals, 1863–64* (New Brunswick, N.J.: Rutgers Universities Libraries [Microfilm, n.d.]).

King, G. Wayne, "Death Camp at Florence" in *Civil War Times Illustrated* 12 (Jan. 1974).

———, "The Emergence of Florence, South Carolina, 1853–1890" in *South Carolina Historical Magazine* 82 (July 1981).

———, "History Lesson: Correspondent Desired Camp" in *Florence Morning News*, Florence, S.C. (May 23, 1976).

———, *Rise Up So Early: A History of Florence County, South Carolina* (Spartanburg, S.C.: The Reprint Company, 1981).

Kirk, John Foster, A *Supplement to Allibone's Critical Dictionary of English Literature and British and American Authors* (Philadelphia: J. B. Lippincott Company, 1908).

Korn, Jerry, *The Fight for Chattanooga: Chickamauga to Missionary Ridge* (Alexandria, Va.: Time-Life Books, 1985).

———, *Pursuit to Appomattox: The Last Battles* (Alexandria, Va.: Time-Life Books, 1987).

Kost, Kathryn, "The Rock Island, Illinois, Civil War Prison: 1863–1865" (Master's thesis, Illinois State University, 1965).

Lassen, Andrew, "A History of the Prisoner of War Camp During the Civil War at Rock Island, Illinois" (Master's thesis, University of Northern Iowa, 1994).

Lawrence, A. (ed.), *Who's Who Among American Authors: Vol. III, 1927–1928* (Los Angeles: Golden Syndicate Publishing Company, 1927).

Leader, Jonathan M., Ph.D., *Walking the Deadline: Recent Archaeological Investigations at the Florence Stockade* (Columbia, S.C.: South Carolina Institute of Archaeology and Anthropology, Prepared for the Florence Historical Society and the City of Florence, South Carolina, July 1999).

Ledoux, Reverend Albert H., "Remarks of the Reverend Albert Ledoux, Memorial Day 1999, Florence National Cemetery, Monday, May 31, 1999."

———, *The Union Dead of the Florence Stockade* (Darlington, S.C.: The Old Darlington District Chapter, South Carolina Genealogical Society, Inc., 2000).

Leonard, Albert C., *The Boys in Blue of 1861–65: A Condensed History Worth Preserving* (Lancaster, Pa.: Leonard, 1904).

Lewis, Lloyd, *Sherman: Fighting Prophet* (New York: Harcourt, Brace and Company, 1932).

Lewis, Stan, "Florence Grave Recalls Story of Great Love" in *The News & Courier*, Charleston, S.C. (Feb. 16, 1941).

Lewis-Jones, S., and D. Baxby, "The History of the Eradication of Smallpox" in *British Journal of Dermatology* 145 (2001, Suppl. 59).

Lewy, Guenter, *America in Vietnam* (Oxford and New York: Oxford University Press, 1978).

Locke, David Ross, *Divers Views, Opinions and Prophecies of Yours Trooly Petroleum V. Nasby, Lait Pastor uv the Church of Noo Dispensashin* (Cincinnati: R. W. Carrol, 1867).

Lonn, Ella, *Foreigners in the Confederacy* (Chapel Hill, N.C.: University of North Carolina Press, 2002. Originally published in 1940).

Lutz, Stuart, "Last Words from Grave 9868" in *Civil War Times Illustrated* 41 (March 2002).

MacDonald, Vic, No Title, Newspaper Clipping (Florence, S.C.: Florence County Library, n.d.).

Marquis, Albert Nelson (ed.), *Who's Who in America: A Biographical Dictionary of Notable Living Men and Women of the United States: Vol. 14, 1926–1927* (Chicago: A.N. Marquis & Company, 1926).

Marten, James, "Exempt from Ordinary Rules of Life: Researching Postwar Adjustment Problems of Union Veterans" in *Civil War History* 47 (March 2001).

Martin, Joe, "Hope of Restoring Confederate Prison Revived" in *Florence Morning News*, Florence, S.C. (Aug. 9, 1959).

Martinez, J. Michael, "'By No Means a Bed of Roses': The Florence Stockade, 1864–65" in *Carologue: A Publication of the South Carolina Historical Society* 17 (Winter 2001).

———, and Robert M. Harris, "Graves, Worms, and Epitaphs: Confederate Monuments in the Southern Landscape" in *Confederate Symbols in the Contemporary South*, J. Michael Martinez, William D. Richardson, and Ron McNinch-Su (eds.) (Gainesville: University Press of Florida, 2000).

Marvel, William, *Andersonville: The Last Depot* (Chapel Hill, N.C.: University of North Carolina Press, 1994).

———, "Johnny Ransom's Imagination" in *Civil War History* 41 (Sept. 1995).

Massey, Helen Woods, "A Sketch of the Life of Walter DuBose Woods" (Darlington, S.C.: Darlington County Historical Commission Files, n.d.).

McAdams, Benton, *Rebels at Rock Island: The Story of a Civil War Prison* (Dekalb, Ill.: Northern Illinois University Press, 2000).

McConnell, Stuart, *Glorious Contentment: The Grand Army of the Republic, 1865–1900* (Chapel Hill, N.C.: University of North Carolina Press, 1962).

McElroy, John, *Andersonville: A Story of Rebel Prisons, Fifteen Months a Guest of the So-Called Southern Confederacy* (Toledo: D. R. Locke, 1879).

McMurry, Richard M., *Atlanta 1864: Last Chance for the Confederacy* (Lincoln and London: University of Nebraska Press, 2000).

McPherson, James M., *Abraham Lincoln and the Second American Revolution* (New York: Oxford University Press, 1991).

———, *Battle Cry of Freedom* (New York: Oxford University Press, 1988).

———, *What They Fought For, 1861–1865* (Baton Rouge: Louisiana State University Press, 1994).

Mendenhall, Marjorie S., "Southern Women of a 'Lost Generation'" in *South Atlantic Quarterly* 33 (Oct. 1934).

Miller, James Newton, *The Story of Andersonville and Florence* (Des Moines: Welch, The Printer, 1900).

Miller, William J., "I Only Wait for the River: McClellan and His Engineers on the Chickahominy" in *The Richmond Campaign of 1862: The Peninsula and the Seven Days*, Gary W. Gallagher (ed.) (Chapel Hill, N.C.: University of North Carolina Press, 2000).

Minnich, J. W., "About Re-Enlistments for the War" in *Confederate Veteran* 15 (Dec. 1907).

———, "The Affair at May's Ferry, Tenn." in *Confederate Veteran* 33 (Feb. 1925).

———, "At Bean's Station, Tenn." in *Confederate Veteran* 36 (Jan. 1928).

———, "The Cavalry at Knoxville" in *Confederate Veteran* 32 (Jan. 1924).

———, "Comment and Correction" in *Confederate Veteran* 37 (June 1929).

———, "Comment on Rock Island Prison" in *Confederate Veteran* 16 (Aug. 1908).

———, "Famous Rifles" in *Confederate Veteran* 30 (July 1922).

———, "Freezing and Fighting, December 10, 1863" in *Confederate Veteran* 27 (Feb. 1919).

———, "Hiding Out" in *Confederate Veteran* 26 (July 1918).

———, "How Some History Is Written" in *Confederate Veteran* 13 (March 1905).

———, "Incidents of the Peninsular Campaign" in *Confederate Veteran* 30 (Feb. 1922).

———, *Inside of Rock Island Prison from December, 1863, to June, 1865* (Nashville: M.E. Church, South, 1908).

———, "Liddell's Division at Chickamauga" in *Confederate Veteran* 13 (Jan. 1905).

———, "Lightning Bugs in Virginia" in *Confederate Veteran* 22 (Sept. 1914).

———, "Picturesque Soldiery" in *Confederate Veteran* 31 (Aug. 1923).

———, "Proposed Design for Woman's Monument" in *Confederate Veteran* 14 (Jan. 1906).

———, "Query Concerning Chickamauga" in *Confederate Veteran* 11 (Nov. 1903).

———, "The Sixth Georgia Cavalry" in *Confederate Veteran* 26 (April 1918).

———, "That Affair at Dandridge, Tenn.," in *Confederate Veteran* 30 (Aug. 1922).

———, "Tunnels to Release Prisoners" in *Confederate Veteran* 17 (Nov. 1909).

———, "Unique Experiences in the Chickamauga Campaign" in *Confederate Veteran* 35 (June 1927).

———, "Unique Experiences in the Chickamauga Campaign [Part II]" in *Confederate Veteran* 35 (Oct. 1927).

———, "With the Louisiana Zouaves" in *Confederate Veteran* 36 (Nov. 1928).

Montgomery, Horace, *Howell Cobb's Confederate Career* (Tuscaloosa, Ala.: Confederate Publishing Company, 1959).

Morgan, Michael, "Libby: Warehouse to Big House" in *Civil War Times Illustrated* 40 (Oct. 2001).

Morris, Roy Jr., "Chickamauga: Pyrrhic Victory for the South" in *Military History* 17 (Dec. 2000).

Mosser, Jeffrey S., "The 5th Georgia's War Record Included Major Western Theater Battles and Guarding Andersonville Prisoners" in *America's Civil War* 15 (March 2002).

Muldrow, Elihu, "The First South Carolina Regiment" in *Confederate Veteran* 18 (May 1910).

Murphy, Richard W., *The Nation Reunited: War's Aftermath* (Alexandria, Va.: Time-Life Books, 1987).

Murray, Alton J., *South Georgia Rebels: The True Wartime Experiences of the 26th Regiment Georgia Volunteer Infantry, Lawton-Gordon-Evans Brigade, Confederate States Army, 1861-1865* (St. Mary's, Ga.: Author, 1976).

"The Mystery of Florena Budwin" in *The State Magazine*, Columbia, S.C. (Dec. 12, 1954).

National Archives & Records Administration, *General Register of Prisoners: 1864–1865* (Washington, D.C.: National Archives Microfilm Publications, n.d. Microcopy 598, Reel 131).

———, *Record of Prisoners of War Who Have Died at Rock Island Barracks, Illinois* (Washington, D.C., National Archives Microfilm Publications, n.d. Microcopy 598, Reel 132).

Nelson, Larry E., "Sherman at Cheraw" in *South Carolina Historical Magazine* 100 (Oct. 1999).

Nevin, David, *Sherman's March: Atlanta to the Sea* (Alexandria, Va.: Time-Life Books, 1986).

"New Museum Honors American POWs" in *New York Times*, New York, N.Y. (April 19, 1998).

"New Museum Honors POWs" in *American History* 33 (March 1998).

Northrop, John Worrell, *Chronicles from the Diary of a War Prisoner in Andersonville and Other Military Prisons of the South in 1864* (Wichita: Author, 1904).

Oates, Stephen B., *With Malice Toward None: The Life of Abraham Lincoln* (New York: New American Library, 1977).

———, *A Woman of Valor: Clara Barton and the Civil War* (New York: Macmillan, 1994).

Olmstead, Frederick Law, *The Cotton Kingdom: A Traveller's Observations on Cotton and Slavery in the American Slave States* (New York: Alfred A. Knopf, 1953. Originally published in 1861).

"One of the C7K" in *Confederate Veteran* 25 (Nov. 1917).

Parker, Elmer O., United States General Services Administration, National Archives and Records Service, Washington, D.C, Letter to H. F. Rudisill, Darlington County Historical Commission, Darlington, S.C. (Darlington, S.C.: Darlington County Historical Commission Files, Oct. 17, 1967).

Parker, Sandra V., *Richmond's Civil War Prisons* (Lynchburg, Va.: H. E. Howard, 1990).

Perry-Mosher, Kate E., "The Rock Island P.O.W. Camp" in *Civil War Times Illustrated* 8 (July 1969).

Phillips, M. V. B., *Life and Death in Andersonville; What I Saw and Experienced During Seven Months in Rebel Prisons* (Chicago: T. B. Arnold, 1887).

Pike, James S., *The Prostrate State: South Carolina Under Negro Government* (New York: D. Appleton & Company, 1874).

Pollard, Edward A., *The Lost Cause: A New Southern History of the Confederacy* (New York: E. B. Treat and Company, 1866).

Poppenheim, Mary B., *The History of the United Daughters of the Confederacy* (Richmond: Garrett and Massie, 1938).

Potter, Jerry O, "A Tragic Postscript" in *American History* 31 (Dec. 1996).

Pullen, P. P., "A Kentucky Hero" in *Confederate Veteran* 31 (Aug. 1923).

Putnam, George Haven, *A Prisoner of War in Virginia, 1864-5* (New York and London: G. P. Putnam's Sons, The Knickerbocker Press, 1912).

Quarles, Benjamin, *The Negro in the Civil War* (2d ed.) (Boston: Little, Brown & Company, 1969).

Quinquennial Catalogue of the Law School of Harvard University, 1817–1904 (Cambridge, Mass.: Harvard Law School, 1905).

Ramsdell, Charles W., "Lincoln and the First Shot" in *Journal of Southern History* 3 (Aug. 1937).

Ransom, John L., *John Ransom's Diary* (New York: Paul S. Ericksson, 1963).

Reid, Whitelaw, *After the War: A Southern Tour, May 1, 1865–May 1, 1866* (New York: Harper & Brothers, 1965. Originally published in 1866).

Rhea, Gordon C., *To the North Anna River: Grant and Lee, May 13–25, 1864* (Baton Rouge: Louisiana State University Press, 2000).

Rigdon, John C., *The Boys of the Fifth* (Augusta, Ga.: Eastern Digital Resources, 1997).

Ripple, Ezra Hoyt, *Dancing Along the Deadline: The Andersonville Memoir of a Prisoner of the Confederacy*, Mark A. Snell (ed.) (Novato, Ca.: Presidio Press, 1996).

Roberts, Edward F., *Andersonville Journey: The Civil War's Greatest Tragedy* (Shippensburg, Pa.: White Mane Publishing Company, 1999).

Roberts, Nancy A., "The Afterlife of Civil War Prisons and Their Dead" (Ph.D. dissertation, University of Oregon, 1996).

Robertson, James I., "The Scourge of Elmira" in *Civil War History* 8 (June 1962).

———, *Tenting Tonight: The Soldier's Life* (Alexandria, Va.: Time-Life Books, 1984).

Rogers, James A., "Good Morning: A Reminder of the Past" in *Florence Morning News*, Florence, S.C. (Dec. 18, 1958).

———, "Pee Dee Pen: Mass Prison Escape Narrowly Averted at Florence Stockade" in *Florence Morning News*, Florence, S.C. (Darlington, S.C.: Darlington County Historical Commission Files, n.d.).

———, "Pee Dee Pen: McClellan Won in Florence" in *Florence Morning News*, Florence, S.C. (Darlington, S.C.: Darlington County Historical Commission Files, n.d.).

———, "Vote at Stockade Opposed Lincoln" in *Florence Morning News*, Florence, S.C. (Aug. 15, 1968).

Rone, John T., "First Arkansas Brigade at Chickamauga" in *Confederate Veteran* 13 (April 1905).

Rousse, Nares H., *Cheniere Caminada: Another Look*, Dian Boudreaux (ed.) (Galliano, La.: Author, 1992).

Rowland, Thomas J., *George B. McClellan and Civil War History: In the Shadow of Grant and Sherman* (Kent, Ohio: Kent State University Press, 1998).

———, "'Heaven Save a Country Governed by Such Counsels!': The Safety of Washington and the Peninsula Campaign" in *Civil War History* 42 (March 1996).

Rummel, Leslie, "History Buffs Fight for Stockade" in *Florence Morning News*, Florence, S.C. (Darlington, S.C.: Darlington County Historical Commission Files, n.d.).

Rusling, Bvt. Brig. Gen. James F., Inspector, Q.M.D., "Report of the Inspection of the National Cemetery at Florence, S.C." (Charleston, S.C.: United States Quartermaster Department, May 27, 1866).

Rutherford, Mildred Lewis, *Andersonville, UDC Monument to Captain Henry Wirz* (Athens, Ga.: Author, 1921).

Rutman, Darrett B., "The War Crimes and Trial of Henry Wirz" in *Civil War History* 6 (June 1960).

Sallee, Scott E., "'Big Pete' McCullough, the Hanging Judge of Andersonville" in *Blue & Gray* 20 (Summer 2003).

Schreckenhost, Gary, "Gaines' Mill: Costly Confederate Victory" in *America's Civil War* 13 (Jan. 2001).

"The Sentiment of Our Memorial Day" in *Confederate Veteran* 1 (June 1893).

"A Serious Error" in *Confederate Veteran* 25 (July 1917).

"Service Record: John W. Minich (sic): Louisiana Confederate Soldiers," *Confederate Research Sources*, Vol. II, M (Baton Rouge: Author, 2002).

Silverman, Jason H., and Susan R. Silverman, "Blacks in Gray: Myth or Reality?" in *North & South* 5 (April 2002).

Simpson, Brooks D., *Ulysses S. Grant: Triumph Over Adversity, 1822–1865* (Boston: Houghton Mifflin, 2000).

Singleton, Burt Jr. and Stan Lewis, "Story of a Great Love Amidst Hell and Horror of Civil War" in *The News & Courier*, Charleston, S.C. (Feb. 9, 1941).

Sitz, Herbert Emil, "The Rock Island, Illinois, Arsenal: Its History and Services to the Government of the United States, Especially During World War II" (Master's thesis, Northeast Missouri State Teachers College, 1967).

Smart, Charles, *The Medical and Surgical History of the War of the Rebellion, Volume 1, Part III: Medical History: Being the Third Medical Volume Prepared Under the Direction of the Surgeon General, United States Army* (Washington, D.C.: Government Printing Office, 1888).

Smith, C. A., *Recollections of Prison Life at Andersonville, Georgia and Florence, South Carolina*, Steven Fenton (ed.) (Raleigh, N.C.: Martini Print Media, Inc., 1997).

Sneden, Robert Knox, *Eye of the Storm: A Civil War Odyssey*, Charles F. Bryan and Nelson D. Lankford (eds.) (New York: Free Press, 2000).

———, *Images from the Storm: 300 Civil War Images*, Charles F. Bryan, Nelson D. Lankford, and James C. Kelly (eds.) (New York: Free Press, 2001).

Speer, Lonnie R., *Portals to Hell: Military Prisons of the Civil War* (Mechanicsburg, Pa.: Stackpole Books, 1997).

Spencer, Ambrose, *A Narrative of Andersonville, Drawn from the Evidence Elicited on the Trial of Henry Wirz, the Jailer, with the Argument of Col. N. P. Chipman, Judge Advocate* (New York: Harper & Brothers, 1866).

Sprague, Homer B., *Lights and Shadows in Confederate Prisons: A Personal Experience, 1864–5* (New York: G. P. Putnam's Sons, 1915).

Stafford, David W., *In Defense of the Flag: A True War Story* (Warren, Pa.: Warren Mirror Print, 1915).

Starnes, Richard D., "Forever Faithful: The Southern Historical Society and Confederate Historical Memory" in *Southern Cultures* 2 (Winter 1996).

State of Louisiana, Secretary of State, Division of Archives, Records Management, and History, "Soldier's Application for Pension: John Wesley Minnich" (Filed February 19, 1915. Reel CP1.98, Microdex 4, Sequence 4).

"Statistics from Rock Island Prison" in *Confederate Veteran* 21 (March 1913).

Stephens, Alexander H., *A Constitutional View of the Late War Between the States: Its Causes, Character, Conduct and Results Presented in a Series of Colloquies at Liberty Hill*, Vol. II (Philadelphia: National Publishing Company, 1868–70).

Stephens, Clifford W. (comp.), *Rock Island Confederate Prison Deaths* (Rock Island: Blackhawk Genealogical Society, 1973).

Stevenson, R. Randolph, "Andersonville Prison" in *Andersonville: The Southern Perspective*, J. H. Segars (ed.) (Atlanta: Southern Heritage Press, 1995).

———, *The Southern Side, or Andersonville Prison* (Baltimore: Turnbull Brothers, 1876).

"Stockade Here Held Over 12,000 Union Prisoners Near War's End" in *Florence Morning News*, Florence, S.C. (Feb. 3, 1959).

"Story of Rock Island Prison" in *Confederate Veteran* 15 (Aug. 1907).

Styple, William B., and John J. Fitzpatricks (eds.), *The Andersonville Diary and Memoirs of Charles Hopkins* (Kearny, N.J.: Belle Grove Publishing Company, 1988).

Swindler, Jumana A., "12,000 Union Prisoners Were Kept on 24 Acres of Misery" in *Florence Morning News*, Florence, S.C. (April 6, 1986).

Tap, Bruce, *Over Lincoln's Shoulder: The Committee on the Conduct of the War* (Lawrence: University Press of Kansas, 1998).

Thomas, Emory M., *Robert E. Lee: A Biography* (New York: W. W. Norton, 1995).

Thomas, Eugene Marvin, "Prisoner of War Exchange During the American Civil War" (Ph.D. dissertation, Auburn University, 1976).

Thompson, Holland, "The Prisons of the War" in *The Photographic History of the Civil War in Ten Volumes*, Vol. VII, Francis Trevelyan Miller (ed.) (New York: The Review of Reviews Company, 1911).

Thompson, Neil (ed.), *A Captive of War: Solon Hyde* (Shippensburg, Pa.: Burd Street Press, 1996).

Thompson, William Y., "The U.S. Sanitary Commission" in *Civil War History* 2 (June 1956).

Tillinghast, B. F., *Rock Island Arsenal: In Peace and in War* (Chicago: The Henry O. Shepard Company, Printers, 1898).

Toppin, Edgar A., "African Americans and the Confederacy" in *Macmillan Information Now Encyclopedia: The Confederacy*, Richard N. Current (ed.) (New York: Simon & Schuster Macmillan Reference USA, 1993).

Townsend, Leah, "The Florence Prison Pen or Stockade" in *Florence Morning News*, Florence, S.C. (Nov. 7, 1937).

"Treatment of Prisoners at Rock Island" in *Confederate Veteran* 15 (Feb. 1907).

Trowbridge, John T., *The Desolate South, 1865–66* (New York: Little, Brown & Company, 1956. Originally published in 1866).

Trudeau, Noah Andre, "'Kill the Last Damn One of Them': The Fort Pillow Massacre" in *With My Face to the Enemy: Perspectives on the Civil War*, Robert Cowley (ed.) (New York: G. P. Putnam's Sons, 2001).

Tucker, Glenn, *Chickamauga: Bloody Battle in the West* (Indianapolis: Bobbs-Merrill, 1961).

Tucker, Gwynn A., "Andersonville Prison: What Happened?" in *Andersonville Prison: Lessons in Organizational Failure*, Joseph P. Cangemi and Casimir J. Kowalski (eds.) (Lanham, Md.: University Press of America, 1992).

Tucker, J. T., "Fifty Exposed as the 'Six Hundred'" in *Confederate Veteran* 7 (Aug. 1899).

Tucker, John, *Florence Prison Pen* (Sullivan's Island, S.C.: U.S. Department of the Interior, National Park Service, Fort Sumter National Monument, 1990).

"Union Officer Who Was in Prison" in *Confederate Veteran* 18 (April 1910).

United States Army, Rock Island Arsenal, *A History of Rock Island and Rock Island Arsenal from Earliest Times to 1954*, Three Volumes (Rock Island, Ill.: Author, 1967).

United States House of Representatives, *Report on the Condition of Returned Prisoners of War at Annapolis, Maryland* (Washington, D.C.: Government Printing Office, Thirty-eighth Cong., 1st Sess., Rept. No. 67, 1864).

———, *Treatment of Prisoners of War by the Rebel Authorities During the War of the Rebellion* (Washington, D.C.: Government Printing Office, Fortieth Cong., 3rd Sess., Rept. No. 45, 1869).

———, *The Trial of Henry Wirz* (Washington, D.C.: Government Printing Office, Fortieth Cong., 2nd Sess., House Executive Document 23, 1868).

United States Sanitary Commission, *Narrative of Privations and Sufferings of United States Officers and Soldiers While Prisoners of War in the Hands of the Rebel Authorities, Being the Report of a Commission of Inquiry* (Philadelphia: King and Baird for the U.S. Sanitary Commission, 1864).

United States War Department, *War of the Rebellion: A Compilation of the Official Records of the Union and Confederate Armies*, 128 Volumes (Washington, D.C.: Government Printing Office, 1880–1901).

Urban, John W., *In Defense of the Union; Or Through Shot and Shell and Prison Pen* (Chicago: Monarch Book Company, 1887).

Urwin, Gregory J. W., "'We Cannot Treat Negroes . . . as Prisoners of War': Racial Atrocities and Reprisals in Civil War Arkansas" in *Civil War History* 42 (Sept. 1996).

"Virtual American Biographies: James Chatham Duane" (http://www.famousamericans.net/jameschathamduane.htm) (September 22, 2002), adapted from James Grant Wilson and John Fiske, *Appleton's Cyclopedia of American Biography* (New York: D. Appleton and Company, 1887).

Walker, T. R., "Rock Island Prison Barracks" in *Civil War Prisons*, William B. Hesseltine (ed.) (Kent, Ohio: Kent State University Press, 1962).

Wallace, Lee A., "Coppens' Louisiana Zouaves" in *Civil War History* 8 (Sept. 1962).

Wallace, W. Stewart, *A Dictionary of North American Authors Deceased Before 1950* (Toronto: The Ryerson Press, 1951).

"Walter D. Woods (Obituary)" in *Southern Christian Advocate*, Darlington, S.C. (Darlington, S.C.: Darlington County Historical Commission Files, Nov. 1, 1917).

Ward, Geoffrey C., *The Civil War: An Illustrated History* (New York: Alfred A. Knopf, 1990).

Watson, Ronald (ed.), *From Ashby to Andersonville: The Civil War Diary and Reminiscences of Private George A. Hitchcock, 21st Massachusetts Infantry* (Campbell, Ca.: Savas Publishing Company, 1997).

Waugh, John C., *Re-Electing Lincoln: The Battle for the 1864 Presidency* (New York: Crown, 1997).

Weigley, Russell F., *A Great Civil War* (Bloomington and Indianapolis: Indiana University Press, 2000).

Westwood, Howard C., *Black Troops, White Commanders and Freedmen During the Civil War* (Carbondale, Ill.: Southern Illinois University Press, 1992).

———, "Captive Black Union Soldiers in Charleston—What to Do?" in *Civil War History* 28 (March 1982).

"What Our Patrons Think" in *Confederate Veteran* 25 (Jan. 1917).

White, William W., *The Confederate Veteran* (Tuscaloosa, Ala.: Confederate Publishing Company, 1962).

Who Was Who Among North American Authors, 1921–1939 (Detroit: Gale Research Company, 1976).

Williams, George W., *A History of the Negro Troops in the War of the Rebellion, 1861–1865* (New York: Harper & Brothers, 1888).

Williams, Sidney S., *From Spotsylvania to Wilmington, N.C. by Way of Andersonville and Florence* (Providence, R.I.: The Rhode Island Soldiers and Sailors Historical Society, 1899).

Williams, Walter L., "Again in Chains: Black Soldiers Suffering in Captivity" in *Civil War Times Illustrated* 20 (May 1981).

Wilson, Charles Reagan, "The Religion of the Lost Cause: Ritual and Organization of the Southern Civil Religion: 1865–1920" in *Journal of Southern History* 46 (May 1980).

Wilson, Joseph T., *The Black Phalanx: A History of the Negro Soldiers of the United States* (Hartford, Conn.: American Publishing Company, 1890).

Winberry, John J., "Lest We Forget: The Confederate Monument and the Southern Townscape" in *Southeastern Geographer* 23 (1983).

Winik, Jay, *April 1865: The Month That Saved America* (New York: HarperCollins, 2001).

Winther, Oscar O., "The Soldier Vote in the Election of 1864" in *New York History* 25 (1944).

"Wirz Monument Dedicated in Kind Spirit" in *Confederate Veteran* 17 (June 1909).

Wise, Stephen R., *Gate of Hell: Campaign for Charleston Harbor, 1863* (Columbia, S.C.: University of South Carolina Press, 1994).

Woods, Walter D., "Confederate Memorial Day" Reprinted from *The News and Press*, Darlington, S.C. (Darlington, S.C.: Darlington County Historical Commission Files, May 4, 1916).

———, "Notes on the Confederate Stockade of Florence, South Carolina, 1861–1865" (Florence, S.C.: Florence Public Library, Typeset Manuscript, circa 1915).

Woodward, Joseph Janvier, *The Medical and Surgical History of the War of the Rebellion, Volume 1, Part II: Medical History* (Washington, D.C.: Government Printing Office, 1879).

Woodworth, Steven E., "Davis, Bragg, and Confederate Command in the West" in *Jefferson Davis's Generals*, Gabor S. Boritt (ed.) (New York and Oxford: Oxford University Press, Gettysburg Civil War Institute Books, 1999).

Wright, Charles, "Rock Island Prison, 1864–5" in *Confederate View of the Treatment of Prisoners Compiled from Official Records and Other Documents*, J. William Jones (ed.) (Richmond: Southern Historical Society, 1876).

Wyeth, John Allan, *That Devil Forrest: Life of General Nathan Bedford Forrest* (New York: Harper & Brothers, 1959).

"The Yankee Prisoners at Florence" in *Camden Daily Journal*, Camden, S.C. (Oct. 29, 1864).

Young, Bennett H., "Treatment of Prisoners of War" in *Confederate Veteran* 26 (Nov. 1918).

"Youngest General of the Confederate Army" in *Southern Historical Society Papers* 35 (1907).

Index

REFERENCES TO PHOTOGRAPHS ARE IN ITALICS